WHAT IS E-BUSINESS?

How the Internet Transforms Organizations

Feng Li

UNIVERSITY OF NEWCASTLE UPON TYNE, UK

Blackwell
Publishing

BLACKWELL PUBLISHING
350 Main Street, Malden, MA 02148-5020, USA
9600 Garsington Road, Oxford OX4 2DQ, UK
550 Swanston Street, Carlton, Victoria 3053, Australia

First published 2007 by Blackwell Publishing Ltd

1   2007

Library of Congress Cataloging-in-Publication Data

Li, Feng.
    What is e-business? how the internet transforms organizations / Feng Li.
        p. cm.
    Includes bibliographical references and index.
    ISBN-13: 978-1-4051-2557-4 (hardcover : alk. paper)
    ISBN-10: 1-4051-2557-8 (hardcover : alk. paper)
    ISBN-13: 978-1-4051-2558-1 (pbk. : alk. paper)
    ISBN-10: 1-4051-2558-6 (pbk. : alk. paper)   1. Electronic commerce.
    2. Strategic planning.   3. Organizational change.   I. Title.

    HF5548.32.L49 2007
    658′.05—dc22
                                                        2005032597

A catalogue record for this title is available from the British Library.

Set in 10/12.5 pt Photina
by Graphicraft Limited, Hong Kong
Printed and bound in Singapore
by Markono Print Media Pte Ltd

The publisher's policy is to use permanent paper from mills that operate a sustainable forestry policy,
and which has been manufactured from pulp processed using acid-free and elementary chlorine-free
practices. Furthermore, the publisher ensures that the text paper and cover board used have met
acceptable environmental accreditation standards.

For further information on
Blackwell Publishing, visit our website:
www.blackwellpublishing.com

Brief Contents

v

Contents

Preface

Today, memories of the dot.com boom and bust are fading, and the euphoria and pessimism have been replaced by more cool-headed rational thinking and coordinated actions, underpinned by various theories and conceptual frameworks. The dot.com bust did not mark the end of the Internet and e-Business, because the underlying rapid growth of the network society and economy, in terms of the number of people and organizations getting online and the business volume of e-Commerce, has continued even during the economic downturn.

As the technology sector recovers rapidly from the dot.com crash, organizations from around the globe are exploring opportunities and challenges brought about by the Internet and related technologies. This is not limited to the private sectors. Public sector organizations are also increasingly exploring new ways of delivering information and services to customers and citizens via electronic channels. Many public sector organizations and agencies are also actively facilitating, stimulating and shaping the development of ICTs (information and communications technologies) infrastructure and services. As the technologies and services continue to proliferate and penetrate into every corner of our economy and daily lives, the boundaries between products, services, channels, industries and organizations are rapidly eroding, and the distinctions between work, leisure, education and play are becoming increasingly blurred. The success of private and public sector organizations in the next few years will depend critically on how effective they are in implementing new ways of working, by innovatively exploiting new capabilities from Internet and related technologies.

In understanding and implementing such radical changes, there is a strong need for theoretical guidance. However, unlike many other business management subjects (such as strategy or marketing), e-Business is still an emerging area, and most scholars active in this area have come from other adjacent, more established disciplines. The views different scholars hold on critical issues are often divergent and incoherent. This creates a serious problem for researchers, teachers, consultants and practitioners alike, as the foundations on which new ideas and new business activities are being built are still not fully established.

In fact, since the dot.com crash, I have been repeatedly asked by publishers and journal editors, as well as by scholars and students: given the pervasive influence of the Internet and e-Business in every aspect of business and management, should e-Business actually be treated as an area of study? In other words, perhaps e-Business-related issues should be subsumed into existing disciplines in business and management, from strategy and marketing to human resource management and information systems. This to some extent is already happening, because the Internet and related technologies are radically reshaping every aspect of business and management. However, these studies do not address – nor exclude – the need for a comprehensive and systematic understanding of *how the Internet transforms organizations*. As will be illustrated in detail in this book, the world has changed profoundly, and many emerging issues in the area of the Internet and e-Business cannot be centrally and systematically addressed within the realms of established disciplines. Some of the most significant developments in e-Business are about reintegrating fragmented and compartmentalized activities and functions within and between organizations: it will provide the basis for a new generation of organization and management theory for the new economy.

Since the late 1990s, numerous books on e-Business and e-Commerce have been published, and new ones are continuously being released. However, most books I have come across are either too broadly focused to contain sufficient details within each topic, or too narrowly focused to give students a full picture of the transformation surrounding e-Business and e-Commerce. More seriously, many textbooks are simply a loose collection of related topics, and the complex relations between different issues are not clearly or coherently articulated. Although several new books have adopted more coherent structures than their predecessors, the detailed content is often generic rather than e-Business specific. For example, even though some authors talk about e-Business infrastructure, e-Business strategy, and organizational innovations for e-Business in the chapter headings, the content within those sections is often primarily generic business information systems theories, traditional strategy literature and frameworks, and standard organizational transformation issues. This contradicts the basic premise that the Internet and e-Business may lead to radical changes and render many existing business management theories and frameworks invalid.

This problem has posed a serious challenge for my teaching and research. With the growing number of students at both postgraduate and undergraduate levels taking e-Business-related modules, the demand for a 'core textbook' that covers most issues in a coherent manner has been growing each year. However, to satisfy this seemingly straightforward (and 'reasonable') request is not easy, because most available textbooks are structured as an accumulation of relevant topics rather than using a theory-driven form of presentation, underpinned by a coherent, robust, yet broadly focused theoretical framework. This concern was echoed by many other academics and book publishers.

As such, the main motivation behind this book is to use a robust and tested, and widely acceptable, theoretical framework to underpin e-Business-related topics, covering issues at three closely intertwined levels:

1. the new business environment as the context for e-Business;
2. emerging strategies and business models as responses to opportunities and challenges in the new business environment, especially those engendered by innovatively exploiting the new capabilities of Internet and related technologies;

3. organizational innovations required to translate new strategies and business models into manageable activities and processes, through innovative exploitation of ICTs in general and Internet and related technologies in particular.

Many other issues can also be effectively integrated into this framework. The purpose is to provide students and other readers with a coherent conceptual framework to integrate the vast range of topics and issues surrounding e-Business with their existing knowledge and experience. This will enable readers to interpret conflicting and rapidly changing business phenomena and make coherent and consistent decisions in the context of rapid technological developments and volatile fluctuations of market conditions and public opinion. They will be able to develop an in-depth understanding of '*what*' is happening, '*why*' it is happening, and '*how*' emerging issues can or should be dealt with, rather than being swayed constantly by fashion and the fad of the month or by the popular media. This may not guarantee 'best' decisions, but it will ensure consistency, coherence and rational justification every time and over time, which is extremely valuable for organizations and business executives in a volatile environment.

Since I first developed, with colleagues, a cluster of four e-Business modules for the Strathclyde MBA in 1997/98, the framework has been tested and refined in the contexts of my research, teaching, consultancy and executive development programmes. In particular, the topics and the underlying theoretical framework have been explored in the e-Business modules for the Strathclyde MBA, and similar modules for the MSc BITS (Business Information Technology and Systems), MSc Operations Research (OR), and Master of Communications Management (MCM). Since I joined Newcastle University Business School in early 2002 the materials have been further developed and refined through a series of e-Business modules in our Executive MBA, MBA, MA IBM (International Business Management), MA HRM and IHRM (Human Resources Management, and International Human Resources Management), a new MSc on E-Business and Information Systems (EBIS), a large undergraduate final year module on Exploring E-Business, and several other programmes. Some of the materials have also been used in my executive development programmes delivered both in the UK and overseas. Feedback and suggestions from students, business executives and colleagues have been incorporated into the framework. The purpose is to provide a solid introduction to the whole area of how business has changed and the key issues involved, rather than an ephemeral treatment of e-Business-related issues and phenomena.

The book has focused primarily on theoretical issues underpinned by a robust conceptual framework. However, at the end of each chapter, some discussion questions and possible assignments are provided, together with suggestions for further reading. These activities will not only help students revise the main issues covered in the chapters, but also enable them to develop relevant skills and interpret various theoretical issues in different contexts and for different audiences. At the end of the book, three appendices illustrate further major assignments that could be adopted by various courses. These assignments could be effectively used to extend the coverage of the book, addressing both theoretical and practical issues.

The first is about applying theories to practice by developing a *launch-ready e-Business plan*. This assignment has worked particularly well in the past. In one of the modules I developed, this element – supported by a series of external speakers (lawyers, accountants, bankers, entrepreneurs as well as representatives from local development agencies) and small group seminars – made up 50 per cent of the total module. Some of the business plans developed by students won various competitions both locally and nationally, and some students even launched their own e-Businesses after graduation. For all students, this assignment enabled them to apply their knowledge and skills in the context of a project, which significantly enhanced their employability and problem-solving skills. It also enables them to appreciate the significance of various theoretical issues in practical contexts.

The second assignment has worked well with several modules I taught, especially at the postgraduate level. By developing an online resource portal on *who is who in e-Business*, this assignment provides a useful vehicle for students to focus on a particular sub-area of e-Business and investigate the key scholars and main issues involved in detail. It also allows students on the course to share their learning with one another, and over time this could be developed into a useful resource for both current and future students.

The third assignment requires students to use *Wiki* and *blogs* to develop and share materials and ideas on different issues in e-Business in the form of an electronic encyclopaedia (Wikipedia). Similar to the second assignment, this assignment can also lead to the development of a useful online resource portal for the course. Wiki is a piece of server software that allows users to freely create and edit webpage content using any web browser. Web logs, or blogs, are a type of web content typically created by independent writers to share views and ideas with others. This assignment will enable students to develop their own e-Business Wikipedia for the course and keep individual blogs on relevant issues. This effort could be extended beyond the duration of the course once the 'community' is built up.

I hope you will find the book informative and useful. Any suggestions, comments and constructive criticisms are welcome. I can be reached by e-mail at Feng.li@ncl.ac.uk.

Feng Li
Newcastle upon Tyne

Acknowledgements

This book has been many years in the making and it would not have been possible without the guidance, support, suggestions, comments, discussions, debates, encouragement and challenges from numerous people. First of all I would like to thank Professor John Goddard OBE, Professor Andy Gillespie and Dr Mark Hepworth, amongst many other 'Newcastle PICT' folks, for introducing me to the concepts of ICTs and the information economy in the late 1980s. It was their pioneer work that inspired me to embark on an exciting journey of investigating new opportunities and challenges in the realm of ICTs and organizational transformation during a period of profound socio-economic change and rapid technological developments.

I would also like to thank Professor Colin Eden, Professor Kees van der Heidjen and Professor Howard Williams at Strathclyde University, not only for being my role models and mentors, but also for encouraging me to organize and articulate my ideas coherently. Back in 1997 when the dot.com boom was about to take off in the UK, the four of us got together one day to discuss emerging business opportunities and challenges associated with the Internet. This discussion led to the subsequent development of a cluster of four e-Business modules for the Strathclyde MBA in 1998:

- The Institutional and Regulatory Settings for E-Business
- New Business Models for the Information Economy
- Organizational Innovations for E-Business
- Developing and Implementing Effective E-Business Solutions.

These modules were delivered both in the UK and internationally to the Strathclyde MBAs, and some aspects of these modules also provided the basis for various executive development short courses and for several other modules for various Master programmes. This book has been significantly shaped by these ideas.

Thanks are also due to all the students, business executives, tutors and guest speakers who participated in and/or contributed to my various postgraduate and undergraduate classes and executive development short courses. Their questions, insights, comments, suggestions, criticisms and challenges have forced me to continue to refine, research and redevelop the overall framework underpinning the book and many of the theories and ideas – a sincere thanks to all of you! The numerous senior executives who contributed guest lectures to my classes over the years – among them, Reinhard Klein, Head of Integrated Technology Services in IBM Europe, Pete Marsden and Tracy Willis, CTO and Customer Technology Director of Egg.Com, Bernie Callaghan, CEO of Leighton Group, Herb Kim, CEO of Codeworks and former CEO of QXL.Com UK, Hemant Sabbat, Senior Vice President and General Manager of Perot Systems (Mobile Communications), and many others. I am extremely grateful to all of them for sharing their valuable experience and insights with me and my students.

Another group of people who strongly influenced my ideas were colleagues involved in setting up the E-Institute (Kelvin Institute) in Scotland. This Institute was a multimillion-pound initiative funded by the Scottish Executive via Scottish Enterprise and some major global companies such as IBM, NTL and Cisco. I was one of the original academics who contributed to the development of the agenda and business plan. I have particularly benefited from the meetings, discussions and collaborations with some leading experts in computing and telecommunications – Professor Richard Connor, Professor Paddy Nixon, Professor Andrew McGettrick, Professor Geoff Smith, Professor John Dunlop and Professor Tariq Durrani, amongst others. This effort enabled me to develop a much deeper understanding of the technological issues in computing and telecommunications. Our discussions with senior managers from sponsoring companies, including IBM, Nortel and National Bank of Australia, also played a key part in informing my assessments of technological developments and emerging opportunities and challenges.

I have also benefited enormously from collaborations with colleagues since I rejoined Newcastle University, where 'informatics' has been a central focus of research for a large number of researchers from multiple disciplines and perspectives. In particular, discussions with colleagues from the School of Computing, the multidisciplinary Informatics Institute, as well as RCID and Schin (Health Informatics), helped me understand many emerging technologies and their applications (e.g. grid computing, web services) – Professor Paul Watson, Professor Mike Harrison, Professor Ian Purves, Dr Rob Smith, Ron Jamerson, Dr Joan Harvey and many others. Most of all I benefited hugely from discussions with colleagues in the Centre for Social and Business Informatics, especially in understanding the differences between private and public sector organizations in implementing e-systems and the wide range of methodologies and approaches deployed in making sense of emerging issues. Special thanks to Professor Ian McLoughlin, Professor Mike Martin and James Cornford. I would also like to thank the Business School for creating space for me to write this book.

My PhDs and researchers have also influenced and challenged my thinking in many ways – in particular, Dr Shahizan Hassan, Dr Alexis Barlow, Irene Yousept, Dr Rahim Ghasemiyeh, Dr Savvas Papagiannidis, Dr James Carr, Joanna Berry, Michael Conyette, Joe Lee, Alawiyah Abd Wahab and Maggie Zeng. The questions they raised and new insights they developed have informed my own research in many ways.

Special thanks are due to Rosemary Nixon, Senior Commissioning Editor at Blackwell. She has been instrumental in this project. Since the late 1990s, I have been approached by several publishers to develop this book, but it was Rosemary who actively encouraged and supported me in putting ideas into action. Without her persistent encouragement and genuine enthusiasm for my work, I would probably not have made the extra effort required to find time to write this book during a very demanding period of my career. It was also she who suggested the sub-title of the book. Many thanks, Rosemary! You are a star. The editorial and production team at Blackwell – Annette Abel, Bridget Jennings and Karen Wilson in particular – also deserve special thanks for their efficient and professional work.

Finally, I would like to thank my family for their continuous support, love and understanding throughout the years. My parents and three sisters have always loved and supported me unconditionally. Most of all, my wife and son, Sarah and Jeffrey, once again put up with my mood swings and the extra hours I have had to put into the development of this book. It was their love, support, understanding and patience – day in, day out – that enabled me to get on with the research and writing. I would like to dedicate this book to them. Any errors remain my own.

Chapter 1

Introduction

The purposes of this book are threefold. It examines the key characteristics of the new business environment, which provides the context for e-Business. It then explores some new strategies and business models that have been developed as responses to changes in the business environment, and highlights the critical role of the Internet and related technologies in the process. Following that, the book introduces a series of organizational innovations that have been developed to translate new strategies and business models into manageable activities and processes, and to improve the efficiency, effectiveness and responsiveness of the organization through innovative application of ICTs. One of the main objectives of the book is to introduce a robust, coherent, yet broadly focused conceptual framework, together with a range of theories and techniques, to help the readers understand and exploit emerging opportunities and challenges posed by the Internet and e-Business in the increasingly networked, information economy.

What Is E-Business? Does It Still Matter?

E-Business is one of those unfortunate concepts where everyone has a view on what it is, but everyone's definition is somewhat different from the next person's. Although this is usually unproblematic in everyday conversations, it creates challenging problems for researchers, policy makers and business practitioners who need to communicate their views precisely and make important decisions on the basis of those views. The problem is particularly acute when measuring the size of e-Business activities, which is like measuring the length of a rubber band: the result depends on how far you stretch it. The next chapter will explore what is (and isn't) e-Business in more detail.

E-Business is not just about dot.com or Internet-only companies; or selling and buying via electronic channels (which is often referred to as e-Commerce). Fundamentally, e-Business is a much broader concept and it is concerned with using the Internet and related technologies to integrate and redesign an organization's internal activities, processes and external relations, and create new ways of working that are significantly different from, and very often far superior to, what was possible (or conceivable) in the past. In other words, e-Business is about developing new ways of working by innovatively exploiting the new capabilities of ICTs in general and the Internet and related technologies in particular.[1]

This means that even though e-Business developments since the mid-1990s have been spectacular in many ways, the origin of e-Business could go back several decades. There have been numerous studies in the past few decades on the use of ICTs and changes in the visions, strategies, business models, organizational designs and inter-organizational relations of private and public sector organizations, supported by robust theoretical conceptualization and intensive and extensive empirical evidence. Despite various step changes in recent years, in many aspects of organizations continuity from the past needs to be maintained. Valuable lessons can be learnt from previous research.

The second part of the question is therefore not *'does it still matter?'* but how it matters, to whom, and most of all, what we can do about it. To answer this question, it is necessary to explore the context for e-Business, the strategic innovations and organizational transformation it generates, and the implications for organizations, their employees and customers, and for society and the economy as a whole.

What Is *New* in the New Business Environment?

There are at least two fundamental changes in the business environment. The nature of the economy has changed, as measured by the informational (intangible) elements of our products, services and production processes; and by the proportion of the workforce whose primary activities are informational rather than physical, often known as information workers or knowledge workers. Information (or knowledge, intelligence) has become the most important resource upon which the efficiency and competitiveness of all organizations depend, and the main source of future 'value-added'. This is true not only in services or high-tech industries, but also in primary and manufacturing industries – and in both private and public sectors. In other words, all activities, products and production processes have become information intensive – even in traditional industries.

In the meantime, the so-called 'Information and Communication Technologies (ICTs) Revolution' continues to gather pace, providing us with increasingly more powerful, versatile, affordable and convenient tools in the forms of technologies, infrastructure and services. From the users' perspective, the *only* purpose of these technologies is to deal with 'information' – to capture, store and retrieve, manipulate, transmit and present information. As a result of the technological advances we are able to deal with information in ways not even possible only a few years ago.

The combination of these two intertwined processes is extremely powerful. On the one hand, the most important resource in the economy has changed, from land, raw materials, capital and money to 'information' (broadly defined). On the other hand, we have at our fingertips increasingly more powerful yet affordable tools and techniques to deal with the most important resource of the economy (i.e. information), often in ways impossible in the past. This combination redefines many basic assumptions about our economy and organizations, creating new rules for all to follow. Most importantly, it means that today, organizations large and small can, should and indeed must do things differently in order to survive and thrive in the new economy. This gives rise to the need for a new generation of organization and management theories. These theories should be embedded in the context of new economics of information, and explicitly exploit the unique capabilities of the Internet and related technologies (and that of ICTs in general). These issues will be discussed in more detail later in the book.

At the foundation of such new theories are what I refer to in this book as the *strategic innovations and organizational transformation*: new visions and strategies, new business models, new organizational designs, new ways of working, and new inter-organizational relations that are intimately related to – supported, enabled or facilitated by – the Internet and related technologies. These technologies have brought about some radical changes in the last few years, although there is also a significant element of continuity from the past. These changes provide the essential context for e-Business.

Strategic Innovations for E-Business

The changing business environment requires organizations to develop new strategies and business models. The rapid development of the Internet and related technologies, combined with the changing nature of the economy, has enabled many organizations to explore new strategies and business models profoundly different from existing ones. In fact, some recent studies are challenging the basic assumptions of many widely used strategic frameworks, such as Porter's five forces of competitive analysis, or Hamel's theory of core competence, because some of the implicit, underlying assumptions and starting points of these frameworks may no longer be valid in today's new business environment.

In the meantime, many new strategies have been advocated, developed and implemented in recent years, including using the Internet to create disruptive innovations in a number of industries: the so-called web strategy or cluster (platform) strategy, where organizations cluster around a particular technological standard or customer segment to collectively deliver unique customer value; and the changing strategic orientations from products, to services, to solutions, and more recently to the co-creation of consumer experience through a network of independent product and service providers. This is not an exhaustive list, but these new strategies will be used to illustrate some radical changes that have been introduced in different industries at strategic levels, by innovatively exploiting the new capabilities of the Internet and related technologies.

Such new strategies are increasingly reflected in the business models of various organizations in a wide range of industries. This book will explore the ontology of e-Business models, and introduce a taxonomy of e-Business models that have emerged in recent years. One particular tendency that will be highlighted in this book is the deconstruction of the integrated business models and business processes through the Internet and related technologies, which is leading to the emergence of virtual organizations and other new organizational forms. These new strategies and business models are increasingly reflected in new organizational designs and emerging forms of organizations.

Organizational Transformation through the Internet and Related Technologies

The Internet and related technologies have enabled organizations to adopt new organizational designs and new ways of working, which are sometimes referred to as organizational transformation or organizational innovations. This book will examine such changes in different facets of organizations – the structure, process, work organization and inter-organizational relations. Some of the changes are incremental but others are radical.

Take structure, for example: a study of confidential compensation data from 300 large American companies gathered between 1986 and 1999 clearly indicated that the organizational hierarchy has been flattened. The number of people reporting directly to the CEO has increased steadily, but the managerial levels between the CEO and the lowest-level managers with profit centre responsibilities have decreased by more than 25 per cent. The study also found that even mergers, acquisitions and diversifications have not significantly added to the number of CEO direct reports, and lower-level managers are taking on more responsibilities. A critical reason for flattened hierarchy is that 'technology has put information at everyone's fingertips' (p. 5).[2] However, the study also concluded that despite significant changes, the fundamental nature and characteristics of the hierarchy have been retained. From a contingency perspective, the new business environment requires organizations to adopt new organizational designs in order to achieve new fit (or alignment) between the organization and its environment. As will be explored in detail later in the book, some very radical changes have been introduced within hierarchies which significantly enhanced their flexibility and responsiveness.

Equally, from a process perspective, organizational changes have been introduced, from continuous, incremental improvements to radical revolutionary business process re-engineering. Many incremental and radical changes have also been introduced in the way people work (work organization) and in inter-organizational relations.

Before we move on to the next section, the approach adopted in this book needs to be explained briefly. Many of us have heard the ancient tale about *Four Blind Men and an Elephant*. There were four blind men who had never seen an elephant before. One day, they decided to find out what an elephant looked like, and the only way to do that was by feeling the elephant with their hands. So the first man walked up to the elephant and embraced one of its front legs with both arms. Then he announced excitedly to the rest of the men that the elephant looked like the trunk of a tree. Eager to find out directly for himself, the second blind man walked up to the elephant and touched its body, so he said that the elephant did not look anything like the trunk of a tree at all. In fact the elephant looked like a spongy wall. The third blind man was standing behind the elephant and managed to grab its tail, so he was absolutely convinced that the elephant looked like a thick rope. Then the fourth blind man touched one ear of the elephant and said the elephant looked like a palm tree leaf. They argued and argued all day long, and nobody could convince the others about their own visions of the elephant.

When studying a complex entity such as the organization, we often face similar problems. Because of our physiological and methodological limitations, we are often unable to see the organization from multiple angles simultaneously. It is important that we do not take a small part of the organization as a true representation of the whole. In other words, we need to understand the limitations of investigating the organization from a particular angle while extrapolating insights into other aspects – and more importantly, of using the findings from one particular perspective to dismiss the validity of findings from other perspectives. One way to address this potential problem is to recognize the limitations, and strengths, of each of our approaches, and intelligently reassemble what we discover from each of these approaches in an attempt to come up with an understanding of the whole organization as close to the reality as we possibly can.

When we look at organizational designs, we often examine their structures (shape) and processes (how work is done), as well as their work organization and their relationships with other organizations. We also examine various other aspects such as production methods, logistics systems and so on. The theoretical and methodological approaches we adopt in exploring each aspect of organizational designs often have different underlying assumptions about organizations and their environments, different starting points, and different purposes and objectives. Comparing the results from different approaches directly can often lead to debates that are seemingly interesting and insightful but fundamentally flawed and meaningless. We need to be acutely aware of such potential problems and limitations when researching organizations.

Emerging Issues and Areas Not Covered in This Book

The rapid development of the Internet and e-Business also raises a series of other issues, including online security and privacy, individual and organizational identities in cyber space and their similarities, differences and relationships with the identities in the physical world. There are also regulatory and legal issues, ethical issues, as well as many other issues related to online marketing – such as e-mail spamming and e-mail 'bombing' (flooding an e-mail address with junk mails), hacking and viruses. Other important topics include m-Commerce and m-Business; e-Government and e-Public Services (including e-Health or health informatics); e-Learning and e-Business-related issues in a wide range of industries and application domains – Internet banking, the changing business models in the telecommunications industries, online stock trading, e-holidays and e-music, to name a few.

Owing to the size of the book, many of these issues will not be investigated here. However, such issues can be effectively explored within the framework introduced in this book. Many of them will also make interesting student assignments and exercises, and provide useful topics for independent research. Some discussion questions and possible assignments – together with suggested further readings – have been provided at the end of each chapter; and three major assignments are suggested at the end of this book (see appendices).

The Structure of the Book

The structure of the book reflects the conceptual framework deployed to integrate and underpin the theories and issues. The next chapter will examine what e-Business is and is not. Following that, the book will be organized into three main sections to discuss changes in the new e-Business environment (Part I); emerging strategies and business models for the network economy (Part II); and organizational innovations through information systems (Part III). Finally, the book will highlight a series of other issues not covered in the book and conclude by highlighting why e-Business matters, in what ways and what we can do about it. I will also speculate on a range of emerging issues and on where things are going. E-Business is still a rapidly evolving phenomenon and new research is clearly needed to make sense of what is happening, the opportunities and challenges it poses and how these opportunities and challenges can be effectively exploited.

Discussion Questions

1   In your view, what is e-Business? Why do you want to study this subject?
2   What main issues should be included in e-Business studies? Why? If you were to write a book on e-Business, what would the table of contents look like? Justify your answers.
3   How do you characterize e-Business as an emerging field of study in relation to other more established disciplines (such as strategy, marketing and human resource management)? Why?

Assignment

Visit the website of five e-Businesses you are most interested in, and investigate the ways these businesses are different from conventional businesses. Write up your main findings (one side of A4, single spaced, for each case) and report your main findings to your class.

NOTES

1   It should be emphasized that 'e-Business' is not limited to the private sector and that Internet technologies are increasingly applied in public sector and other non-business institutions, although more recently other terms are increasingly used to describe those specific activities, such as e-Government, e-Learning, e-Health and so on. This issue will be discussed in more detail in the next chapter.
2   Rajan, Raghuram G. and Julie Wulf (2003) The flattening firm: evidence from panel data on the changing nature of corporate hierarchies. Reported in *Sloan Management Review*, 44(4), 5. Full paper available from Wulf@wharton.upenn.edu.

FURTHER READING

I will not suggest any particular e-Business or e-Commerce books for this chapter. Instead, visit a bookshop and/or the library, and do some quick research on amazon.com. Flip through all books on this subject you can find and pay particular attention to the table of contents and the introductions. Identify the main themes – and the key issues – covered by these books.

Chapter 2

What Is E-Business and Does It Still Matter?

What Is E-Business: Where Do We Draw the Line?

Before we define what e-Business – and e-Commerce – is or isn't, first let us explore the following scenarios.

You need a piece of new software so you log onto the website of the firm that developed the software or a third-party vendor. After paying for it by credit card online, you then download the software via the Internet and install it on your PC. The entire process – including payment and delivery – is conducted electronically. Is this e-Business (or e-Commerce)? Everyone will agree that the answer is yes.

Now let's imagine you go to Amazon.com and find a book you want. You pay for the book by credit card electronically. Amazon.com takes the money and then despatches the book either via a third-party book distributor, or directly from one of its own warehouses, physically. You receive the book the next day. Given that the distribution is done physically, would this be e-Business or e-Commerce? Most people would probably still say yes. After all, Amazon.com has been the bellwether of e-Business and e-Commerce.

Now imagine you want to buy a new hi-fi. You search the Internet to find out about various product features and the best deals from various companies. Rather than buying it via the Internet, you telephone the call centre of a retailer and order the product. They despatch the product physically, and you pay off the invoice by posting the retailer a personal cheque. The transaction is not conducted electronically even though the Internet played a part in the deal. Would this still be e-Business or e-Commerce?

What about buying a new car? You search the Internet for product features and best deals. Then you print off the best deal and take it to the local car dealer and demand the same offer. You then conclude the deal with the local dealer in person. Would you consider this e-Business or e-Commerce?

Although most people have a view on what e-Business or e-Commerce is, it becomes problematic as soon as we start measuring it. In fact, if we include all the above scenarios as e-Business or e-Commerce, then it would be difficult to find anything that can be excluded from the definition. Where do we draw the line? The way we define the concept will have significant implications for the total size of e-Business activities. This is perhaps one major reason for the vastly different statistics and forecasts on the size of e-Business in various contexts. It has been said that measuring the size of e-Commerce and e-Business is like measuring a rubber band – the result depends on how far you stretch it.

From a business perspective, this is a significant issue. For example, in the UK many people conduct desk research through the Internet when choosing a mortgage. However, once they have found one or several acceptable deals, rather than completing the transaction online most people will then visit either a bank branch or an independent personal financial adviser to confirm the details of the deal and then complete the transaction in person or by phone. For a bank or building society, the Internet channel is perhaps not profitable since only a tiny percentage of customers complete the transaction online. However, people who have researched product information through the Internet are much more likely to complete a deal than someone just walking into a branch without such preparation. According to some banks and building societies we have studied in the UK, the chance of concluding a deal increases from one in twenty for those who did not undertake any research to one in three for those who have studied product information beforehand via the Internet. So the significance of the Internet in selling mortgages cannot be underestimated. Even though, strictly speaking, the Internet channel itself is perhaps not profitable, it significantly increases the conversion rate in the branches and on other channels. Closing down the Internet channel for mortgages (because of its low profitability) will affect the profitability of other channels.

This is in fact a generic issue for all multi-channel retailers. Gartner analyst Adam Sarner told the *E-Commerce Times* that multi-channel retailers learnt that e-Commerce does not necessarily mean a transaction in an online shopping cart. 'J. Crew knows that someone going to jcrew.com is 27 per cent more likely to visit a J. Crew store soon afterwards . . . The Web is a powerful influence.'[1] As such, defining what is and isn't e-Business is extremely important, with profound theoretical and practical implications.

What Is E-Business and E-Commerce?

E-Business was a phrase first coined by IBM in its advertising campaign in the 1990s. It was defined as 'the transformation of key business processes through the use of Internet technologies'. Today, e-Commerce is commonly defined as electronic transactions conducted by business partners, which can be both organizations and individuals. In contrast, e-Business is much broader, referring not only to buying and selling, but also to servicing customers, collaborating with business partners, and conducting electronic transactions *within* an organization.

Jelassi and Enders defined e-Business as the use of electronic means to conduct an organization's business internally and/or externally. They specifically emphasized the inclusion in their definition of internal e-Business activities, including the linking of an organization's employees with each other through an Intranet to improve information sharing, facilitate knowledge dissemination and support management reporting. E-commerce is regarded as a subset of e-Business, which deals with the facilitation of transactions and selling of products and services online, either via the Internet or via any other telecommunications network. They went on further to define mobile commerce or m-commerce as a subset of e-Commerce, and it refers to online activities similar to those mentioned in the e-Commerce category, but the underlying technology is limited to mobile telecommunications networks which are accessed through wireless hand-held devices such as mobile phones, hand-held computers or personal digital assistants (PDAs).[2] A similar definition was also adopted by Chaffey.[3]

Such definitions are, however, not universally accepted. For example, Turban et al. defined e-Commerce and e-Business interchangeably, to include transactions both within and between organizations.[4] They used e-Commerce to describe the process of buying, selling, transferring, or exchanging products, services and/or information via computer networks, and specifically emphasized e-Learning and conducting electronic transactions within an organization as part of e-Commerce.

In contrast, Laudon and Traver defined e-Commerce as digitally enabled commercial transactions between and amongst organizations and individuals, whereas e-Business is used to refer primarily to the digital enablement of transactions and processes within a firm, involving only the information systems under the control of the firm.[5] In other words, e-Business refers to those activities other than 'buying and selling' via electronic channels.

In this book, a broad definition of e-Business is adopted, which encompasses all internal and external electronically based activities and processes – both in the private and public sectors. [E-commerce is part of e-Business, which focuses on electronic commercial transactions between and amongst organizations and individuals.] ？ ？

As the application of Internet and related technologies extends to new areas of activities, many other terms have increasingly emerged, including e-Government, e-Public Services, e-Health, e-Learning, e-Democracy and so on. Although they are regarded by many researchers as subsets of e-Business, there are also unique issues and specific challenges within each of these areas, and some of these sub-areas are increasingly becoming self-contained research and application domains that overlap with, but go beyond, the realm of e-Business.

Whichever definition we adopt, one common theme among all of them is that the origin of e-Business could go back a long time, and there is a wealth of knowledge already available, much of it based on large, comprehensive research programmes and practical applications in private and public sector organizations throughout the world. Even though the phrase has only been popular since the 1990s, the origin of the phenomenon can be traced back much further. This also means that the focus of e-Business is not only about dot.coms and Internet-only companies, but also – perhaps more significantly – [about transforming existing businesses through the innovative use of Internet and related technologies.]

ICTs and Business Transformation: The Evolution of E-Business

There have been numerous studies on the evolution of ICTs and the associated business transformation in various contexts. Long before the arrival of computers, use of the telegraph and the widespread adoption of the telephone resulted in considerable changes in organizational structures and processes. Back in the 1970s, Goddard studied how the use of the telephone led to the development of new organizational structures, where control was increasingly concentrated into large cities in the core regions while production and other low-level functions were increasingly decentralized into the peripheral regions and developing countries.[6] A large body of research then followed which lasted until the early 1980s, when the focus was increasingly shifted from voice communications via the telephone to data communications via computer networks. By enabling computers to communicate with other computers over space and people to communicate with computers over distance as part of their work-related activities, and, most of all, by providing the means of acquiring information, analysing and transmitting it over space at speed and volume not possible in the past, the technologies were challenging the prevailing production processes and organizational structures, resulting in significant changes in the organization of work and the nature of the workplace.[7] Many such changes have been reflected in the literature on ICTs and organizational transformation.[8]

Organizational changes are often divided into incremental or evolutionary changes, and those that are more radical or revolutionary in nature. Incremental changes normally refer to changes that are continuous, take place in small steps and often affect only a small part of the organization. In contrast, radical changes often entail rule-breaking, large-scale changes that happen in a short period of time and often redefine some significant aspects of the organization. Transformation is often related to radical changes and it usually affects the entire organization. However, transformation is not an on–off event and it does not necessarily happen in sudden bursts. According to Farhooman, transformation is usually accompanied by a series of continuous progressions that involve putting in place fundamental technologies, creating new structures and processes, developing new products and services or creating entirely new markets for the organization.[9] Sometimes, the term organizational innovation is used to illustrate the radical nature of the organizational changes.[10] Many such changes are underpinned, facilitated, enabled by, or simply intimately related to ICTs.

Business computing and organizational transformation

The evolution of computing in a business context has been well documented, and it has often been divided into several different eras.[11] Back in the late 1950s, mainframe computers were introduced into a few large companies. These computers were very expensive, with low levels of accessibility, reliability, capacity and versatility. The focus was on automating a number of information-intensive tasks, particularly those of a clerical, repetitive nature. There was a strong demand for networking technologies to share the expensive equipment and software over space and time in order to achieve scale economy. In the case of large, multinational firms this was particularly facilitated by the demand for more effective means of coordination and control as their activities increasingly spread over space.

From the 1960s this demand pull was gradually met by rapid technological developments, and the volume of data transmission expanded rapidly and continuously. The introduction of microelectronics greatly improved memory capacity, reliability and, above all, reduced costs for using computers; the introduction of computer peripherals and terminals led to greater accessibility; the combination of telecommunications and computers made the remote use of mainframe computers possible; the replacement of electro-mechanical switching with electronic exchanges meant that the telephone network could be used to transmit electronic data; and further technological development in transmission technologies significantly increased telecommunication capacity so as to cope with the growing demand for rapid data exchange over long distances.

From the mid-1970s, minicomputers became increasingly affordable, supported by user-friendly software, which marked the beginning of end-user computing. By the end of the 1970s and early 1980s microcomputers began to appear on the market, advancing towards modern-day personal computers (PCs) in the 1980s. During this period, corporate computer networks with distributed processing were implemented in a wide variety of organizations, which accelerated considerably from the mid-1980s with the introduction of the so-called client–server architectures. The volume of data transmission expanded rapidly and continuously throughout the 1980s and 1990s, and the trend has been projected to continue in the foreseeable future. A flow of incremental innovations, such as packet switching, timesharing, distributed networking and tele-software, has served to reduce the costs of using large-scale computers dramatically. The increasingly powerful and 'intelligent' terminals mean that complex tasks can be carried out collectively and/or independently over space. The rapid development of the Internet and grid computing are opening up many new possibilities and dimensions, as are mobile communications and hand-held devices. The worldwide ICT infrastructures are enabling a large number of organizations and individuals to have remote access to large-scale computers with enormous capability at low costs. The combinations of these developments are resulting in radical changes in the way that information is collected, processed, presented, transmitted, stored, retrieved, used and traded.

The application of ICTs also expanded rapidly from their original use in rapid calculation to a wide range of tasks in which the capture, processing, storage and retrieval of data cover almost every aspect of their operations. In particular, corporate networks provided large organizations with new capacity in the control and coordination of various flows and activities by transcending the limitations of space and time for the transmission of information. Such new capabilities are leading to the development of powerful innovations in production, organization, transaction and management in a wide variety of organizations.

However, until the rapid commercial application of the Internet and related technologies from the mid-1990s onwards, most ICT-based innovations were integral to particular institutional structures and these innovations could not be divorced from the particular institutions in which they were embedded. Private 'corporate networks' played a vital role in linking up technological developments with organizational innovations. This situation was to change in the e-Business era begun in the mid-1990s, although the critical role of (virtual) private computer networks (even though they increasingly use public networks and facilities) remains fundamental to many strategic and organizational innovations.

The Internet opened up new possibilities for transforming activities and relationships within, between and amongst organizations. The origin of the Internet could go back to 1969 when the US government funded ARPnet, a network of high-speed links between supercomputers in research and educational sites primarily in the USA. However, it was when large commercial Internet Service Providers (ISPs) assumed responsibility for the Internet backbone in the mid-1990s that the surge in Internet usage and commercial applications began. Different from corporate networks which are largely proprietary in nature and private in their usage, a large part of the Internet is an open, public communications infrastructure, and it enables organizations to develop the capabilities needed to improve the flows of information and business intelligence amongst all their stakeholders. A company can now exchange information with any customer, supplier or business partner without the need to establish and maintain costly proprietary networks. In particular, with the rapid reduction in costs, the Internet is increasingly becoming a public infrastructure and even small and medium-sized enterprises (SMEs) and individuals have increasing access to the vast resources and capabilities embedded in it.

The boom and burst of the Internet bubble

The evolution of e-Business since the mid-1990s has been well documented. Jelassi and Enders used the theory by Carlota Perez on technological revolution to analyse the evolution of e-Business.[12] They found that the evolution of e-Business followed a similar cycle to other technological revolutions in the past.

Perez defined a technological revolution as a 'powerful and highly visible cluster of new and dynamic technologies, products and industries, capable of bringing about an upheaval in the whole fabric of the economy and of propelling a long-term upsurge of development' (p. 8).[13] A technological revolution can be divided into two consecutive periods – the installation period and the deployment period, which are further divided into five stages: irruption, frenzy, crash, synergy and maturity. Jelassi and Enders used this framework to analyse the evolution of e-Business. Using data from Nasdaq and many real-life examples, Jelassi and Enders classified the evolution of e-Business into four periods, which correspond to the first four stages of Perez's model of other technological revolutions.

The first period was before the widespread commercial use of the Internet, which Jelassi and Enders called the grassroots of e-Business. In fact, the commercial application of EDI (electronic data interchange) in some sectors, as well as several other similar technologies and services, such as Minitel in France, could go back several decades, and long preceded the commercial application of the Internet. There were many well-documented examples of innovative applications,[14] but between 1983 and 1993 the Nasdaq barely doubled from 350 to 700. This period corresponds to Perez's irruption period.

The rise of the Internet, the second period, started in 1995 with the launch of Amazon.com, which corresponded to the frenzy period in Perez's technological revolution model. This period was characterized by great exuberance and belief in the seemingly unlimited potential of the Internet. The fundamental belief was that the Internet would increase value creation significantly by lowering costs and increasing customer benefits simultaneously, leading to a rapid expansion of market volume. Between 1995 and the dot.com crash in March 2000, investors and managers artificially inflated the market size for dot.com companies and overlooked many important issues that led to the subsequent dot.com crash.[15] The Nasdaq rose sharply from under 1,000 in 1995 to well over 4,500 in March 2000! At the peak of this period, the P/E (price/earnings) ratio on Nasdaq reached an incredible 62, compared with the fact that between 1973 and 1995 the P/E ratio never exceeded 21.[16] Also, during the dot.com boom, the profitability and economic viability of companies and their business models did not seem to matter. Instead, metrics such as the click-through rate or the number of unique visitors to a website were the main determinants for stock market success and media coverage. Many companies ignored business fundamentals in pursuit of rapid growth and market share, which ultimately resulted in the spectacular dot.com crash in 2000 and 2001.

Between 10 March and 14 April 2000, the crash period, the Nasdaq dropped a staggering 1,727 points (34 per cent), and by the end of 2000 it had fallen 45 per cent. This market crash was not unexpected, but the frenzy prior to the crash and a series of other conditions meant that the momentum continued until it became unsustainable. In fact, during the Internet boom, many investors did not necessarily believe in the future of the start-ups they funded. Yet they hoped that as long as the stock market kept going up and people kept buying Internet stocks, they could always sell the stock to someone else at an even higher price – known as the 'Greater Fool Theory'. Such perverted incentives contributed significantly to the build-up of the Internet bubble which eventually burst.

The fourth period, the consolidation phase, began in late 2000 following the bursting of the Internet bubble. All key stakeholders, including investors, entrepreneurs and managers as well as the media, were forced to reflect on the harsh reality and the reasons behind so many spectacular failures of Internet ventures, and why many of the anticipated benefits failed to materialize. A return to business fundamentals ensued and critical issues such as cost, efficiency, revenue generation and business models, as well as customer retention and, most of all, profit, were addressed. Since 2002 and 2003, many of the survivors of the dot.com crash have turned profitable and the stock market has started to recover steadily. The emphasis is no longer on technological innovation but instead on how to make the technology easy to use, reliable, secure and cost efficient. This phase is still continuing today.

The duration and scale of the Internet bubble

Given the profound impact of the Internet bubble on the evolution of the Internet and its applications, it is necessary to examine it in more detail. The Nasdaq Composite index exploded in the late 1990s, more than doubling in value in the year up to the early 2000 peak, followed by a spectacular crash from March 2000 to September 2002 as the index lost three-quarters of its value. Interestingly, recovery during the aftermath of the crash was remarkably fast, and productivity growth recovered very rapidly to its previous levels faster than even the most optimal forecasts.

In a comment by Brad Delong, a professor of economics at the University of California, Berkeley, and Konstanin Magin, post-doctoral fellow at the Center of Integrated Nanomechanical Systems, published on 19 April 2005 in the *Financial Times*, it was revealed how surprisingly short the stock market bubble actually was.[17] Their calculations showed that when Netscape launched its IPO (initial public offering) in 1995, the stock market was not in a bubble, because those who invested in the Nasdaq in March 1995 and then shadowed the index would have earned real returns averaging 9.3 per cent per year by early 2005; and those who invested in the Nasdaq in September 1995 (the month after Netscape's IPO) would have earned 7.3 per cent annually. Compare this with the average 8.8 per cent real return on the Nasdaq since the start of the 1970s, there is no evidence that the market in 1995 was significantly overvalued. Their calculations also revealed that by the end of 1996 when Alan Greenspan, Chairman of the US Federal Reserve, warned that 'irrational exuberance has unduly escalated asset values', the market was in fact still rational. Investing in the Nasdaq then would have produced a real return of 8.1 per cent per year in early 2005.

The beginning of the Internet bubble is difficult to pinpoint because, since 2000, the Nasdaq has been hit by two major developments. One was the 11 September 2001 terrorist attack on the USA, and the other was the increasing realization that it is extremely difficult to translate technological excellence in ICTs into durable profits. The main beneficiaries of innovations in ICTs have been business users, such as Wal-Mart and its shareholders and customers, rather than the workers, entrepreneurs and financiers of Silicon Valley.

To pinpoint the beginning of the Internet bubble, they used four separate measures. The first benchmark was the long-run historic average of 6.5 per cent per year, and for the Nasdaq to be in a bubble, returns from the start of that bubble period would need to be less than the 6.5 per cent per year. Cumulative real returns on the Nasdaq only lagged behind 6.5 per cent per year since April 1997: the bubble lasted for less than three years before the Nasdaq peaked. The second benchmark states that a bubble can be defined as a period during which real returns do not match the 3 per cent per year expected from investment in bonds. The realized Nasdaq real return only dropped below 3 per cent per year in October 1998. The third and most stringent yardstick would define a bubble as a period in which returns are negative. This only happened in November 1998. According to these two benchmarks, the bubble was remarkably short: the Nasdaq was overvalued for less than a year and a half before its peak in March 2000. They also used Fischer Black's definition that a large bubble is when assets are twice their fundamental values or more: the Nasdaq bubble became a large one only in September 1999, less than half a year before its peak.

Based on such analysis, they concluded that market valuations were remarkably close to the fundamental values of the underlying assets. Despite rapid technological change with very uncertain long-term consequences and the fact that humans are prone to irrational exuberance, the stock market kept doing a good job of feeding the real economy an appropriate shadow value of capital, and did not succumb to irrationality until 1997 or 1998. 'Financial markets were not as dumb as we feared then, and so are probably not as dumb as we fear now.' However, they did concede that the short duration of the Internet bubble did not mean small magnitude: people who invested during the peak of the bubble at the end of February 2000 would still not have recouped even 50 per cent of their investment by early 2005.

Other issues

Before moving to the next section, several points need to be emphasized here. The first is that the evolution of e-Business is much more than the rise and fall of Internet start-ups, despite the intense media focus on them. E-business is perhaps more importantly about using the Internet and related technologies to transform established businesses large and small, enabling them to conduct business and manage internal activities and processes and external relations in ways superior to, and often impossible, in the past. In fact, during the consolidation period after the dot.com market crash, many of the successful firms were not Internet start-ups but instead established incumbents.

Secondly, as has been discussed in the Preface, the dot.com bust did not mark the end of e-Business. The underlying rapid growth of the network society and economy, in terms of the number of people and organizations getting online and the business volume of e-Commerce, has continued even during economic downturns. The Internet has become an increasingly important part of consumers' everyday lives – shopping, banking, amusement and education. Furthermore, the Internet has become part of mainstream business culture, fulfilling its promise as a medium that can connect consumers and organizations and cut red tape from transactions. This is not limited to the private sector, and developments in the public sector have been particularly fast since the dot.com crash. The debate on pure-plays (Internet-only companies) versus multi-channel organizations remains unresolved, but today websites are necessary for almost any business – even if the online arm loses money. In fact, the return to business fundamentals after the dot.com crash has produced visible and significant results both in the surviving dot.com companies and in established private and public sector organizations across regions, sectors and organizational sizes. Many organizations are leveraging the potential of the Internet to deliver significant value to their customers and at the same time being highly profitable. The stock market valuation of some successful Internet ventures has already recovered to levels during the Internet boom years. Perhaps it is indeed not the end, but just the beginning of a golden age.

E-Business Classifications

E-business can be classified into many different categories, but the most commonly used classification is by the nature of transactions or relationships amongst participants. As the areas of application extend to new sectors and new activities, and as the underpinning technologies continue to develop rapidly, new categories are being invented – many of which are subgroups within the main categories.

Business to Business (B2B): E-business activities between two or more organizations. These organizations can be from both the private and public sectors, but more recently, as the application of Internet technologies gather momentum in public services (which are referred to as e-Government and e-Public Services), B2B is increasingly used to refer to activities between business organizations. Despite rapid developments in other e-Business activities, B2B still makes up the lion's share of the total e-Business volume today.

Business to Consumer (B2C): As the name indicates, this is primarily about retail e-Commerce between individual consumers and businesses. Similar to B2B where the organization could be in either the private or the public sector, today it refers particularly to commercial transactions between a consumer and a private sector organization.

A sub-category of this category is the so-called *C2B (Consumer to Business)*. Examples include an individual selling products or services to organizations; or individuals who seek sellers to bid on products or services they need. One example in this category is Priceline.com, also known as Reverse Auction.

Consumer to Consumer (C2C): This category refers to situations where consumers sell directly to other consumers via the Internet. The most prominent example of this is eBay, the auction site, but this category also includes other e-Business activities such as individuals selling houses, cars and other items via online advertisements. Strictly speaking, this category should be referred to as *C2B2C* because the transactions between individuals are often facilitated or enabled by a business in the middle.

Also related to this category are the so-called *Peer to Peer (P2P)* applications. This category started with online music swapping (Napster.com) but the technology is also increasingly used in B2B and B2C applications. Usually P2P focuses on free transactions between individuals, whereas C2C focuses on commercial transactions.

Intra-organizational e-Business: this category includes all internal activities and processes that are enabled by Internet technologies. Many intra-organizational e-Business activities are conducted on a corporate intranet or via corporate portals.

With the rapid development of e-Government and e-Public Services (many public services are increasingly provided by private sector organizations in countries such as the UK), several other categories of e-Business are also worth mentioning. Key categories include the following.

Government to Business (G2B): E-Business activities between government agencies or departments and business organizations, which include a government entity buying products or services from private sector organizations, or providing or receiving information to/from them.

Government to Citizens (G2C): Electronic communications and information exchanges between government agencies and individuals or citizens. This could involve commercial transactions (such as paying for council tax, or parking fines), or other communications or information exchanges.

Also in this arena is *Citizens to Citizens (C2C)*, whereby citizens communicate with one another directly to exchange information or address issues of common concern.

There are many other categories – such as Internet-enabled activities between and amongst other non-business institutions and individuals. Examples include academic institutions, not-for-profit organizations, religious organizations, hospitals, charities and other social organizations. Such organizations increasingly use Internet technologies to reduce costs and improve efficiency, information provision and quality of services. The terms used to describe such activities include *e-Learning* or *e-Education*, *e-Health*, *non-business e-Business or e-Commerce* and so on. There are also many other common terms to describe e-Business activities in particular domains or sectors, such as *e-Tailing*, *e-Music*, *e-Banking (Internet banking)*, *e-Books*, *e-Publishing*, *e-Library* and so on. Most such terms are self-explanatory. Many other e-Business and e-Commerce textbooks provide detailed explanation of such concepts.

The Context for E-Business: Why E-Business? Why Now?

Many factors have led to the rapid development of e-Business, but some fundamental changes in the business environment make up the key context for e-Business. As has been discussed briefly in chapter 1 of this book, the changing nature of the economy, combined with the rapid development and proliferation of Internet and related technologies in particular and ICTs in general, are perhaps the most significant. Other changes such as government initiatives and targets have also fuelled the development.

The nature of the context for e-Business is a complex one, and people's views have evolved considerably over the years. The advent of the new economy was first noticed as far back as 1962 when Machlup published his seminal book on the knowledge element of the US economy,[18] but when Peter Drucker perceived the arrival of knowledge workers in 1969, interest in the phenomenon increased significantly. The new economy is often referred to as the Information Economy, because of information's superior role (rather than material resources or capital) in creating wealth.

However, in his article 'New rules for the new economy', published in *Wired Magazine* in 1997, Kevin Kelly explained why he preferred the term Network Economy, because *information* is not enough to explain the discontinuities we see:

> We have been awash in a steadily increasing tide of information for the past century. Many successful knowledge businesses have been built on information capital, but only recently has a total reconfiguration of information itself shifted the whole economy . . . The grand irony of our times is that the era of computers is over. All the major consequences of stand-alone computers have already taken place. Computers have speeded up our lives a bit, and that's it . . . In contrast, all the most promising technologies making their debut now are chiefly due to communication between computers – that is, to connections rather than to computations. And since communication is the basis of culture, fiddling at this level is indeed momentous.[19]

This view was echoed in 2002 by Peter Drucker when the profound impact of the Internet Revolution was felt. He argued that this impact was not fuelled by information or artificial intelligence, nor by the effects of computers and data processing on decision making, policy making or strategy. It was the explosive emergence of the Internet as a major worldwide distribution channel for goods, services and information that was profoundly changing economics, markets, industry structure, products and services, work flows, consumer segmentation, value and behaviour, as well as jobs and labour markets. He went on to say that the impact may be even greater on society and politics, and above all on the way we see the world.[20]

In late 2002 the think-tank GBN (Global Business Network) published an interview with its new member Clay Shirky on the next big phase of the Internet. In the interview, Shirky argued that the essence of the Internet and early generations of software innovations like e-mail was that they allowed groups to work together more effectively. It was not just another one-to-many broadcast medium like television or a one-to-one medium like the telephone. It did both those things *and also* allowed for many-to-many communications – something that could never be done before outside of physical gatherings: 'The Internet was the first new tool to help convene group conversations since the invention of the table.' Shirky believed that this ability to hold groups together and make them work effectively across distance holds one of the keys to the power of the Internet in the coming years.

This is one of the main reasons why in this book the phrase information and communications technologies (ICTs) – rather than information technology (IT) – is used to emphasize the critical importance of not only information but also the communication and distribution of information over space and time.[21] The transition to the knowledge-based, information economy is a basic condition for many of the profound changes enabled by the Internet technologies to materialize. It is the changing nature of the economy, characterized by the growing proportion of information content in our products, services and production processes, and the growing proportion of information labour in the total make-up of our workforce, that has made information, as opposed to material inputs, the most important resource of our economy. The need for accurate, up-to-date, relevant information has created an enormous demand pull for new technologies as well as new techniques to manage and deploy the most important resource of the economy (i.e. information) efficiently – when and where it is required, in the form it is required. This is not only true in the developed economies, but also increasingly in many developing economies.

This demand pull has increasingly been met by rapid technological development in ICTs, and most of all, by the Internet Revolution. Computing processing power and telecommunication transmission capacity have both been growing extremely rapidly in the past few decades, but the most critical technological innovation remains the convergence between computers and telecommunications, which enables computers to exchange information with other computers at the global scale, and people to exchange information with computers over distance as part of their job-related activities. What is especially important about the Internet is that it is based on an open standard, and is very quickly becoming a public infrastructure accessible by, and increasingly affordable to, all.

The information and communication capabilities afforded to us by the Internet technologies, in a context where information – not physical materials – is key to economic and business success, have unleashed the potential for unprecedented new economic, social, political and individual developments. The extension of the technological convergence between computers and telecommunications to areas such as the media has kick-started – and perhaps legitimated – the beginning of the integration of these two great forces: a trend to combine the capabilities of Internet technologies with the content (which happens to be the most important resource in the new economy) that the technologies are developed to deal with. Regulations (more precisely – deregulation) and policies played a key part in this process, enabling the convergence of different industries. Government initiatives and targets in various areas – such as in the UK, where 100 per cent of government services that can be provided online must become available online by 2005 – have also facilitated the rapid development of e-Business infrastructure, activities and services, and huge improvements in the e-Business environment. Regional development agencies (RDAs) and other government departments also provided essential support for UK businesses to get online and actively promoted awareness and the proliferation of best practices in various areas.

This still leave the question of 'why now'? As with many other technological revolutions, it takes time for the technology to proliferate and become widely accessible and affordable. More importantly, it is not sufficient just to have the appropriate technology in place. Managers and workers need to be willing and able to abandon previous ways of doing things and start using the new technology in such a way that it actually creates value. This takes time and requires a lot of experimenting and fine-tuning. Only when the development has reached a critical point can the revolutionary effects be widely felt.

The widespread proliferation of networking technologies only started to gather momentum in the 1980s with the development of distributed computing. However, before the advent of the Internet technologies, most computer networks were proprietary in nature and were expensive to develop and maintain – and most of all they were private networks integral to particular organizations. This remains the case today but, since the 1990s, the Internet has increasingly become a mass public infrastructure accessible and affordable to a rapidly growing proportion of organizations and individuals.

To explain this point, let us consider the example of boiling a kettle of water. The boiling point for water is 100 °C. Before the water temperature reaches that point, the water in the kettle is relatively calm despite louder and louder noises. However, as soon as the temperature reaches 100 °C, big bubbles begin to erupt out of the water surface. This critical point is reached through a gradual accumulation of heat in the water, but the major effect is only clearly visible when the critical point is reached. This analogy perhaps can explain the gradual growth of the information content in our economy and labour composition, and the gradual proliferation of ICTs in general and Internet technologies in particular, accumulating to a critical point to unleash the enormous potential of the Internet Revolution.

This perhaps can also explain why, more than 50 years since computers began to be used in business, computerization had so little effect on industrial productivity for four decades and then, in the mid-1990s, it suddenly seemed to become the driving force behind a sharp acceleration in the productivity of the US economy (although this was not reflected in most European economies or Japan).[22] It perhaps can also explain why the recent productivity gains have been unevenly distributed across industries and regions. The e-Business phenomenon is perhaps the manifestation of the Internet Revolution which marked the eventual arrival of the networked information economy.

The implications are profound. Today, all industries have become information intensive as measured by the critical importance of information in production and distribution. Accurate and adequate information has become crucial to the success of all industrial and commercial activities, and to the effective provision of public services and the efficient management of public sector organizations; in other words, a critical strategic resource in all sectors of the economy. The Internet technologies enable us to capture, store, search, manipulate, communicate and retrieve information in ways not possible or even imaginable in the past. This not only provides rapidly growing demand for products and services from the information and ICT industries, but also enables organizations and individuals to do many things in ways impossible in the past, with profound implications for what activities are located where, how territories are administered, markets served, and linkages maintained between customers and suppliers. Such a new capacity is increasingly reflected in the emerging strategies, business models and organizational designs in both the private and public sectors.

Implications of E-Business: Emerging Strategies, Business Models and Organizational Designs

The nature of the economy has changed, as measured by the informational (intangible) elements of our products and services and production processes, and the proportion of the workforce whose primary activities are informational rather than physical. Information has become the most important strategic resource upon which the efficiency and competitiveness of all organizations depend. In the meantime, the Internet Revolution continues to gather pace, providing us with increasingly powerful, versatile and affordable tools whose sole purpose of existence is to deal with 'information' – to capture, store and retrieve, manipulate and communicate information. This combination is extremely powerful, because we have increasingly powerful tools to deal with the most important resource of the economy, often in ways impossible in the past. Organizations large and small today can, should and, indeed, must do things differently in order to survive in the new economy.

This gives rise to the need for a new generation of organization and management theories. These theories should be embedded in the new economics of information and should explicitly exploit the unique capabilities of ICTs. At the centre of such studies should be the continuous search for strategic and organizational innovations, including new visions and strategies, new business models, new organizational designs, new ways of working and new inter-organizational relations that are intimately supported by ICTs in general and Internet and related technologies in particular. These issues will be addressed in detail in this book.

We have already seen some radical changes in the past few years, and there is also a significant element of continuity from the past. ICTs have changed the way organizations carry out many important activities, but it remains debatable whether these changes have led to any fundamental alterations to the essential form or size of corporate organizations. ICTs have delivered great benefits to some firms and public sector organizations, even propelling a few companies into industry leadership, but for many other businesses and organizations, ICTs and the associated organizational transformation have been a main source of frustration and disappointment. ICTs have allowed many companies to cut labour costs and working capital substantially, but ICTs themselves have become the largest of all capital expenditure and an intrinsic element of almost all critical business processes, often without clear, measurable returns on such investments. In fact, many such investments continue to be made without a clear conceptual understanding of the ultimate strategic or financial impact. Furthermore, even when ICTs have made organizations more efficient and competitive, they have also made them more vulnerable because of their dependency on such technologies, without which they simply could not function. Despite more than 50 years having passed since computers began to be used in business (and over a century for the telephone), there remains much that we do not know about their influence on organizations and on our economy and society. This book will address some of these issues and provide a conceptual framework for understanding and evaluating them.

Discussion Questions

1   Illustrate the dot.com boom and bust since the mid-1990s. What are the main causes for the dot.com boom and bust? What lessons can be learnt by business executives? Support your views with evidence and explanations.

2   What is e-Business? Study the definitions of e-Business in five different textbooks, and compare and contrast their similarities and differences. Discuss some of the potential problems associated with the main differences among these definitions.

3   It has been argued that ICTs in general and the Internet in particular are having pervasive impacts on people's lives. In what ways have the technologies affected your own life over the past five years? Ten years? What are the possible implications for businesses and government agencies that provide products and services to you?

Assignment: Essay

In your own words, write a 1,000-word essay clearly explaining what e-Business is, illustrating its main categories, and explaining in what ways it is relevant to today's organizations.

NOTES

1   LeClaire, Jennifer (2005) Online retailers learned valuable E-Lessons in 2004, *E-Commerce Times* 01/24/05. http://www.ecommercetimes.com/story/39785.html [accessed 26 January 2005].

2   Jelassi, Tawfik and Albrecht Enders (2005) *Strategies for E-Business: Creating value through electronic and mobile commerce.* Pearson Education Ltd, Harlow.

3   Chaffey, David (2002) *E-Business and E-Commerce Management*. Pearson Education Ltd, Harlow.

4   Turban, Efraim, David King, Jae Lee and Dennis Viehland (2004) *Electronic Commerce: A managerial perspective 2004*. Pearson Prentice Hall, New Jersey.

5   Laudon, Kenneth C. and Carol Guercio Traver (2003) *E-Commerce: Business, technology and society*. 2nd edn. Pearson Addison Wesley, Boston.

6   Goddard, John (1975) *Office Location and Urban and Regional Development*. Oxford University Press, London.

7   Hepworth, Mark (1989) *Geography of the Information Economy*, Belhaven, London; Li, Feng (1995) *The Geography of Business Information: Corporate networks and the spatial and functional corporate restructuring*, John Wiley & Son, Chichester.

8   Yates, JoAnne and John Van Maanen (2001, eds) *Information Technology and Organizational Transformation: History, rhetoric, and practice*. Sage, Thousand Oakes, CA.

9   Farhoomand, Ali (2005) *Managing (e)Business Transformation: A global perspective*. Palgrave Macmillan, Basingstoke.

10 Li, Feng (1997) From compromise to harmony: organizational innovations through information systems. *International Journal of Information Management*, 17(6), 451–464 .

11 Li (1995) op. cit.

12 Jelassi and Enders (2005) op. cit.

13 Perez, C. (2002) *Technological Revolution and Financial Capital: The dynamics of bubbles and golden ages*. Edward Elgar, Cheltenham.

14 Li, Feng and H. Williams (1999) Inter-firm collaboration through inter-firm networks. *Information Systems Journal*, 9(2), 103–117.

15 Although the stock market peaked in March 2000 and industrial production began to decline in September 2000, the National Bureau of Economic Research, which officially dates business cycle turns, set the start of the recession at March 2001. Please see *The Economist*, 8 December 2001. Also see Adams, F. Gerard (2004) *The E-Business Revolution & the New Economy: E-Conomics after the dot.com crash*. Thomson (South-Western), Mason, Ohio.

16 Jelassi and Enders (2005) op. cit.

17 Delong, Brad and Konstantin Magin (2005) Comment: The last bubble was brief, but it was still irrational. *Financial Times*, 19 April, p. 19.

18 Machlup, F. (1962) *The Production and Distribution of Knowledge in the United States*. Princeton University Press, Princeton, NJ.

19 Kelly, Kevin (1997) 'New rules for the new economy'. *Wired Magazine*, Issue 5.09, September. http://www.wired.com/wired/archive/5.09/newrules.html.

20 Drucker, Peter (2002) *Managing in the Next Society*. Truman Talley Books, New York.

21 Today, IT and ICTs are often used interchangeably in the literature to refer to computers and their telecommunications networks. This is limited not only to the hardware and software, but also to the human activities and management systems deployed to regulate their development and use. Generally speaking, European researchers and policy makers prefer to use the term ICTs instead of IT, but in the USA and many other countries, IT instead of ICTs is often used to refer to the same notion. In this book these two terms are used interchangeably.

22 Adams, F. Gerard (2004) op. cit.

FURTHER READING

Chaffey, David (2002) *E-Business and E-Commerce Management*. Pearson Education Ltd, Harlow.

Farhoomand, Ali (2005) *Managing (e)Business Transformation: A global perspective*. Palgrave Macmillan, Basingstoke.

Jelassi, Tawfik and Albrecht Enders (2005) *Strategies for E-Business: Creating value through electronic and mobile commerce*. Pearson Education Ltd, Harlow.

Laudon, Kenneth C. and Carol Guercio Traver (2003) *E-Commerce: Business, technology and society*, 2nd edn. Pearson Addison Wesley, Boston.

Turban, Efraim, David King, Jae Lee and Dennis Viehland (2004) *Electronic Commerce: A managerial perspective 2004*. Pearson Prentice Hall, New Jersey.

Part I

The New E-Business Environment

Introduction

In order to make sense of the e-phenomenon and understand the interplays between ICTs and changes at different levels of organizations, first of all we need to examine the nature and characteristics of the business environment. Has the business environment changed? In what ways? What evidence do we have of such changes? Are they radical, revolutionary, step changes, or simply gradual evolutions from the past? What are the implications of these changes for organizations and individuals? Answers to these questions will provide the essential context for e-Business. These issues are addressed in this part of the book.

There are three chapters in this part. In chapter 3, comprehensive evidence on the changing business environment will be explored. The reasons for and against the proclaimed transition from the industrial to the information economy, and key developments in ICTs in general and Internet and related technologies in particular, will be critically examined. Available evidence suggests that some of the changes in the business environment are revolutionary in nature, and in fact some basic rules of the economy have been redefined. Chapter 4 will discuss some of the changing rules and the implications for organizations and individuals. In chapter 5, the theory of transaction cost economics will be used to illustrate why and how Internet technologies could affect organizational boundaries and industrial and organizational structures. The profound implications of the changing business environment for contemporary organizations will be highlighted.

Chapter 3

The 'ICT Revolution' and the Information Economy

E-Business has developed in the context of a rapidly changing business environment. The business environment has always been evolving – sometimes slowly but at other times more rapidly. For many years we have been talking about new global political and economic orders; demographic changes in various countries; rapidly improving educational attainments of the general population; the development and opening up of new markets; global and regional economic integration as well as localization of production; lowering of trade barriers both regionally and globally; European integration and enlargement; growing environmental concerns; shifting political ideologies and growing pressure on public sectors to be more efficient, to improve quality of services and meet targets, and to demonstrate value for money; deregulation; rapid technological developments, especially in ICTs but also in other areas such as life sciences, new materials and nanotechnologies; and more recently, terrorist attacks and war on terrorism; and corporate governance as well as corporate social responsibilities and business ethics after the WorldCom and Enron scandals. The rapid development of China and India – as the 'factory of the world', and the 'call centre' and 'software coding centre' of the world, respectively – have also posed new opportunities and challenges for businesses from all over the world. The list can go on, and new factors are continually being added to this list.

Despite different interpretations of these factors and their implications for businesses and various economies, from a business perspective it is generally agreed that some of these factors are driving forces, whilst others are merely facilitating or inhibiting factors. Two changes that have been repeatedly singled out for their profound roles in the current transformation are the changing nature of the economy and the rapid development and proliferation of ICTs, even though different terminologies have often been used to illustrate them. There is no doubt that ICTs in general and the Internet in particular are facilitating profound changes in the structures and operations of businesses, but the debate continues on whether we are now indeed living in a *new* economy. The ICT Revolution, like the Industrial Revolutions of the 18th and 19th centuries, promises to transform the economy and society, but some people believe that ICTs have changed barely anything – especially after the Internet bubble was deflated in 2000–1. Using evidence both for and against such claims, this chapter highlights some of the critical issues in these two broad areas, which provide the essential context for e-Business.

The 'ICT Revolution': Convergence between Computing and Telecommunications

One of the key driving forces in the business environment is the continuous rapid development and proliferation of ICTs. Although computers have been used in business since 1951 when British catering firm J. Lyons & Company built and installed a mainframe computer in its head office, it was originally used only for routine activities such as processing payrolls or performing rapid calculations. The reprogrammable microprocessor invented by Intel engineer Ted Hoff in 1969 began to unleash the full potential of computers, 'allowing the computers to be used by all sorts of people to do all sorts of things in all sorts of companies' (p. 2).[1] Today, ICTs have pervaded virtually all forms of human endeavour – work, education and leisure, communication, production, distribution and marketing. The story of how computers and their networks evolved and how they were used to reshape our society and economy has been told in a vast range of books, reports, articles and TV programmes, reflecting the full range of views from naive optimism to unmitigated pessimism.

Nicholas Carr gave a detailed chronicle account of critical technological advances in ICTs in his book *Does IT Matter?* After the invention of the microprocessor in 1969, Bob Metcalfe created Ethernet in 1973 which provided the basis for local area networks (LANs). Mass-produced personal computers appeared in 1975, and since then a whole range of desktop computing programs have been developed – including word processing, spreadsheet and so on. In 1982, the introduction of TCP/IP networking protocols paved the way for the modern Internet. The Apple Macintosh, launched in 1984, provided an easy-to-use graphical user interface. E-mail over the Internet began in 1989, followed by the explosive growth of the Internet and World Wide Web in the 1990s. Corporate websites and Intranets were developed, and commercial transactions are increasingly conducted online. Sophisticated software has been developed to manage both internal and external activities. Nicholas Carr concluded that over the past forty years ICTs have been the major force shaping businesses, and ICTs have become the backbones of commerce at least in the developed world. A brief discussion of the evolution of ICTs and e-Business was given in chapter 2 of this book. The ICT Revolution has been underpinned by several closely interrelated developments. Some of the major developments are discussed here.

Network connectivity

At the heart of the ICT Revolution is network connectivity.[2] The critical technological innovation, the convergence of the *within*-workplace technology of computing with the *between*-workplaces technology of telecommunications, enables computers to communicate with other computers over space, and people to communicate with computers over space as part of their work-based activities. By providing the means of acquiring vital information, analysing and transmitting it over space at a speed and volume never before possible, ICTs are challenging the existing production processes and organizational structures – leading to new forms of organizations and new ways of working.[3]

With the rapid development and proliferation of Internet infrastructure and technologies, the network has increasingly become the market in which transactions take place. The connections between computers at different levels of the supply chain and between businesses and consumers have bypassed many steps that previously required human intervention and paperwork. These new opportunities for efficiency have important implications for how business is organized and conducted. In some fields, the result has been spectacular. In others we are only beginning to witness radical transformations, and there is room for significant improvements across the entire economy and society.[4] The transformation is not limited to the private sector alone, and the Internet is also fundamentally transforming the public sector and the provision of public services, and indeed, the way we live.

Moore's Law and Gilder's Law: exploding capacity and shrinking price

Another critical development underpinning the ICT Revolution is the rapid and continuous cost reduction in the use of computers and telecommunications, as a result of rapid increases in their processing power and transmission capacity. In 1965, Gordon Moore, a founder of Intel, famously predicted that the number of transistors embedded in a chip is likely to double every 18–24 months. Although his forecast was slower than what has actually been happening, this has been widely known as 'Moore's Law'. Experts predict that there is potential for this trend to continue for another ten to twenty years. Beyond that, when we have reached the physical limit of the current technologies, new developments and technological breakthroughs in nanotechnologies, bio-computing and quantum computing may lead to even faster growth in computing processing power.[5] Closely related to the rapid doubling of processing power in microprocessors is the halving of its price. Since the 1970s microprocessor chips have been halving in price, or doubling in power, every 18 months; and the trend is still continuing today!

What has been less well known is the so-called 'Gilder's Law' – a similar trend that has been taking place in telecommunications. George Gilder forecasted that for the foreseeable future the total bandwidth of telecommunication systems will triple every 12 months – much faster than the breathtaking speed at which microprocessors have developed. The rapid increase in capacity and reduction in price in computing and telecommunications have resulted in what is sometimes known as 'inverted pricing', i.e. rather than paying a premium for improved performance, people expect to pay less, or the same amount, for more powerful computers and faster and higher quality telecommunications over time. This is extremely important because the exponential developments have resulted in rapid reduction in prices for using computing and telecommunications, making it increasingly affordable by every organization and individual. There has already been talk of computing processing power and telecommunications bandwidth becoming 'free' – in terms of cost per unit data processed and transmitted diving towards zero.[6] Without this trend the explosive growth of the Internet since the 1990s would not have been possible.

This trend has led to several other important developments in recent years. One example is so-called utility computing. A typical organization has hundreds of functions that all use computing power. Utility computing allows an organization to look at all those functions in terms of the total computing power they use, and then buy and use computing power in bulk for the entire company instead of having each department administering its own computing resources. IBM calls it *On Demand Computing*. Hewlett-Packard calls it the *Adaptive Enterprise*. Electronic Data Systems calls it the *Agile Enterprise*. At the simplest level, these buzzwords are all ways to describe a service that technology experts call 'utility computing' or 'virtualization'.[7] Computing processing power is increasingly treated as a utility just like electricity and water, although the embedded applications still vary significantly from organization to organization. This point will be discussed again later.

Heavy investments by private and public sectors

The ICT Revolution is also characterized by heavy and continuous investment in both private and public sector organizations, and rapid development of infrastructure and services. Data from Gartner indicate that today IT represents the largest capital expenditure by American companies. In 1965, less than 5 per cent of the capital expenditure of American companies went into IT. In the 1980s, with the rapid adoption of personal computers, the percentage increased to 15 per cent. By the 1990s it had reached 30 per cent and by the turn of the century the dot.com boom pushed the percentage to over 50 per cent. Even after the bursting of the technology bubble in 2001, the average American company still invests as much in IT as in all other capital expenditure combined. The trend is similar in Europe and the Far East, and even developing countries are catching up fast. Worldwide IT spending by businesses has surpassed US$1 trillion which includes hardware, software and services. If telecommunications services are included the figure increases to over US$2 trillion![8] In the UK, around 90 per cent of businesses have access to the Internet (for businesses with over 50 employees, the figure is almost 100 per cent). This figure has been stable for several years and is unlikely to grow further.[9] Various government initiatives have facilitated this trend.

The investment in the public sector has been equally significant in the past few years. Back in 2000 *The Economist* famously announced that after e-Commerce and e-Business, the next Internet Revolution would be e-Government.[10] The UK government set itself an ambitious target for the provision of public services electronically, that everything that can be online should be online by the end of 2005. It also wanted to make the UK the best place in the world for e-Commerce. Billions of pounds have since been invested in central and local governments, the health services and other public sector organizations in order to achieve the target (£14 billion per year on computer systems and services).[11] Similar initiatives have been launched by governments from all over the world, not only in developed countries but also in an increasing number of developing countries.

Metcalfe's Law: explosive growth of the Internet

The explosive growth of the Internet has been well documented, and the trend has demonstrated the so-called Metcalfe's Law in practice. Robert Metcalfe, a founder of 3Com, once said that the value of a network is proportional to the square of the number of users, so the more people there are on a network, the greater the value of the network to each user. In other words, the experienced utility of belonging to an electronic network increases exponentially with the growing number of users. Furthermore, a small increase in the number of nodes on the network will significantly increase the total value of the network. This means that once the network reaches a critical mass, it becomes irresistible and simply explodes.

The number of websites on the Internet and the number of Internet users has exploded since the mid-1990s. It started off as a North America dominated phenomenon, because a large proportion of the websites and Internet users resided in the USA and Canada. However, the rest of the world soon caught up, and by March 2000, of the 300 million Internet users in the world, over 160 million of them were outside North America, compared to less than 140 million inside North America (table 3.1). The year 2000 is significant not only because of the dot.com crash, but also because for the first time in history the Internet became a global phenomenon. Internet growth has also been faster in Pacific Asia and Europe than in North America. Today, there are well over one billion Internet users in the world, and more and more people from developing countries are joining the Internet. This is especially the case when many users are accessing the Internet via mobile devices (such as the mobile phone or cell phone).

Not only are individuals getting online, but businesses, governments and all other types of organizations are also getting connected to the Internet at astonishing speeds. In most developed countries one can hardly find any organization not connected to the Internet. The issue today is no longer simply getting connected: the dynamics are now around speed (broadband) and type of access (e.g. wireless). The focus is

Table 3.1 Number of people online (in millions)

	Mar-99	Mar-00	Level increase	Percent increase
Africa	1.1	2.6	1.5	136
Asia/Pacific	27.0	68.9	41.9	155
Europe	40.1	83.4	43.3	108
Middle East	0.9	1.9	1.0	111
Canada & USA	97.0	136.9	39.9	41
South America	5.3	10.7	5.4	102

increasingly on smart deployment of the technologies to unlock their full potential and deliver real value to stakeholders.

Several other developments are equally spectacular, and by any measure the technological leaps made in the past few decades have been immense. Just when we think the development is about to mature and slow down, many other new innovations emerge and proliferate at even more astonishing speed. One such development is mobile phones (cell phones), which experienced an even faster rate of growth than the wired Internet. In most developed countries the proportion of people owning a mobile phone has already reached maturity, and many developing countries are catching up fast. In fact, in countries such as China and Thailand, many households have by-passed the stage of owning a landline and mobile phones are often their first phones.

People did not wake up in the seventeenth century one morning and shout that they were in the middle of the Industrial Revolution. It was only with hindsight that people realized that technologies developed extremely rapidly during a relatively short period of time and their widespread application in subsequent years led to radical changes in society and the economy. Today the convergence between telecommunications and computers has been extended to other areas such as the media, and ICTs have penetrated into every corner of our society and economy – including our work, leisure, education and personal lives. We are indeed in the middle of a 'Technological Revolution'. The ICT Revolution has already led to some profound changes, and many more radical changes may yet come. The Internet is particularly important because it is the contemporary platform on which many of the exciting developments are taking place.

The Information Economy

The ICT Revolution would have been far less significant if the nature of the economy had not changed in parallel. Today, information has become the most critical strategic resource upon which the competitiveness and future development of any organization depend.[12] The information content has been growing steadily in almost all products, services and in all the activities and processes involved in the development, production, delivery and even consumption of these products and services – they have all become information intensive as measured in quantitative terms. At the same time information labour represents an increasingly large proportion of the total workforce – at least in, but not limited to, all developed economies. Furthermore, most new value added has been derived from information (intangible) rather than material inputs. It is in this context that the profound potential of ICTs – and the Internet – is being realized.

The origin of the concept and its key characteristics

The concept of the information economy has been used for decades, although until very recently there perhaps was an underlying doubt, unconscious or even deliberate, that it was perhaps not true. Sceptics argued that the critical role of information or knowledge in economic activities was nothing new. Previous technological developments, in the printing press, and in television and radio, significantly increased our ability to store, acquire and disseminate information. What made things different this time round is that the scale and speed of information creation, dissemination and deployment have reached a scale unimaginable before and this ability is still growing exponentially. Many other phrases – network economy, knowledge economy, post-industrial economy, for example – have also been used to illustrate the new economy.

The concept of the information economy is associated primarily with the work of Porat in 1977, but its clear antecedents lie in Bell's model of the post-industrial society in 1973, Peter Drucker's perception of the arrival of knowledge workers in 1969, and Machlup's work on the knowledge base of the US economy in 1962.[13] The emergence of the information economy has been regarded as a key feature of recent development in all developed economies. It is within this context that the ICT Revolution has originated, its processes have taken place, and its impacts have been clearly felt.[14] This development is also profoundly affecting developing economies all over the world.

The growth of the information economy has been defined in relation to several key processes, and it is in these processes that the role of ICTs has been highlighted.[15] Most of these processes are still valid today. First, information is coming to occupy centre stage as the strategic resource for the effective production and delivery of goods and services in all sectors of the economy. Second, this economic transformation is underpinned by the technological convergence of telecommunications and computers, which is transforming the means of information exchange within and between organizations. Third, ICTs are facilitating the growth of the tradable information sector in the economy. Finally, the growing 'informatization' of the economy is making possible the global integration of national and regional economies, and ICTs are being widely used to maximize the benefits to firms and regions in the process of localization and globalization.

The crucial characteristic of the information economy is that information, both as commodity and resource, has become the strategic resource upon which the competitiveness of all firms depends. The information content in all economic activities has been growing steadily as measured in quantitative terms, and information labour accounts for an increasingly large proportion of the overall workforce in all developed economies. These changes clearly have demonstrated that the nature of the economy has been transformed from an industrial economy to an information economy with several fundamental new characteristics.

The quantitative evidence and real-life examples

Porat declared that even in 1967, the USA could be described as an information economy, because 46 per cent of the GNP was bound up with information activities (both marketed and non-marketed goods and services); nearly half of the labour force held informational jobs – that is, occupations primarily engaged in the manipulation of symbols (information), either with a high intellectual content (e.g. a nuclear scientist), or at a more routine level (e.g. a data entry clerk); and these workers earned 53 per cent of labour income. By the beginning of the 1980s, it was estimated that between 40 and 50 per cent of the workforce in all industrialized countries were involved in information-handling occupations.

In Great Britain, information labour on average accounted for 45.2 per cent of the total national workforce in 1981, with that in the highest region, Greater London, at 58 per cent. Even in the least information-intensive region of Northern England, the figure was still as high as 38.9 per cent, implying that even the most peripheral regional economy of Britain had become information intensive by the early 1980s.[16]

The information elements in the economy have continued to grow since, and it is estimated that in most developed countries, the proportion of information labour today is over 60 per cent. In a modern company today, 70–80 per cent of what people do is now done by way of their intellects. This is not just limited to high-tech or information sectors, but also in manufacturing. Seventy per cent of the value of a new car lies in the intangibles – and an average car nowadays has more computing power than the computers used to send the first person to the moon. In General Electric, the undisputed king of heavy industry, over two-thirds of its revenue came from financial, information and product services by the late 1990s. Manufacturing competitively today depends critically on utilizing ICTs to manage logistics and supply chains, design and produce superior products, provide efficient and high-quality service support, and communicate efficiently internally and externally with suppliers and consumers. In other words, even for industrial products, the value lies not in the plastics and metal but in the intangibles embedded in them.[17]

Information Workers in All Sectors of the Economy

Tom Peters in his book *Re-imagine!* told an interesting story about work in the London docks. In the 1970s, when a timber ship pulled into the docks, it took 108 men five days to unload it. By the turn of the century, it only took eight men one day to unload it. Most people who now work in a modern port are doing 'white-collar' work. The same is true in most manufacturing sectors, because 'well over 80 per cent (perhaps 90 per cent) of people who work in "manufacturing" don't do any manufacturing'.[18] As Jonas Ridderstrale and Kjelle Nordstrom put it, '[w]e are increasingly competing on competence. A company such as Ericsson is more than 50 per cent service and pure knowledge work, and at Hewlett-Packard and IBM this figure is closer to 80 and 90 per cent. They are all being transformed, whether they like it or not, from manufacturing companies with a little service to service companies with a little manufacturing. Today, all companies are, or should be, brain-based.'[19]

Knowledge 'Soldiers'

Informatization is not limited to the business world: when the US Army fought the Vietnam War, only 15 per cent of the soldiers had a college degree. However, during Operation Desert Storm (the first Iraqi war), 99.3 per cent of the soldiers were college graduates.[20]

The significance of the information (intangible) elements of the economy is also clearly reflected in the comparison of the stock market capitalization of a company and the physical assets it owns. Depending on the sector, it is not uncommon for the market value of a company to be several times the physical assets it owns. Today, the market value of e-Bay is worth more than McDonald's; Microsoft is worth more than the three major car manufacturers in the USA put together. The irony is that even today, many organizations and business executives still spend most of their time and effort to ensure the tangible assets are fully and efficiently utilized, while leaving the intangibles to sort themselves out.

Tangible versus Intangible: The Value of Companies

Some years ago, when Philip Morris purchased Kraft (a food company) for $12.9 billion, it was regarded as a fair price which was verified by the financial performance of the company in subsequent years. What was less publicized then was the fact that the assets of Kraft were worth only $1.3 billion. The rest, $11.6 billion in total, was for 'others' – the intangibles, goodwill, brand equity, employee knowledge and so on.

Ford Motors paid $6.46 billion to acquire Volvo. However, the manufacturing facilities owned by Volvo were not worth a great deal, and neither were its offices and warehouses. What was valuable was the intangibles embedded in Volvo, including its brand, its relationships with suppliers and customers, the knowledge and know-how that exists within the company, and its IPs (intellectual properties). There are numerous other examples – Bacardi-Martini paid £1.5 billion for Dewar's four distilleries, 49 employees and a 15-year supplier contract!

A further indication of the value of intangibles is a study by Deloitte Consulting of selected Fortune 500 companies, which showed the proportion of each firm's share price on 21 August 2002 that was attributable to cash generated by existing assets, versus cash that investors expected to be generated by new investments – something that has not yet happened. Dell computers' share price was $28.05, of which only 22 per cent was justified by the profits it generated from the company's present assets, leaving 78 per cent of the valuation coming from the company's future growth. The figures for Procter & Gamble were 38 per cent versus 62 per cent, for Intel 51 per cent versus 49 per cent, Boeing 70 per cent versus 30 per cent, but for General Motors, 95 per cent versus 5 per cent. In fact, Microsoft has only a fraction of the physical assets owned by General Motors, but Microsoft's market capitalization is several times more than General Motors'.

For many organizations, their employees' skills, organizational culture and brands are worth far more than their tangible assets. More importantly, sustainable competitive advantages often depend on such intangibles because they are difficult for competitors to imitate. Furthermore, the same intangible asset is often worth very different amounts to different people and organizations, which is particularly significant when companies are contemplating mergers and acquisitions, or when talented individuals and groups move between organizations. The sad truth is that most existing organization and management theories and techniques – and management efforts – are geared towards managing the full utilization of tangible assets.[21]

Nike: What Are We Paying for?

Look at the products we buy – what proportion of the money we pay is actually for the materials? I recently bought a pair of Nike trainers (shoes) for my son. When he made his choice in the shop, he said 'Could I have this pair? They are very comfortable and look really cool.' While I was paying for the shoes, I wondered how much of the £65 was actually for the leather and rubber used to make the shoes – probably less than a few pounds. In fact, Nike probably paid the manufacturers in China only a few pounds for both the materials and the labour in producing those shoes.[22] Where did the rest of the money go – and for what? My son wanted that pair of trainers because of the design, the comfort, and most of all the 'tick' representing a particular kind of image associated with Nike. No wonder Nike, the shoe company, is consigned to Fortune's Service 500 list, not the industrial one. The company created its enormous stock market value through its superb design and marketing skills, which created a brand image that is associated with a particular lifestyle that many people want to identify with. It is such information-intensive activities that add most value to its products. The low value-added activities, such as production, are subcontracted to factories around the world.

Furthermore, like most other companies, Nike is under pressure from shareholders to generate growth. The company may be able to persuade people to buy ten pairs of trainers each year instead of three – through innovative marketing and promotions – but beyond that, further growth will become more difficult. This means that to achieve continued revenue growth, Nike will need to extract more value from each pair of shoes it sells. This can only be achieved not by adding more materials to the shoes but by adding more intangible elements – new designs, new images, new features – perhaps with even fewer materials. The production cost of making a £65 pair of trainers is probably not much more than those costing £20, but my son wanted me to pay the extra because they are 'very comfortable and really cool'.

Nike is not an isolated example, and Benetton, the Italian clothes company, provides another superb example. Today, organizations, services and products are becoming more and more similar in almost all industries, and differentiation is increasingly difficult to achieve. When we purchase a car, what tips the balance is no longer just how good the engine is (because almost all engines are good enough nowadays), but also, perhaps more importantly, other things associated with the car – the image, the design, the warranty, the service deal and the financial package. It is often the intangibles that make products competitive.

In the information economy, companies have to work hard to get noticed, and what it takes to attract the interest of customers often surpasses the actual cost of producing the customer offering. As is today well known, information about money is more valuable than money itself; and information about products and services is often worth more than the underlying offering. Bloomberg is one example that comes to mind.[23]

Today, it is generally accepted that we are living in a knowledge-based, information economy. The reality is that in most developed economies, well over 50 per cent of the labour force are information workers, more than 50 per cent of the gross national product (GNP) is bound up with information activities, and over 50 per cent of the value of most products and services is made up of information content; most of all, for most products and services the future value-added will come from intangible, informational rather than material inputs; and all production processes have also become increasingly information intensive. The quantitative changes in the composition of capital and labour indicate that all industries have become information intensive as measured by the growing importance of information in production and distribution – *all* industries and sectors, including primary and secondary industries. Accurate and adequate information has become crucial to the success of all industrial and commercial operations. For this study in particular, it is in the context of the information economy that the enormous potential of ICTs is highlighted, understood and realized.

The ICT Revolution and the Information Economy: The Solow Productivity Paradox

Despite the evidence provided in the last two sections about the ICT Revolution and the information economy, one question I was repeatedly asked during executive programmes and MBA classes was that if the development took a very long time to accumulate – over several decades – why it is suddenly such a big deal now? Today, opinions about the significance of these developments cover the whole spectrum, from extreme true believers to absolute non-believers. Whilst some commentators emphasized the accelerated rate of productivity growth, low unemployment, and low inflation in recent years in the USA and several other developed countries as evidence of the arrival of the new economy, others questioned if productivity growth has actually accelerated, and indeed, if the new economy could measure up to the great inventions of the past. During the dot.com boom, many argued that ICTs, and the Internet in particular, would change everything. After the deflation of the dot.com bubble, however, some commentators have argued that ICTs have barely changed anything. Between such extreme views are the majority of scholars, business executives and policy makers, who welcome rapid economic changes but recognize that some conventional principles still apply and some continuity from the past has been, and needs to be, maintained.

F. Gerard Adams, in his book *The E-Business Revolution & The New Economy: E-Conomics after the Dot-Com Crash*, reviewed a large body of existing studies and systematically examined the statistical evidence both for and against the new economy. By examining evidence about productivity growth, price, cost and output measurement, high employment rate without inflation, and changes in the business cycle, as well as the nature and processes of technological revolution and its interactions with the structure and operation of business, he concluded that statistical evidence of a new economy is probable but still inconclusive. While there are many changes, the underlying structure of the economy probably has not changed radically. He also argued, however, that the technological revolution and the tremendous gains in electronics and networks are affecting business operations and organization in many fields, and because of this, further rapid economic growth is likely.[24]

A major debate about the new economy is whether the rate of productivity growth has accelerated owing to the widespread diffusion and rapid development of ICTs. Back in 1987, Robert Solow famously argued that 'you can see the computer age everywhere but in productivity statistics'.[25] To examine this issue, Adams first reviewed evidence about the trend towards high productivity in the US economy. The average annual growth of real gross domestic product (GDP) in the USA indicated that between 1973 and 1995, the economy grew by an average of 1.4 per cent; but between 1995 and 1999, growth accelerated to 2.9 per cent per annum.

However, by looking at the percentage change in output per worker, the cyclical nature of productivity growth was clearly revealed. The upward swing in productivity growth since 1996 corresponded closely to a business upswing, making it doubtful whether there was actually a new upward trend in productivity. Also, improvements in semiconductor technologies clearly led to rapid productivity improvement in electronic hardware production, but very little productivity gain has been measured in older sectors of the economy. Nevertheless, the continued rapid productivity growth in 2001, 2002 and 2003 when the economy fell into recession tentatively supported the hypothesis that there is indeed a new economy.

There have also been several studies about the total factor productivity (TFP), which represents productivity gains that could not be explained in terms of production inputs. It is usually but not exclusively related to technological change. Adams reviewed several studies, all of which suggested that, comparing the period 1995–2000 with 1973–1995, labour productivity increased around 1 per cent. In other words, during 1995–2000, average annual output per person-hour increased by 2–2.5 per cent, compared to an annual average increase of 1.4 per cent during 1973–1995. Further analysis indicated that 0.5 per cent of the improvement can be attributed to the effect of greater capital intensity, especially through IT investments, including both hardware and software. Changes in labour quality have only slightly more impact in recent years than in the past. The remainder represents TFP, the gains in productivity that cannot be explained by capital-deepening or changes in labour quality. TFP accounted for 0.4 per cent of annual productivity growth of 1.4 per cent during 1973–1995. It increased to around 0.75 per cent during the 1995–2000 period. The extra gains perhaps could be attributed to the arrival of the new economy.

A significant proportion of this gain can be attributed to the ICT sectors themselves, and the spillover to the rest of the economy remains unclear. However, it may take time for the effects of ICT investments to affect productivity. Geographically, similar productivity gains were identified only in Australia and a few other countries, but not in the major European countries, Japan and other East Asian countries. However, business cycle weakness in some of these countries may have offset the positive effect of the ICT Revolution on productivity growth.

Furthermore, by looking at firm-level data, Brynjolfsson and Hitt argued that the aggregate statistics greatly underestimate the actual gain in productivity.[26] They are concerned with the complementarities between hardware costs and the organizational costs of computerization. Large investments in intangible assets are necessary to make computerized systems work effectively. They include investments not only in software but also in reorganizing business processes and in training personnel. There are also substantial costs in hiring consultants and in compensating employees for additional time and skills. Such upfront costs, which are usually measured as current expenses, are counted against current output at the firm level. Yet most of these investments for improving business processes and improving working skills will pay off over time, often over periods as long as seven years. These intangible investments should be counted as part of input and depreciated later. They estimated that this underestimation of the productivity growth rate could exceed 1 per cent per year.

Other statistical evidence also indicated the arrival of the new economy in the mid-1990s. One dimension of the new economy is the improved trade-off between inflation and unemployment. When the unemployment rate reduces to a certain level, inflationary pressure often increases dramatically. This trade-off is sometimes illustrated by the so-called Phillips Curve. The Phillips Curve represents the relationship between the rate of inflation and the unemployment rate; A. W. H. Phillips discovered the trend and published a study in 1958 showing that there was a consistent negative relationship between the rate of wage inflation and the rate of unemployment in the United Kingdom from 1861 to 1957. When unemployment was high, wages increased slowly; when unemployment was low, wages rose rapidly.

By plotting the actual inflation and unemployment data on a two-dimensional chart, clear clusters emerged, and the rates of both inflation and unemployment since the mid-1990s were lower than before, indicating a shift of the Phillips Curve downwards. One explanation for this shift is that technological progress was producing increased gains in productivity which offset increased wages. In other words, the new economy factors have had a significant impact which was reflected in the shift in the Phillips Curve. Figure 3.1 shows the shifting Philips Curve in the UK; similar tendencies have been identified in the USA.[27]

It should also be noted that the Phillips Curve represented the average relationship between unemployment and wage behaviour over the business cycle. However, the relationship between wages and unemployment changed over the course of the business cycle. When the economy was expanding, firms would raise wages faster than normal for a given level of unemployment; and when the economy was contracting, they would raise wages more slowly than normal. As indicated by figure 3.2, the Philips Curve actually shifted outwards between the 1970s and the period of the 1980s. Could the downward shifting of the Philips Curve simply reflect an upswing in the economic cycle?

In terms of the end of the traditional business cycle, the 2001 recession perhaps proved that the business cycle is here to stay, but the period 1991–2001 represented one of the longest periods of uninterrupted expansion. The new recession was also

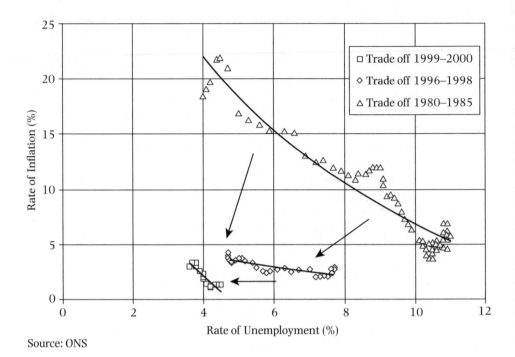

Source: ONS

Figure 3.1 The shifting Philips Curve in the UK (1980–2000)
Source: http://www.tutor2u.net/economics/content/topics/inflation/philips_curve.htm.
Reproduced with permission of Tutor2u.net

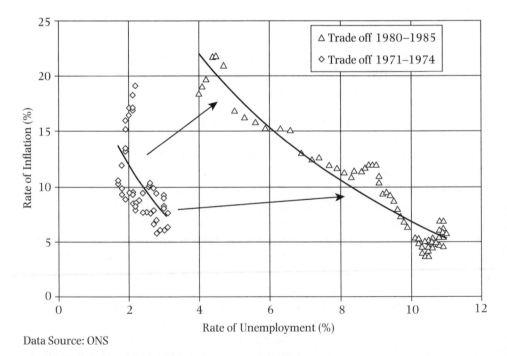

Data Source: ONS

Figure 3.2 The shifting Philips Curve in the UK (1971–1985)
Source: http://www.tutor2u.net/economics/content/topics/inflation/philips_curve.htm.
Reproduced with permission of Tutor2u.net

short-lived and the recovery has been well under way since 2003, even though the recession was also significantly affected by several dramatic events, including the 11 September 2001 terrorist attack on New York and the SARS outbreak in China. One view is that ICTs will result in faster inventory adjustments, leading to shorter business cycles where a recession may be more abrupt but recovery will come more rapidly. This again supports the new economy hypothesis.

'The Real *New* Economy' \ared

McKinsey Global Institute studied labour productivity and its connection to corporate IT spending and use in the USA, Germany and France, and they concluded that a new economy did come into being in the 1990s. However, unlike popular views that the new economy emerged from the Internet, they found that the new economy emerged from intensifying competition and a resulting surge of managerial innovations. The role of IT is more complicated than previously assumed: 'IT is of great, but not primary, importance to the fate of industries and individual companies.'[28]

Farrell argued that the productivity statistics indicated that something did change in the economy in the late 1990s. Between 1973 and 1994 US labour productivity increased only 1.4 per cent per annum, but between 1995 and 1999 the figure rose to 2.4 per cent. Even though the figure was reduced from 2.9 per cent in 2000 to 1.1 per cent in 2001 owing to the dot.com crash, it recovered impressively to 4.8 per cent in 2002. The productivity surge coincided with major increases in IT spending in US companies, when they increasingly integrated IT into the fabric of their operations. Overall, the proportion of GDP accounted for by IT goods increased from 2 to 12 per cent during the 1990s.

However, the relationship between IT investment and productivity gains is not straightforward, and the McKinsey study found little direct correlation between them. Although most industries invested heavily in IT, the rates of productivity growth varied enormously. In the USA, productivity gains were concentrated in six sectors, including retailing, securities brokerage, wholesaling, semiconductors, computer assembly and telecommunications. Many other sectors also invested heavily in IT but saw very little productivity growth, such as hotels and television broadcasting. Farrell went on to argue that it was the intensifying competition that led to productivity-boosting innovations in the six key sectors. In other words, it was innovations in products, business practices and technologies that led to gains in productivity:

> In fact, an important dynamic of the new economy – the real new economy – is the virtuous cycle of competition, innovation and productivity growth. Fierce competition spurs innovation, in both technology and business processes. These innovations spread quickly, improving productivity across the sector. As productivity rises, competition intensifies further, bringing a fresh wave of innovation. (p. 106)[29]

This, however, does not mean that IT is not important in the new economy. On the contrary, during the 1990s IT proved to be particularly powerful. It enabled the development of attractive new products and efficient new business processes; facilitated the rapid diffusion of innovations both within and between industries; and also exhibited strong scales economy as the benefits multiplied rapidly when its use expanded. The power of IT in promoting innovation was not evenly distributed across industries: productivity boomed only in sectors with highly complex operating processes, heavy transaction loads or technically sophisticated products – in other words, those most dependent on intensive information processing.

The implications are very significant. Companies must target their IT investments at the key factors that affect the productivity of their industry and themselves, rather than simply following broad IT trends. The sequence and timing of their investment are also very important, because the benefits of certain critical IT investments can only be realized if the groundwork has been laid in other routine applications. Most of all, successful companies and industries pursue technological innovations in tandem with managerial innovations, because technological innovations are often of little use until managerial practices adapt to them. It is also important to note that the success of IT investments hinges on the particular characteristics of different industries and the particular practices of different companies. As Farrell put it: 'IT is not a silver bullet. But if it is aimed correctly, it can be an important competitive weapon' (p. 112).[30]

Extracting the Business Value of ICTs: From Deployment to Usage

Despite ICTs' enormous potential in transforming organizations, many organizations have failed to extract the expected business value from their investments. In fact, many business-oriented ICT projects have not lived up to expectations or even failed spectacularly. Blame is often shared between the business executives and ICT specialists. Also, despite many years of discussions and debates about the void between managers who, for the most part, lack the technical expertise of ICT specialists, and ICT experts who lack the business acumen of managers, the gap does not seem to be getting narrower. There remains a huge gap between what the ICT industry promises (namely, ICT investments would lead to 'competitive advantage') and what ICTs in industries and companies have delivered – sometimes described as 'competitive necessity' where most firms competing in the same industry are deploying the same ICTs and using them more or less for the same purposes, often supplied by the same technology providers and advised by the same consultants. Many business executives know that their companies must spend on ICTs, but want to invest no more than is necessary to keep up with competitors. This is one of the major reasons why the ICT function is under continuous pressure to reduce costs and deploy standardized systems and processes.

The competitive advantage versus competitive necessity debate has recently gained considerable momentum owing partly to a short article by Nicholas Carr in *Harvard Business Review* entitled 'IT doesn't matter'. Carr argued that since ICTs are equally available to all firms, they are now more of a commodity than value-delivering technology. In other words, ICTs are now a utility just like electricity and water. The fierce criticisms from numerous camps – management consultants, academics, IT directors and business executives from the ICT industries – served only to fan the flame.

However, during the past ten years, ICT investments by companies have contributed to their increased productivity and also significantly increased price competition in many industries. The chief beneficiaries of ICT deployments have been customers who have been able to buy more products and services from companies with less, and the ICT industry itself which has directly benefited from heavy ICT investments in all sectors. This has created a huge dilemma for business executives. If ICTs are a commodity, then deploying them should be done as economically and efficiently as possible. For most business managers, the actual usage of information and ICTs in their companies is a 'black hole', consuming human energy, time, attention and resources, its business value is rarely fully realized, and often it is not even measured or fully understood.

In addressing this issue, Donald Marchand[31] of IMD made a significant distinction between the 'usage' – as apposed to 'deployment' – of ICTs and information, which has been largely ignored or overlooked by business managers. He argued that busines managers routinely spend 90 per cent of their attention on planning ICT projects, aligning ICTs with the business needs, budgeting and investing in ICTs, and dealing with the ICT function and external suppliers. Many managers also naively seek to solve business problems with ICT solutions. What many business managers do not see clearly is that ICT investments have to be accompanied by significant behavioural and cultural changes in the ways that information and ICTs are used by people in business functions such as sales, marketing and servicing. These soft factors of how people in a company behave with information and use ICTs have not been measured very well, or managed effectively with the introduction of information systems. This has led to business disappointments over the results obtained from major ICT investments and deployments.

Marchand also argued that only 20–25 per cent of the business value of ICTs is linked to deployment and investments, whereas 75–80 per cent of the business value of ICTs and information is linked to so-called soft factors. However, most managers devote 90 per cent of their time and attention to ICT investments and deployment that account for only 20–25 per cent of the business value of ICTs and information! The focus on the effectiveness of information and ICT usage by people receives much less managerial time and attention. Thus the potential business value residing in increased usage of information and ICTs in the company by people is largely lost. The result is that business managers often overlook the largest potential payoff from ICTs by not focusing on how effectively information and ICTs are used by people in their companies. To achieve the full value of ICTs we need to exploit strategic and organizational changes, and changes in the mindset and behaviour of managers and employees. These issues will be explored in detail later in this book.

Capital versus Talent: The Battle that is Reshaping Business

One other significant change in the transformation from the industrial to the information economy is the battle between capital and talent. In a *Harvard Business Review* article in July 2003, Roger L. Martin and Mihnea C. Moldoveanu argued that for a century, capital fought labour for the biggest share of profits. Now knowledge workers have gone to war with investors, and the outcome remains unclear today.[32]

> For much of the twentieth century, labor and capital fought violently for control of the industrialized economy and, in many countries, control of the government and society as well. Now, before the wounds from that epic class struggle have fully healed, a fresh conflict has erupted. Capital and talent are falling out, this time over the profits from the knowledge economy. While business won a resounding victory over the trade unions in the previous century, it may not be as easy for shareholders to stop the knowledge worker-led revolution in business.

One example cited concerning this new battle is the recent outcry about CEO compensation, which has grown very rapidly and shows no sign of slowing down despite a rising global outcry from shareholders. Martin and Moldoveanu argued that in the knowledge-based economy, value is the product of knowledge and information. Companies cannot generate profits without the ideas, skills and talent of knowledge workers, and they have to bet on people, not technologies, factories or capital.[33]

For much of the twentieth century, capital and labour have been struggling for a greater share of the profits from industrialization. Overall, capital has won the battle despite the efforts of trade unions. However, a new battle has already started in the knowledge-based economy, where talents are demanding – and getting – a large share of the profits. Martin and Moldoveanu cited the example of the chairman of Walt Disney Studios, Jeffrey Katzenberg, who wrote a memo in 1991 about the spiralling irrationality of the movie business and leaked it to the media. Katzenberg argued that the studios put up all the capital and took all the risks, but movie stars, scriptwriters and directors – the 'talents' – stripped off most of the profits. Similar examples were also cited from investment banking when investment bankers fought shareholders for the returns on investments. As the Information Age supplanted the Industrial Age, managers sensed that knowledge would be more important than capital in producing wealth. Knowledge assets – the managers themselves – would soon be more valuable to a company than its capital assets. Because they invested skills and knowledge in companies, managers felt that they should earn returns on those investments. CEOs, in particular, began to flex their muscles.

Furthermore, the continued rise of the knowledge worker will create tensions not just between talent and capital but between talent and labour. Workers entered the capital market through pension funds so that they could get a share of the profits they help companies make. Ironically, by the time they did so, talent started taking more of the profits from capital. As the talent class cashes in on the knowledge it creates, the knowledge-creation process will become a battlefield. Martin and Moldoveanu suggested that ultimately both capital and labour may ask lawmakers to regulate the returns to talent just as policy makers regulated the returns to utilities in the 20th century. In the end, capital, labour and talent will need to learn to live together as labour and capital did after the great battles of the past century. The manner in which capital and talent fight this war will decide the nature of the peace.[34]

In the UK, the situation remains unclear. There have been increasingly loud outcries about excessive executive pay packages – even when the executive failed to deliver positive results. Several high-profile rows broke out, including Sir Peter Davis of Sainsbury, the UK supermarket chain in July 2004; Michael Green of Carlton Group, who received £1.8 million compensation for loss of office in October 2003, in addition to £13.2 million in share awards through the merger of Carlton with Granada; Jean-Paul Garnier of GSK whose £22 million 'platinum parachute' should he lose his job was voted down by shareholders; and Jonathan Bloomer of Prudential whose pay package and a £4.6 million bonus were withdrawn after opposition by shareholders.[35] Although symbolically the shareholders are winning, the government believes that investor activism is curbing the so-called 'fat cat' deals and has decided against new legislation for the time being. Patricia Hewitt, former Secretary of the Department of Trade and Industry in the UK, called on the main industry lobby groups to draw up a common set of best practice guidelines on directors' contracts by the end of 2005, but in doing so leading investors and business lobby groups have signalled that the government risks reopening their divisions.[36] Fund managers are talking to companies more, but shying away from confrontation over corporate governance.[37] Trade unions are unhappy with the situation, and Brendan Barber, general secretary of the Trade Union Congress, said: 'Top directors still award themselves pay rises many times those given to staff and continue to give themselves VIP pensions when many employees are seeing their schemes close.'[38]

This battle is extremely significant as it raises serious issues about the value of information workers; and for many talented individuals, they are the business and without them there is no business. Some of the major talents are worth hundreds of millions – and sometimes billions – of dollars. This is not just restricted to CEOs, but also film stars, pop singers and sports talents; and many other stars are also commanding a growing share of commercial returns on their talents – consultants, writers, web and system developers, and scientists. In the global network economy, the top talents in any fields are in short supply and heavy demand – and it is easier than ever before for such talents to extract more value and more returns for the service of their talents. Perhaps this is yet another sign of the arrival of the information economy.

Business Implications

There is little doubt that the nature of the economy has changed as measured by the informational (intangible) elements of our products/services and production processes, and the proportion of the workforce whose primary activities are informational rather than physical (both over 50 per cent in developed countries). Information (or knowledge, intelligence etc.) has become the most important resource upon which the efficiency and competitiveness of all organizations depend – and this includes public sector organizations. In the meantime, the so-called 'ICT Revolution' continues to gather pace, providing us with increasingly powerful, versatile and affordable tools, infrastructure and services whose sole purpose of existence is to deal with 'information' – to capture, store and retrieve, manipulate, transmit and present information. Despite some inconclusive evidence in several other aspects, including the productivity paradox and the cyclical nature of the economy, some of the radical changes that have taken place cannot be ignored.

The transformation to an information economy has resulted in a rapid expansion of demand for ICT products and services and a fast-growing ICT industry. This industry is occupying an increasingly large proportion of the overall economy. Some leading ICT companies are also in the vanguard of creating and experimenting with strategic and organizational innovations based on the new capabilities afforded by network technologies, and some of these innovations are proliferating into other sectors. In the meantime, since all sectors have become more information intensive, ICTs, by linking up workplaces both within and between organizations, are having profound effects on what activities are located where, on how territories are administered or markets served, and on how linkages are maintained between customers and suppliers at different locations. These developments are also having profound implications for how – and where – individuals work and also work with one another. Empirical evidence indicates that as a source of product, process and managerial innovations, ICTs in general and the Internet in particular are being widely used to exploit spatial differentiations in sophisticated ways, facilitating radical restructuring of business processes and functions and inter-organizational relations. Many of these changes will be explored in detail in the rest of this book.

This combination is extremely powerful. One the one hand the most important resource in the world economy has shifted from materials and capital to 'information'. At the same time we have at our disposal increasingly powerful tools to deal with the most important resource of the economy (i.e. information), often in ways impossible or not even imaginable in the past. This means that organizations large and small today can, should and, indeed, must do things differently in order to survive and thrive in the new economy. This gives rise to the need for a new generation of organization and management theories. These theories should be embedded in the new economics of information and should explicitly exploit the unique capabilities of ICTs. At the centre of such studies are the 'strategic and organizational innovations' – new visions and strategies, new business models, new organizational designs, new ways of working, new inter-organizational relations, new production and supply chain management systems and so on – that are intimately supported by ICTs. ICTs have already brought about some radical changes but there is also a significant element of continuity from the past. These changes provide the essential context for e-Business.

Discussion Questions

1   Has there been an 'ICT Revolution'? What evidence do you have to support your view? Illustrate the most significant technological developments in ICTs in recent years, and discuss the implications of these developments for contemporary organizations.

2   It is widely believed that all Western developed economies have been transformed from an industrial economy to an information economy. Is there any concrete evidence to support this view? Discuss the main characteristics of the information economy. Critically evaluate the implications of this transformation for contemporary businesses.

3   Many talented individuals are making huge sums of money each year – not only film stars, pop singers and sports personalities, but also talented scientists and senior executives. Could their high incomes be justified? How do you determine the value of a talent?

4   Has the business environment changed? Illustrate the main changes in the business environment; and critically discuss their implications for today's business organizations.

Assignment: Executive Briefing Report

The debate on whether we are in a 'new' economy continues today. You have just joined a large company (please choose a sector you are familiar with). Your first task is to prepare a briefing report to senior executives about the new economy as part of the changing business environment. The report should be around 2,500–3,000 words, including an executive summary; you will need to present clearly the evidence for and against the claim, and highlight the potential implications for this company.

NOTES

1   Carr, Nicholas G. (2004) *Does IT Matter? Information technology and the corrosion of competitive advantage*. Harvard Business School Press, Boston, p. 2.

2   Adams, F. Gerard (2004) *The E-Business Revolution & the New Economy: E-Conomics after the dot-com crash*. Thomson South-Western, Mason, Ohio.

3   Hepworth, Mark (1989) *Geography of the Information Economy*, Belhaven, London; Li, Feng (1995) *The Geography of Business Information: Corporate networks and the spatial and functional corporate restructuring*, John Wiley & Son, Chichester.

4   Adams (2004) op. cit.

5   Adams (2004) pointed out that it is not certain that such gains in computing processing power will actually be needed, so future technical improvements may emphasize other aspects of computer technology.

6   Kelly, Kevin (1997) 'New rules for the new economy'. *Wired Magazine*, Issue 5.09, September. http://www.wired.com/wired/archive/5.09/newrules.html.

7   Harrison, Crayton (2004) Tech firms tout utility computing. *The E-Commerce Times*, 14 July. http://www.ecommercetimes.com/story/35105.html.

8   Carr (2004) op. cit.

9   DTI (2003) *Business in the Information Age: International benchmarking study 2003*. Booz Allen Hamilton, London.

10   *The Economist*, 28 June 2000.

11   Cross, Michael (2005) Public sector IT failures. *Prospect*, October, pp. 48–53.

12   In this book, information is defined broadly. Some authors may argue about the distinctions between data, information, knowledge, intelligence and so on. In this book, information refers to the intangible elements of activities, products and services, which either may be embedded in a physical entity, or do not have a physical existence at all. It can be very sophisticated with a high intellectual content, or simple with low intellectual content.

13   Bell, D. (1973) *The Coming of the Post-Industrial Society*, Basic Books, New York; Machlup, F. (1962) *The Production and Distribution of Knowledge in the United States*, Princeton

University Press, Princeton, NJ; Porat, M. (1977) *The Information Economy: Definition and measurement*, US Department of Commerce, Office of Telecommunications, Special Publication 77–12(1), USA.

14 Li, Feng (1995) *The Geography of Business Information*. John Wiley & Son, Chichester

15 Goddard, J. (1992) New technology and the geography of the UK information economy. In Robins, K. (ed.) *Understanding Information: Business, technology and geography*. Belhaven, London.

16 Hepworth, M., A. Green and A. Gillespie (1987) The spatial division of information labour in Great Britain. *Environment and Planning A*, 19, 793–806.

17 Nordstrom, Kjelle and Jonas Ridderstrale (2002) *Funky Business: Talent makes capital dance*, 2nd edn. FT Prentice Hall, London.

18 Peters, Tom (2003) *Re-imagine! Business excellence in a disruptive age*. Dorling Kindersley, London, p. 50.

19 Nordstrom, Kjelle and Jonas Ridderstrale (2002) op. cit., p. 111.

20 Ibid.

21 Kaplan, Robert S. and David Norton (2004) *Strategic Map*. Harvard Business School Press, Boston.

22 Not long after I wrote this chapter, I read the award-winning book by Joel Balkan who vividly described how Charles Kernaghan of the National Labor Committee, an organization with a mandate to stop American corporations using sweated labour, uncovered the secret of Nike in the Dominican Republic. The production of a shirt, for example, was broken down into twenty-two separate operations. A time was allocated for each task, and each shirt takes a maximum of 6.6 minutes to make, which translates into 8 cents worth of labour for a shirt that Nike then sells for $22.99 in the USA. Bakan, Joel (2004) *The Corporation: The pathological pursuit of profit and power*. Constable & Robinson, London, p. 66.

23 Nordstrom, Kjelle and Jonas Ridderstrale (2002) op. cit.

24 Adams (2004) op. cit.

25 Solow, Robert (1987) We'd better watch out. *New York Times Books Review*, 12 July, p. 36.

26 Brynjolsson, E. and L. Hitt (2002) Intangible assets: Computers and organizational capital, MIT Sloan School of Management, Center for eBusiness, Working Paper (October).

27 Adams (2004) op. cit.

28 Farrell, Diana (2003) The Real New Economy. *Harvard Business Review*, October, 105–112, p. 104. Farrell used IT to illustrate information systems, which covers both computing and telecommunications, and it is similar to the phrase 'ICTs' used in this book. IT and ICTs are used interchangeably in this book.

29 Ibid., p. 106.

30 Ibid., p. 112.

31 Marchand, Donald A. (2004) Extracting the business value of IT: It is usage, not just deployment that counts! *Journal of Financial Transformation*, September, pp. 125–131.

32 Martin, Roger L. and Mihnea C. Moldoveanu (2003) Capital versus talent: The battle that's reshaping business. *Harvard Business Review*, July, 36–41.

33 Ibid.

34 Ibid.

35 Tucker, Sundeep (2005a) Show of hands packs punch in boardroom. *Financial Times*, Wednesday 26 January, p. 3.

36 Tucker, Sundeep and David Turner (2005) Lobby groups cool on executive pay pact. *Financial Times*, Wednesday 26 January, p. 3.

37 Tucker, Sundeep (2005b) Fund managers choose to engage in dialogue rather than confrontation. *Financial Times*, Wednesday January 26, p. 3.
38 Tucker, Sundeep (2005a), op. cit.

FURTHER READING

Adams, F. Gerard (2004) *The E-Business Revolution & the New Economy: E-Conomics after the dot-com crash*. Thomson South-Western, Mason, Ohio.

Carr, Nicholas G. (2004) *Does IT Matter? Information technology and the corrosion of competitive advantage*. Harvard Business School Press, Boston.

Cohn, Jeffrey M., Rakesh Khurana and Laura Reves (2005) Growing talent as if your business depended on it. *Harvard Business Review*, October, pp. 62–71.

Farrell, Diana (2003) The Real New Economy. *Harvard Business Review*, October, pp. 105–112.

Hepworth, Mark (1989) *Geography of the Information Economy*. Belhaven, London.

Kaplan, Robert S. and David Norton (2004) *Strategic Map*. Harvard Business School Press, Boston.

Martin, Roger L. and Mihnea C. Moldoveanu (2003) Capital versus talent: The battle that's reshaping business. *Harvard Business Review*, July, 36–41.

Nordstrom, Kjelle and Jonas Ridderstrale (2002) *Funky Business: Talent makes capital dance*, 2nd edn. FT Prentice Hall, London.

Peters, Tom (2003) *Re-imagine! Business excellence in a disruptive age*. Dorling Kindersley, London.

Schlenker, Lee and Alan Matcham (2005) *The Effective Organization: The nuts and bolts of business value*. John Wiley & Son, Chichester.

Chapter 4

The Network Economy:
New Rules of the Game

As illustrated in the last chapter, the economy has been transformed from an industrial to an information economy, where information has become the most critical strategic resource upon which the operation and success of all organizations depend. In this new economy, the rapidly developing information and communications technologies have become the most critical underpinning infrastructure – and one of the most crucial driving forces – for strategic and organizational innovations. ICTs enable organizations and individuals to manipulate and communicate the most important resource of our economy (i.e. information) more easily and more cheaply than ever before, often in ways impossible in the past. The combination of these two forces has redefined many basic rules of our economy, and organizations and individuals have no choice but to readjust their behaviours and change the way they think, work and relate to each other. In this chapter, some of the new rules of the new economy are illustrated and discussed.

According to some scholars, the changes currently taking place in our society and economy are extremely profound. In the follow-up to her ground-breaking book *In the Age of the Smart Machine*, Harvard Business School Professor Shoshana Zuboff teamed up with her businessman husband James Maxmin to explore what they referred to as the failing of the institutionalized practices and logic that have been shaping managers' work, and investigate the relationships between new markets, new technologies and the new enterprise logic – one based on advocacy, mutual respect and trust.[1] They argued that people have changed more than the commercial organizations upon which they depend, highlighted the chasm between individuals and organizations, and explained why corporations are failing individuals. They went on to argue that this chasm is not limited to the business world, because it also exists between citizens and their public institutions, and worshipers and their religious institutions. Today, corporations continue to operate according to a logic invented one century ago – known as managerial capitalism. However, this logic was invented for the production and distribution of 'things', and it has been uneasily adapted to the delivery of services. Today, neither goods nor services adequately fulfil the needs of markets. So a new logic is desperately needed for a 'new support economy' based on what they refer to as the new distributed capitalism. This entails a fundamental transformation in the nature and purpose of business, as well as in the underlying logic of capitalism itself – in other words, new rules need to be invented and followed. Electronic communications (ICTs) play a critical role in this transformation.

Similarly, C. K. Prahalad and Venkat Ramaswamy in their book *The Future of Competition* also highlighted a fundamental change in the logic of the economy.[2] They argued that traditional notions of value creation are no longer sustainable, and organizations must learn to co-create unique value with customers in the new experi- ence economy. The new economic logic needs to be transformed from a company- centric perspective to a customer-centric perspective, because in the network economy, consumers are connected, informed and active. Information is easily accessible to anyone, and knowledgeable consumers can make informed decisions. Consumers can access information on firms, products, technologies, performance and prices as well as consumer actions and reactions from around the world. Advances in the Internet and in messaging and mobile phone technologies mean that consumers can easily communicate with one another in various communities, and these consumers are also able to experiment with new ideas and new products and services before these ideas, products and services are fully developed. In this context, the traditional notion of value and its creation are challenged, and in the new economy 'joint efforts of the consumer and the firm – the firm's extended network and consumer communities together – are co-creating value through personalized experience that are unique to each individual consumer' (p. x). The authors regarded interaction – increasingly through electronic means – as the basis for co-creation of consumer experience, which is at the crux of the emerging reality. This has been increasingly reflected in emerging strategies and organizational structures and processes, which will be discussed in more detail later in the book. Even though Prahalad and Ramaswamy do not believe there is a revolution, they do recognize 'wide departures from traditional ways of sensing, thinking and doing' (p. x).[3] They argued that the old established corporations would not necessarily disappear, and the new dot.coms would not necessarily survive, but what is interesting is that a new class of firms is emerging in a subtle yet sig- nificant way, which reflects a profound change in the balance of influence between individuals and the institution. These ideas will be discussed in more detail later in the book.

These are just examples of some serious attempts to make sense of and conceptual- ize the current transformation. Despite apparent continuities from the past in many aspects, the new economy has done more than change the way business is conducted: it has rendered obsolete several fundamental economic assumptions on which busi- nesses have been based. In the new economy, several assumptions that were the basis for the success of historic market leaders have crumbled. This chapter will explore some of these changes and highlight their implications for business strategies and organizational designs.

Have Any Basic Rules Been Changed in the Business Environment?

Compared with the industrial economy, the new business environment is fundamentally different in several aspects. For example, in the industrial economy interaction and collaboration costs are high and they need to be carefully balanced with savings in production costs when using external suppliers. However rapid development of the Internet and related technologies has significantly reduced the costs for interaction and collaboration under certain circumstances. This has led to changes in the cost structure of organizations, with profound implications for industrial structures and organizational boundaries. In the industrial economy, high collaboration and interaction costs drove high levels of vertical integration. It was often easier and more cost-effective for organizations to own many of the pieces of the value chain, from raw materials to customer delivery services. Today, however, ICTs have made it possible, and often more desirable, to employ a virtual organization. By assembling a network of best-in-class partners that specialize and excel in the links of the value chain, and by performing only those functions that customers value most, it is possible for organizations to achieve new levels of quality, flexibility and cost savings. This issue will be explored in detail in the next chapter.

In the industrial economy, market returns were derived primarily from physical assets. Property, plant and equipment were key metrics in the valuation of an enterprise. Intangibles, such as brand, technological innovation and customer relationships, contribute considerable value, but existed only in the context of physical products. Intangibles were not themselves a source of revenue. Today, their roles have reversed, and intellectual property and customer relationships move to the forefront. In an increasing range of industries, physical assets can be easily and cheaply leveraged across a global customer base, and intangible assets have become a freestanding source of revenue and value.

In the industrial economy, where maximizing profits meant limiting production capacity, the only way to meet total demand was through multiple organizations. This rule still applies to businesses based on physical assets, but for many businesses, their main assets – information, intellectual property and customer relationships – are not limited by plant capacity. So the rule of decreasing returns is reversed, and an organization can grow – at least theoretically – without limit, incremental unit costs can approach zero, and unit value to the customer can increase exponentially. This could mean that one player, maybe two, can dominate a market. Once a strong lead is established, that leader will only increase momentum, establishing a lead that may be insurmountable. In this environment some established organizations can quickly fall behind a new entrant and never recover.

For buyers and sellers in the industrial economy information was often difficult to get, expensive, or both. Few sources of product information for consumers were accessible. Manufacturers and retailers needed to conduct expensive market research to learn about buyer needs and behaviours, which they could only determine in aggregate. Today, with the Internet technologies, information is easier and cheaper to get. As a result, manufacturers can offer customers more and better choices tailored directly to their preferences, and customers have much more information to evaluate these expanded choices. Partly because of this, customers are becoming more demanding. Organizations are under increasing pressure to continuously create innovative, valued offerings to counter price-based competition.

In the industrial economy, penetrating new markets was difficult. It took years to conduct market research, construct and deploy physical assets, identify and deliver market-specific inventory, and put production and sales capabilities in place. Some of these issues remain true today, but virtual channels can increasingly be used to source, promote, sell, deliver and support goods and services in new markets which can be opened much more quickly. As a result, established organizations are seeing new competitors rapidly entering markets and stealing market shares from them.

These are just some of the changes that are taking place in the business environment. Such changes offer significant opportunities to increase revenue through new value propositions, channels and customer relationships; to reduce operating costs and the costs of raw materials and physical goods; and to decrease dependence on physical capital and inventory. Equally significant is the strategic and operational shift necessary to realize these benefits fully.

Despite such obvious changes, continuity in many aspects of the business environment should not be overlooked. Many fundamental rules of the old economy still apply today. During the dot.com boom, many traditional rules were simply ignored, but since then investors and entrepreneurs have learnt – at huge expense – that even for e-Businesses, profitability remains the rule rather than the exception. Many other good business practices – such as brand building, acquiring and keeping good customers, and setting realistic business goals – are more important than ever.

Kevin Kelly: Twelve New Rules for the Network Economy

One of the most systematic conceptualizations of the new rules for the new economy is perhaps the work by Kevin Kelly, who in 1997 first published his famous article in *Wired* magazine on 'twelve dependable principles for thriving in a turbulent world'.[4] The paper drew on many studies by distinguished scholars and business consultants, and it was later extended into a book published by Harvard Business School Press.

Kelly argued that despite all the headlines on the digital revolution, what is truly significant about the revolution is the arrival of the network economy. He deliberately did not use the phrase 'information economy', because despite information's superior role (rather than material resources or capital) in creating wealth, information is not enough to explain the discontinuities we have seen. He went on to argue that the era of computation is over, and we are entering the age of communication.

The arrival of the network economy has profound implications, which made many traditional rules obsolete – making way for a set of new rules. Kelly argued that the new rules governing the current global restructuring revolve around four axes:

- First, wealth in this new regime flows directly from innovation, not optimization; that is, wealth is not gained by perfecting the known, but by imperfectly seizing the unknown.
- Second, the ideal environment for cultivating the unknown is to nurture the supreme agility and nimbleness of networks.
- Third, the domestication of the unknown inevitably means abandoning the highly successful known – that is, undoing the perfected.
- Finally, in the network economy, the cycle of find, nurture, and destroy happens faster and more intensely than ever before.

Along these axes, Kelly discussed twelve new rules that he believes will take hold of our new economy once networks have penetrated into every space in our lives. Some of these twelve rules are perhaps exploring different facets of the same phenomenon (hence there may not be twelve new rules), but some of the profound changes they highlighted cannot – and should not – be ignored. Many emerging strategies, business models and organizational innovations have been developed to exploit some of these new rules, which will be discussed later in the book.

Rule 1 The law of connection: embrace dumb power

Kelly pointed out that in the network economy, it is not just 'computers' that are being connected together via the Internet. More profoundly, as the size and cost of silicon chips continue to shrink rapidly we are also connecting to chips embedded in everything – from hotel room doors to cans of baked beans in the supermarkets (with the intro-duction of radio frequency identification (RFID)). The basic principle behind this new rule is that the whole is more than the sum of the parts, and when dumb components are connected together properly they can yield smart results. The net is 'the collective interaction spun off by a trillion objects and living beings, linked together through air and glass'. In doing so we connect everything to everything else, enabling the dumb power of ubiquitous computing and pervasive connections to produce enormous intel-ligence we were unable to obtain previously.

Rule 2 The law of plenitude: more gives more

The value of a network increases exponentially when the number of nodes in the network increases arithmetically – a well-known mathematical principle, sometimes known as 'Metcalfe's Law' which was briefly illustrated in chapter 3. When we con-nect everything to everything else, the network effect can be extremely dramatic, and adding a few more members can significantly increase the value for all. Kelly used the infamous example of fax machines (and e-mails) to explain this rule. The first fax machine had no value to the user at all because there was nobody else to send a fax to, but the second fax machine immediately made the first fax machine have some value because now it could be used to send a fax to one recipient. The more fax machines there are in the world, the more valuable each fax machine becomes to its owner because it can be used to communicate with more people. Each additional fax machine added to the network increases the user value of all fax machines already on the network – not linearly but exponentially.

This is very different from a fundamental business principle we have always adhered to in the industrial economy: the more plentiful things become, the cheaper and less valuable they become. In the industrial economy, value came from scarcity; things such as diamonds, gold, oil and university degrees were precious because they were scarce. When things were made plentiful, they became devalued. This rule has been turned upside down in the network economy: value is derived from plenitude. This principle explains why universal standards are so valuable to control and many new business strategies have been developed to exploit this.

Rule 3 The law of exponential value: success is nonlinear

Rule 2 is clearly reflected in the development trajectory of many companies in the network economy. During its first ten years, Microsoft's profits were negligible, and only began to rise around 1985. However, once they began to rise, they exploded. This trend is also reflected in the success of Federal Express, Amazon.com, Dell, Intel and Cisco, to name but a few. Perhaps the most spectacular example of this new rule is the exponential growth of the Internet itself. Mobile phones have followed an even steeper growth trajectory. Drawing upon the work of McKinsey consultant John Hagel III, Kelly used this rule to highlight the fact that the proliferation of technological innovations and the growth of many companies in the network economy followed the exponential growth trajectory of biological systems. Value explodes exponentially with membership, while this value explosion sucks in even more members. The virtuous circle inflates until all potential members are joined. The fact that the explosion did not ignite until approximately the late 1980s indicates that something profound happened then. However, Kelly cautioned readers that the same forces that feed on each other to amplify network presences into powerful overnight standards can also work in reverse to unravel them in a blink. Some new business strategies today have been developed to exploit this rule, which will be discussed later in the book.

Rule 4 The law of tipping points: significance precedes momentum

This rule explains a different facet of Rules 2 and 3. In retrospect, when examining the growth trajectory of companies and the proliferation of new technologies, a point exists where the momentum was so overwhelming that after this point, success became a runaway event. Success became infectious and spread pervasively to the extent that it became difficult for the uninfected to avoid succumbing. 'How long can you hold out not having a phone?', asked Kelly.

Kelly borrowed a phase from epidemiology, where there is a point at which a disease has infected enough hosts that the infection moves from local illness to raging epidemic. This point is referred to as the tipping point. There has always been a tipping point in any business, industrial or network, after which success feeds upon itself. However, in the network economy the low fixed costs, insignificant marginal costs (the cost of making a copy) and rapid distribution depress tipping points below the levels of industrial times. This means that the threshold of significance – the period before the tipping point during which a movement, growth or innovation must be taken seriously – is also dramatically lower than it was during the industrial age. Just like the lily leaf that doubles in size every day, the day before it completely covers the pond the water is only half covered, and the day before that, only a quarter covered, and the day before that, only an eighth. Detecting events while they are beneath this threshold has become absolutely essential in the network economy, because by the time something has become significant it is already too late for any effective actions, a very important point that all decision makers should remember.

Rule 5 The law of increasing returns: make virtuous circles

We are all familiar with the economic law of decreasing returns in the industrial economy. In the network economy this has been reversed to the law of increasing returns. Value explodes with membership, and the value explosion sucks in more members, compounding the result. Kelly pointed out that this is different from the notion of economies of scale, because industrial economies of scale increase value linearly, while in the network economy value increases exponentially. More importantly, industrial economies of scale stem from the efforts of a single organization to outpace the competition by creating more value for less, and the expertise developed by the leading company belongs to the innovators. By contrast, the networked increasing returns are created and shared by the entire network, and the value of the gains resides in the greater web of relationships. A critical aspect of the network development is a common standard. Once a common standard is formed, members of the network can operate within the safety net provided by the network to develop innovations and unleash the power of increasing returns. However, those who own or control the standard are often disproportionately rewarded. Hence the fierce battle in many fields, ranging from platforms for computer games to DVD formats.

Rule 6 The law of inverse pricing: anticipate the cheap

Throughout history people have come to accept that you get what you pay for, and value for money has become an overused phrase not only in the private sector but also in public services. In the industrial economy, consumers experienced slight improvements in quality for slight increases in price, but today consumers expect drastically superior quality for less money over time – and the very best gets cheaper each year (or each month/week). Just think about the price of computers and all the home electronics, for example. The technological innovations underpinning this trend are shrinking chips and exploding networks. The principle of inverse pricing of computing and telecommunications has been illustrated by Moore's Law and Gilder's Law discussed earlier in the book. The trend has led Gilder to speak of bandwidth becoming free – the price per bit transmitted slides down an asymptotic curve towards the free. Because microchips and the Internet are so pervasively proliferated in our society and economy, many other products and services they touch are also following this trend. Kelly used such examples as unit data processing cost (MIPS – millions of instructions per second) and transaction costs, and the cost of information itself – headlines and stock quotes – all plunging towards the free, to illustrate this point. He went even further to claim that 'all items that can be copied, both tangible and intangible, adhere to the law of inverted pricing and become cheaper as they improve'. Whilst he admitted that cars will never be free, the cost per mile will dip towards the free, and 'the function per dollar continues to drop'.

This is great news for consumers but bad news for profit: prices will continue to dive towards free but we expect quality to continue to improve or at least be maintained. This raises fundamental questions about the viability of existing strategies, business models and organizational designs. Radical innovations in business and management theories are urgently needed.

Rule 7 The law of generosity: follow the free

Extrapolating from Rule 2 that a service or product becomes more valuable when more people use it, and Rule 6 that over time better products and services will cost less, the extension of this logic leads to Rule 7: 'the most valuable things of all should be those that are given away'.

This rule explains why many companies are giving away products that cost them millions to develop: Internet Explorer by Microsoft, Eudora by Qualcomm (for e-mail), McAfee's antivirus software, and Java by Sun. This is not limited to the software industry – other examples include free newspapers and magazines, free mobile phones, free satellite receivers, and 'any object with which the advantages of being plugged in exceed the diminishing cost of replicating the object'. While certain products are not yet handed out free, they are sold to customers at or below factory costs – such as the more advanced mobile phone handsets and computer game consoles. The logic behind this rule is that the marginal cost of an additional copy (intangible or tangible) is near zero but value appreciates in proportion to abundance. A flood of copies increases the value of all the copies. When it reaches a certain scale, the spread of the product becomes self-fulfilling. Once the product's worth and indispensability are established, the company can sell auxiliary services or upgrades to generate profits.

To survive in this new business environment, companies need to make significant changes in their mindset and in their strategies and business models. 'The only factor becoming scarce in a world of abundance is human attention ... Giving stuff away garners human attention, or mind share, which then leads to market share.' One business model increasingly adopted in different industries is that of using free products and services to lock in customers, and then leveraging this position to sell other new and more advanced products and services. This new business model will be discussed in detail later in the book.

Rule 8 The law of the allegiance: feed the web first

One choice that organizations have to make in the network economy is whether to have a large slice of a small pie (market) or a small slice of a large pie. Evidence since the 1980s suggests that the big winners are the latter. To succeed in the network economy, many companies need to shift their focus from maximizing the firm's value to maximizing the value of the whole network. The rise of Microsoft and the fall of Apple in the late 1980s and 1990s is an example that comes to mind. McKinsey consultant John Hagel III conceptualized a new strategy – the web strategy – to illustrate this trend which will be described later in the book. He argued that game companies have to devote as much energy to promoting the web – users, developers, hardware manufacturers and so on – as they do to their product. Their success depends critically on how successful the whole platform is – Sony PlayStation, Nintendo or Xbox – not just on how innovative or efficient each individual company is. In order to be successful, feed the web first to establish and grow the market.

Rule 9 The law of devolution: let go at the top

Kevin Kelly believes that the network economy behaves ecologically. 'The fate of individual organizations is not dependent entirely on their own merits, but also on the fate of their neighbors, their allies, their competitors, and, of course, on that of the immediate environment.' The search for the optimal fit (alignment) between an organization and its environment faces multiple uncertainties. The harsh reality is that sooner or later a product will be eclipsed at its prime. Because 'the cycle of find, nurture, destroy happens faster and more intensely than ever before', all organizations must systematically phase out still successful business activities, and leave behind products and technologies before they start to decline, making way for the next innovation. This is more easily said than done, but some companies seem to have mastered this – Intel periodically phases out their still profitable processors, and Microsoft used a similar strategy to introduce new versions of the Windows software. In the network economy, 'the ability to relinquish a product or occupation or industry at its peak will be priceless.'

Rule 10 The law of displacement: the net wins

The new rules of the network economy are not only evident in the software and computer industries; we have also witnessed the gradual displacement of materials by information. This trend has been observed in all sectors of the economy, including heavy industries such as steel, oil, car manufacturing and farming. To illustrate this new rule, Kelly used the new logic of cars as outlined by energy visionary Amory Lovins. Today, a car weighs many times the weight of its passengers, and the energy is mainly used to move the car itself. The use of new materials and other innovations can significantly reduce the weight and improve the safety of cars, thereby reducing its energy consumption. Most cars already boast more computing power than the computers used to send the first person to the moon, and before long our view of cars may shift from 'wheels with chips' to 'chips on wheels' driving on an increasingly wired road system. For many people the car is already the office on the go. 'Once we see cars as chips with wheels, it's easier to imagine airplanes as chips with wings, farms as chips with soil, houses as chips with inhabitants. Yes, they will have mass, but that mass will be subjugated by the overwhelming amount of knowledge and information flowing through it, and, in economic terms, these objects will behave as if they had no mass at all. In that way, they migrate to the Network Economy.'

Although this vision overly simplifies the car as a mere object (it is also a status symbol, a toy, and even a childhood ambition for many drivers), this new business logic will certainly open up numerous new opportunities – and challenges – for organizations and individuals.

Rule 11 The law of churn: seek sustainable disequilibrium

The network economy resembles an ecosystem, and it is constantly in flux as organisms and the environment transform each other. Kelly believes 'change' is not the right word to describe this – instead he used the word 'churn' – 'a creative force of destruction and genesis'. The sustained vitality of a complex network requires that the net keep provoking itself out of balance. If the system settles into harmony and equilibrium, it will eventually stagnate and die. He believes that innovation is a disruption; constant innovation is perpetual disruption; and the goal of a well-made network is to sustain a perpetual disequilibrium. Paraphrasing the work of the economists Paul Romer and Brian Arthur, he described the network economy as operating on the edge of constant chaos. The dark side of churn is that the new economy builds on the constant extinction of individual companies as they are outpaced or morphed into yet newer companies in new fields. Industries and occupations will also experience this churn. He went even further to argue that 'promoting stability, defending productivity, and protecting success can only prolong the misery' and the prime task of the network economy is to destroy the industrial economy. 'While it undoes industry at its peak, it weaves a larger web of new, more agile, more tightly linked organizations between its spaces.' Like it or not, dynamic equilibrium is becoming a fact of life in many facets of our lives. For example, in some of the rapid growing regions of the world economy, new employment opportunities come from more new companies being created than reductions in the number of companies that fail during the same period. These regions often have high rates of business failure but they have even higher rates of new company creation.

Rule 12 The law of inefficiencies: don't solve problems

Kelly argued that in the network economy, productivity is the wrong thing to measure. A Hollywood company that produces longer movies per dollar is not more productive than one that produces shorter movies. In the industrial age, the task for each worker was to discover how to do the job better, but in the network economy the question is 'what is the right job to do?' Today, doing the right thing is far more important than doing the same thing better, but this vital sense of exploration and discovery is difficult to measure and is not reflected in productivity statistics. Drawing on the work of Peter Drucker, Kelly argued that when we are solving problems, we are investing in our weaknesses; but when we are seeking opportunities, we are banking on the network. 'Our ability to solve our social and economic problems will be limited primarily by our lack of imagination in seizing opportunities, rather than trying to optimize solutions.'

These new rules have profound implications for organizations and individuals in the network economy. Although some of them are illustrating different facets of the same phenomenon, and we may not even agree with Kevin Kelly on some or all of these new rules, his work has shed considerable light on the profound transformation that is taking place in our economy and society. In fact, as will be illustrated later in the book, some of these new rules are clearly reflected in some emerging strategies, business models and organizational designs. A main conclusion that can be derived from this is that if the business environment is undergoing such profound changes, organizations and individuals living in this environment need to adapt and change, or we may face extinction.

Peter Schwartz: Future Scenarios of the Network Economy

The analyses in chapter 3 and this chapter have indicated that something profound is happening in the business environment, but the evidence on the exact nature of the transformation remains inconclusive. Is this an evolutionary or revolutionary transformation? To what extent has the economy maintained continuities from the past, and where have discontinuous, step changes taken place? Has the transformation been completed or is it still ongoing? What are the implications of the transformation for organizations and individuals around the world? How do we make consistent decisions when so many uncertainties are surrounding us?

The world economy has successfully recovered from the technological downturn of 2000/2001 – much more quickly than many feared, and the Internet and related technologies continue to spread around the world. New business formations both before and after the dot.com bust have already led to a host of new industries and new companies. Yet at the same time many incumbents have successfully fended off the onslaught of new entrants in many industries, from banking to supermarkets, by successfully combining 'click and mortar', and they are growing larger and stronger.

One might reasonably ask – what is the big deal if there really is a new economy? Peter Schwartz, co-founder of think-tank Global Business Network (GBN), believes it answers the question of whether there really is a high potential for growth. It tells us what the real risks are. 'Are they mainly upside risks of potential unrealized? Or are they downside risks of overshoot and hubris?'[5] The new technology is proliferating into every significant economic, social and political relationship, and it is the engine of prosperity driving the new economy. However, because it is new we are inevitably unsure of its destiny. One way to answer this question and explore some of the other issues is to investigate the main possible scenarios of the future and make decisions based on our judgements on the likelihood of each scenario. Schwartz outlined four possible future scenarios based on different theories and the fundamental uncertainties of our theory of change.[6]

Scenario one is the new economy scenario, that we are indeed entering a brand-new economy. Fundamentally this scenario is about the reorganization of the economy into new ways of working and living, with enormous future potential. It is driven by new knowledge and the future is much richer. We experienced similar changes at beginning of the twentieth century with the introduction of electricity, telephones, the railway, cars and steam power. Many incumbent companies may not survive this transformation but there will be many new types of player in the international economy. Companies that exploit the unique characteristics of the Internet will do especially well.

Scenario two is the incremental scenario, where something new is indeed happening but it is a much more modest transformation and the new economic order is going to take a long time to establish. Many of the old established incumbents and our old ways of doing things will slow the transformation down considerably. During the transition most incumbent companies are likely to make the transition successfully into the new economy. It is a world that resembles today for quite a long time. This is perhaps the most likely scenario because established companies with a physical presence and a strong brand can make the transition cheaper, better and faster than the ones starting from scratch, but some new start-up companies will grow rapidly.

Scenario three regards the new economy as mostly an illusion. Robert Gordon of Northwestern University in the USA believes that most productivity gain is focused on the ICT industries themselves; and Steve Roach of Morgan Stanley argued that by getting ICTs to knowledge workers, we are working longer and harder, not more productively. Under this scenario, tomorrow resembles today in most important respects, and the key players will be some of the old companies and a few new ones.

Scenario four, crash and burn, is where the new economy is just hype and so are most of the new technologies. There is no real gain in productivity and a stock market crash is inevitable, bringing down the world economy and the average consumer with it.

These scenarios are very useful for us when making decisions – about our organizations, our individual choices and our investment strategies. The important thing is to make an educated judgement about the likelihood of each scenario and make our decisions in the context of such judgement. For example, under different scenarios, our decisions to invest in the stock market would be very different. Telecommunications infrastructure companies will make sense under every scenario. If the most likely scenario is the new economy scenario, we should carefully consider promising Internet companies. However, if we believe in the incremental scenario, then the decisions would be similar to the new economy scenario but we may need to be much more selective and choose established companies that are innovatively exploiting the Internet and related technologies. If the new economy is really an illusion, then we should invest in established old blue chip companies and avoid high-tech and Internet companies. If we believe in scenario four, then we should keep our money or invest in bonds and get out of the stock market altogether. On balance, Schwartz believes the safest bet is the incremental scenario, but he also believes that the evidence weighs much more heavily towards the new economy.[7] However, after the dot.com crash, the strong comeback of many of the incumbents and the rapid growth of 'clicks and mortar' as opposed to 'Internet pure-plays' could mean that the incremental scenario is most likely to materialize. More research and more time are needed to ascertain where the future lies.

Summary

In this chapter, some of the new rules of the network economy were discussed and their implications for organizations and individuals were highlighted. For this book in particular, this chapter illustrated some of the radical changes in the business environment, which together with the trends highlighted in the last chapter, provide the essential context for our assessment of e-Business.

Strong evidence suggests that something profound is happening in our economy, although disagreements and uncertainties remain about the exact nature of the transformation. Whatever the future holds, some of the changes in our economy and society cannot be ignored. We may not agree with some of the new rules discussed in this chapter and those highlighted by Kevin Kelly, and we may disagree with Peter Schwartz's scenario analysis of the future, but one important judgement we all have to make is the nature of the current transformation, based on available evidence we have seen. This will provide the essential context for us to make decisions about our organizations and personal lives. It may not guarantee 'best' decisions, but at least it will ensure consistent and coherent decisions in a period of enormous uncertainty.

Discussion Questions

1 Illustrate Kevin Kelly's twelve new rules of the network economy. Do you agree with each of them and why? Discuss in what ways they are relevant to today's organizations. Are there any new rules not illustrated by Kelly?

2 In analyzing the future of the new economy, Peter Schwartz highlighted four possible scenarios and discussed their implications for investing in the stock market. In your view, which scenario is most likely to materialize and why? What are the implications of this scenario for contemporary organizations? Could you come up with alternative scenarios not illustrated by Schwartz?

Assignment: Newspaper Article

You are an expert on the new rules of the new economy. Write a short article for the business section of a broadsheet newspaper (such as the *Financial Times*), clearly illustrating some of the most significant new rules and highlighting who needs to know about them and why (1,000–1,500 words).

NOTES

1 Zuboff, Shoshana and James Maxmin (2002) *The Support Economy: Why corporations are failing individuals and the next episode of capitalism.* Allen Lane, The Penguin Press, London.
2 Prahalad, C. K. and Venkat Ramaswamy (2004) *The Future of Competition: Co-creating unique value with customers.* Harvard Business School Press, Boston.
3 Ibid.
4 Kelly, Kevin (1997) New Rules for the New Economy: Twelve dependable principles for thriving in the turbulent world. *Wired*, September, pp. 140–197, http://www.wired.com/wired/archive/5.09/newrules.html.
5 Schwartz, Peter (2000) The future of the new economy. Global Business Network Scenarios Columns by Peter Schwartz. 1 July, http://www.gbn.org [accessed 4 February 2005]. He

later extended this article to two separate pieces and discussed the implications for our investment strategies. Also available from the GBN website.

6   Ibid.
7   Ibid.

FURTHER READING

Kelly, Kevin (1997) New Rules for the New Economy: Twelve dependable principles for thriving in the turbulent world. *Wired*, 7 September, pp. 140–197, http://www.wired.com/wired/archive/5.09/newrules.html.

Kelly, Kevin (1998) *New Rules for the New Economy: 10 radical strategies for a connected world*, Viking Penguin, Harmondsworth.

Prahalad, C. K. and Venkat Ramaswamy (2004) *The Future of Competition: Co-creating unique value with customers*. Harvard Business School Press, Boston.

Schlenker, Lee and Alan Matcham (2005) *The Effective Organization: The nuts and bolts of business value*. John Wiley & Son, Chichester.

Schwartz, Peter (2000) The Future of the New Economy. Global Business Network Scenarios Columns by Peter Schwartz. 1 July, http://www.gbn.org [accessed 4 February 2005]. He later extended this article to two separate pieces and discussed the implications for investment strategies. Also available from the GBN website.

Shapiro, Carl and Hal R. Varian (1999) *Information Rules: A strategic guide to the network economy*. Harvard Business School Press, Boston.

Zuboff, Shoshana and James Maxmin (2002) *The Support Economy: Why corporations are failing individuals and the next episode of capitalism*. Allen Lane, The Penguin Press, London.

Chapter 5

How the Internet Redefines Organizational Boundaries: A Transaction Cost Analysis

In the last two chapters, comprehensive evidence was presented to illustrate some radical changes in the business environment. In particular, the rapid development and proliferation of ICTs in general and the Internet in particular, combined with the changing nature of the economy, are leading to the emergence of a whole set of new rules that are significantly different from the tried and tested rules of the industrial economy. If the rules of the game are changing, all players in the game – including both private and public sector organizations – need to re-evaluate and transform their strategies, business models and organizational designs.

From a contingency perspective, the business environment has changed significantly, and those organizational species that survived and thrived in the business environment of the old industrial economy need to evolve in order to achieve new alignment (fit) with the new environment. In this process, some existing organizational species will not survive, while new and different ones will emerge. It is in this context that e-Business has originated and emerged. To develop a comprehensive understanding of e-Business we need to understand this evolving context.

One question I have been repeatedly asked by business executives and MBA students is as follows: they have been led to accept – with a leap of faith sometimes – that the changing business environment requires organizations to evolve, therefore their organizations have to adopt strategic and organizational innovations by exploiting the new capabilities from ICTs. However, it remains unclear how the Internet could, or should, have such effects on business strategies and organizational designs. Are there any theories or evidence that could demonstrate, or prove the necessity, or even inevitability, of this logic and uncover the underlying mechanisms linking the Internet with strategic and organizational changes?

To answer this question, this chapter will use the theory of transaction cost economics to illustrate the relationships between the Internet and changes in industrial structures and organizational boundaries. There are limitations to this approach but it clearly demonstrates that from a cost perspective, the rapid development of the Internet and related technologies puts enormous pressure on organizations to adapt their structures and boundaries and the way they relate to each other.

Transaction Cost Economics

The theory of transaction cost economics, also known as institutional economics, is well established and its origin can be traced back to 1937 when Ronald Coase proposed that under certain conditions, the costs of conducting economic exchange in a market may exceed the costs of organizing the exchange within a firm.[1] This theory was further developed by Oliver Williamson from 1975 when he explained the existence of firms in terms of comparative transaction cost advantages.[2] Transaction cost includes *ex ante* costs such as drafting and negotiating contracts and *ex post* costs such as monitoring and enforcing contracts. One important strategic decision for the firm is therefore a choice between a market transaction (market) and vertical integration (hierarchy).

In additional to Ronald Coase, another important strand of work that influenced Williamson's work was Alfred Chandler's historical study of the strategy and structure of seventy large firms in America in 1962.[3] In Chandler's study, three major findings were reported: namely, that organizational structure follows the growth strategy of a firm; the strategy and structure of American enterprises have experienced a stage-wise developmental sequence; and organizations do not change their structures until they are provoked to do so by inefficiency. Similar analyses were duplicated in the UK, France and Japan, and the idea that strategy and structure are closely linked was quickly picked up in a number of disciplines.[4]

Among the most successful followers of Chandler was Oliver Williamson, although Williamson claimed that Chandler was only one of four teachers who inspired his research. He argued that in the past, economists had been preoccupied with markets as the only institution through which efficient economic transactions could take place. However, institutional economics insists that the market and hierarchy are alternative institutions in conducting economic transactions. The efficiency of different institutional arrangements varies, and a firm should choose the form that is most efficient or that provides the least-cost vehicle for conducting economic activities. These two mechanisms for transactions were described by Malone and colleagues:

> Markets coordinate the flow through supply and demand forces and external transactions between different individuals and firms. Market forces determine the design, price, quantity, and target delivery schedule for a given product that will serve as an input into another process. Hierarchies, on the other hand, coordinate the flow of materials through adjacent steps by controlling and directing it at a higher level in the managerial hierarchy. Managerial decisions, not the interaction of market forces, determine design, price (if relevant), quantity, and delivery schedule at which products from one step on the value-added chain are procured for the next step. (p. 485)[5]

The theory is based on three key assumptions: bounded rationality, opportunism and assets specificity. Bounded rationality is the assumption that our cognitive capabilities are limited in such a way that we cannot process all possible information perfectly, which implies that our intent of a rational choice is limited to the information we are able to process. Under environmental uncertainty, in which the circumstances surrounding an exchange cannot be specified *ex ante* and performance cannot be easily verified *ex post*, bounded rationality is a problem. Opportunism is the assumption that decision makers may unscrupulously seek to serve their self-interests, sometimes through malicious behaviour such as lying, cheating, deceit, and violations of agreements. Opportunism poses a problem to organizations when transactions are supported by transaction-specific assets. Transaction-specific assets are things that are uniquely suited to a specific exchange relationship and lose the value outside of the focal relationship.

When there are exchange circumstances characterized by uncertainty, limited information, small numbers and opportunistic behaviour, market price and market substitutes such as contracting are inefficient. Instead, it is more efficient to use an administrative process that takes an adaptive approach to uncertainty by making a sequence of decisions and transmitting the newly acquired information between the interested parties. By internalizing a market transaction firms replace market forces with organizational control, which serves both to safeguard specific assets and facilitate adaptation to uncertainty. Internal organization and administrative processes are regarded as the result of 'market failures' – that is, the invisible hand of the market fails to do its job efficiently. Therefore, adopting an administrative form to replace the market can result in increased efficiency. However, Williamson emphasized that merely converting organizational structure is not enough to improve efficiency. It has to be accompanied by strategic directions, internal controls and incentives, and new management styles.

Williamson's theoretical dimensions permitted much rigorous analysis of the implications of Chandler's initial findings, and the combination of their work stimulated a large number of studies on strategy–structure–performance links. Factors such as strategy, structure, firm size, external contingencies such as competition, technology and market structure, and most of all the harmonization (fit or alignment) between them were all proven to have significant influences on the performance of the firm.[6]

Transaction cost economics regards the market and hierarchy as alternative institutions in conducting economic transactions, although the adoption of one instead of the other is the result of interactions between a whole series of factors (including transaction costs). Using the dichotomy between market and hierarchy, trading parties such as buyers and sellers determine a binary choice on governance mechanism between market and hierarchy to economize on transaction costs. On the one hand, a market mechanism is the optimal solution for buyers and sellers when the transaction does not require specific investment and is conducted under stable circumstances. On the other hand, confronted with high transaction costs posed by high levels of asset specificity and environmental uncertainty, buyers and sellers need to choose vertical integration (hierarchy) to minimize transaction costs.

However, sometimes even if assets involved in a transaction between a buyer and a seller become specific, many transactions are made outside of a vertical integration. Buyers and sellers engage in transactions with highly specific investments under conditions of great uncertainty, but deliberately forgo the opportunity of a vertical integration and remain independent before and after the transaction. A hierarchical integration is replaced by a middle-range governance mechanism. At the moderate level of assets specificity, a middle-range solution incurs lower transaction costs than market-based exchange by reducing incentives to act opportunistically. Individual firms might increase their resources and capabilities by coordinating their resources and achieving mutually beneficial relationships with their trading partners. It may be a more realistic assumption that opportunism is far rarer and trust is far more common than they are assumed in theory. As such, a third alternative form of governance mechanism, sometimes referred to as the 'hybrid', fills the gap between the extremes of markets and hierarchies. A wide range of hybrid forms exist on the continuum between the market and the hierarchy.

Institutional economics is akin to orthodoxy in its insistence that efficiency is central to economic organizations. It focuses on issues that arise, or which can be regarded, as a problem of contracting. It assumes that an economic organization is not only a response to technological or other physical features (such as the economies of scale and scope), but also often has the purpose of harmonizing relations between parties that may otherwise be in actual or potential conflict. Complex institutions are regarded as serving a variety of objectives, but institutional economics insists that for many purposes the firm is more appropriately regarded as a governance structure, rather than as a production function. Therefore, this approach is 'often best used in conjunction with, rather than to the exclusion of, other ways of examining the same phenomena' (p. xii).[7] This theory can clearly explain how the rapid development of the Internet and related technologies can lead to changes in organizational boundaries and market structures.

The Internet and Changing Organizational Boundaries: 'A Revolution in Interaction'

From a transaction cost perspective, the market and the hierarchy are alternative institutions in conducting economic transactions. Although organizations need to consider multiple factors when determining their strategies and organizational designs, and for strategic reasons, it is often important for the organization to take full control of some activities even though those services or components could be more cheaply obtained from the market. Nevertheless, minimizing costs is one important principle that most (if not all) organizations need to adhere to. It is therefore useful to examine the appropriateness of organizational designs from the perspective of cost and efficiency.

To make or to buy: the boundary between the organization and its market

When setting boundaries and determining strategic focus, organizations trade off the value of specialization against the interaction costs associated with external suppliers. The costs to an organization can be divided into two main categories: transaction costs of arranging and coordinating exchanges (sometimes referred to as interaction costs); and transformation costs of production and delivery. Generally, transaction costs are lower within the organization than outside it, because the organization could use administrative means to reduce uncertainty and minimize and even eliminate some of the costs associated with the transaction. However, transformation costs are normally lower outside the organization by using specialist suppliers than within it, because of scale economy and other factors relating to specialist suppliers (please see next subsection). Transaction and transformation costs are incurred both within and outside the organization. When setting its boundary, the organization needs to compare the total costs of transaction and transformation within its boundary for a component or service, with the total costs of the transaction and transformation incurred by obtaining the same component or service from outside its boundary (i.e. the market). If overall it is cheaper to make the component or provide the service internally, then the associated activities should be part of the organization's hierarchy and they should be managed within its boundary. However, if it is cheaper to buy overall, then the organization should leave the associated activities to specialist suppliers outside the organization's boundary – because the component or service can be more efficiently and cheaply obtained from the market. The structure of the organization and industry at a given time is designed to minimize the total costs of transformation and transaction, which sets the boundary between the organization and its market.

Why are production costs lower with specialist suppliers?

It is relatively easy to understand why transaction costs are lower when everything is brought within the boundary of the organization than when dealing with outside suppliers, but why do production costs tend to be lower with external specialist suppliers? One of the main reasons is scale economy, where the suppliers can get inputs more cheaply through bulk purchase and they tend to have more specialist expertise in the area of the specific component or service. To illustrate this point, let us use a hypothetical example. This is obviously highly simplified but it demonstrates that even the largest car manufacturers could not manufacture their own tyres as cheaply as the outside specialists.

To Make or to Buy: That is the Question

Assume there is a major car manufacturer with an annual production of one million cars globally. An important decision for the car manufacturer is whether to make the 5 million tyres (four tyres each car plus one spare), or to buy them from a specialist tyre manufacturer.

Assume the material cost for each tyre is £5. The depreciation of capital equipment works out at £1 per tyre, and labour cost is £1 per tyre. The company invests £5 million each year in R&D. The total annual production costs to the company for 5 million tyres are £40 million, or £8 per tyre.

In contrast, a specialist supplier with an annual production of 50 million tyres will be able to produce better quality tyres at lower costs. The material costs will be lower through bulk purchasing, so each tyre will cost £4.50 (10 per cent discount) rather than £5. Capital depreciation and labour costs could be lower too but assume they are the same as the car manufacturer. Being a tyre specialist, its investment in tyre technologies (R&D) needs to be significantly higher in total than the car manufacturer's – say, five times the investment by the car manufacturer (£25 million). The annual costs for the tyre manufacturer would work out at £225 million for materials, £100 million for depreciation and labour, and £25 million for R&D, a grand total of £350 million – £7 per tyre, which is £1 cheaper than the car manufacturer. Moreover, because of the larger scale of its investment in R&D, the tyre manufacturer could introduce tyres with more advanced features more frequently, and produce tyres of higher quality at lower costs.

'A revolution in interaction' and the changing cost structure of industries

The rapid development of the Internet and related technologies is redefining the cost structure of many industries. This is a direct extension of Moore's and Gilder's laws discussed earlier in the book, when the costs of computing and telecommunications decrease and the capacity increases exponentially. This development is leading to a revolution in interaction in our society and economy, with profound implications for organizational designs and industrial structures, consumer behaviour and, indeed, an organization's strategies and business models.

According to a McKinsey study, interactions account for an increasingly large chunk of our economic activities at the levels of the economy, industry, firm and individual.[8] Individuals and organizations interact to find the right party to exchange goods and services; to arrange, manage and integrate the activities associated with the exchange; and to monitor performance. Interactions occur both within and between organizations and between organizations and the individuals they serve. The forms that such interactions can take include meetings, phone calls, problem-solving sessions, reports, memos and so on, and the underlying purpose is to enable the exchange of goods, services and ideas.

Interactions are not free, and in fact they are very expensive. At the economy level, the McKinsey study found that in the USA, interactions represent 51 per cent of all labour activities. Even in developing countries such as India, the figure is still as much as 36 per cent of all labour activities. At an industry level, interactions account for over 50 per cent of all labour activities in services and over a third in mining, agriculture and manufacturing. At the firm level, interactions make up a large part of an individual firm's activities (58 per cent in the USA); and at the individual level, managers and supervisors spend over 80 per cent of their time in interactions.[9] A study by Philip Evans and Bob Wolf also concluded that in the year 2000, cash transaction costs alone accounted for over half of non-governmental GDP in the USA: 'We spend more money negotiating and enforcing transactions than we do fulfilling them' (p. 103).[10]

Without getting into a long debate about their overlaps and differences, many of the costs associated with interactions can be classified under transaction costs, as opposed to transformation or production costs. To simplify the arguments, the terms transaction costs and interaction costs are used interchangeably in this book, and so are transformation costs and production costs. As highlighted earlier, interaction costs are lower when production occurs within the boundary of the organization, whilst transformation costs are lower for specialist outside suppliers. The decision to make or to buy a particular component or service depends on the total cost of transformation and interaction associated with obtaining it – if it is cheaper to make, then make it; and if it is cheaper to buy from an external specialist supplier, then buy it. From a cost perspective, the structure of the organization and the industry at any given time is designed to minimize the total costs of transaction and transformation. This logic has been explained in detail earlier in this chapter.

McKinsey predicted that with the rapid development of the Internet and related technologies, our capacity to interact would increase significantly, and it is still set to increase by a factor of two to five in the near future. The rate of data transmission capacity will continue to increase rapidly – as much as 45-fold in next ten years! The efficiency of data gathering could increase by a factor of at least three; written and oral communication by a factor of two; and group problem-solving interactions by a factor of at least 1.5. Straightforward searches can be conducted in a fraction of the time they used to take. In fact, even without further technological developments, if current technologies are broadly applied, our economic capacity to search can increase over tenfold; and our capacity to coordinate and monitor can grow by a factor of 2–10. Associated with such rapidly increasing capacity, the costs associated with interactions will decrease dramatically.

Even if we do not totally agree with the scale of these predictions, it is clear that our capacity to interact is exploding and that the costs associated with it are decreasing dramatically. This is happening at all levels of the economy. The collapsing transaction costs in many activities mean that the cost structures of industries and organizations are being redefined, significantly increasing the relative importance (or share) of transformation costs in the total costs. Although transaction costs decrease both within and between organizations, this change generally favours more activities being conducted by specialist suppliers outside the organizational boundary. It therefore puts enormous cost pressure on organizations to outsource peripheral and generic activities and focus only on their core competences. This gives rise to the need to deconstruct the integrated business models, leading to the emergence of virtual organizations in a wide range of industries.

The implication of the revolution in interaction goes far beyond organizational boundaries and industrial structures. Customers' behaviour will also change. When customers choose products and providers, they trade off the interaction costs of additional search against the marginal gains expected from it. The more they search the market, the more likely they will be to locate a supplier that could provide the product of the same quality at lower costs. When interaction costs are high, market imperfection serves to protect many providers, because when the customer locates a supplier that is acceptable (good enough) it will soon become uneconomic to continue the search because the additional costs incurred in the additional search will exceed the potential gains of locating a better supplier. However, when the interaction costs collapse and our interactive capacity increases multi-fold, any minute differences in price and other features may result in dramatic changes in customer behaviour, because the market is far more transparent than before. The change will also significantly affect distribution economics, manufacturing scales, in-sourcing versus outsourcing and a range of other decisions.[11]

Deconstruction of the Integrated Business Model

The changing cost structure of organizations and industries has put enormous pressure on organizations to focus on their core competences and outsource the rest from the market. This has resulted in the integrated business model in many industries being unbundled and deconstructed, and some scholars and business consultants went even further to prescribe how the unbundling should take place.[12] A more detailed discussion will be provided in the next section of the book when exploring emerging strategies and business models.

Until recently, the search for scale economy by internalizing interactions between different business activities led to the widespread adoption of the integrated business model, where many different activities are managed within the same organization. For most organizations, their activities can be classified into the following three categories, each illustrating the nature of activities they actually do:[13]

- customer relationship management;
- product innovation and commercialization;
- infrastructure management.

These activities have very different features and require different styles of organization and management. When they are unnaturally bundled together within one organization, none of these activities can operate at the optimum level. The emphasis for customer relation management is scope – i.e. each customer should be treated as an individual and the offering the organization provides should match the requirements of the customer as far as possible. In contrast, the emphasis for product innovation and commercialization is speed – innovate fast and get the innovations to market as quickly as possible. For infrastructure management, the key word is scale – full utilization of capacity and increase throughput as far as possible. In the past, the compromise was tolerated because of the savings garnered from the efficiency gains associated with the internalization of transactions. However, with the rapid development of computing and telecommunications and the 'revolution in interactions', interaction costs have been reduced significantly both within and between organizations. Organizations are increasingly reassessing the situation to determine if this is still the most efficient business model, and many organizations have been unbundled. In fact, many organizations are also increasingly outsourcing strategic activities from specialist suppliers, such as the whole or part of the IT, accounting or human resource functions, sometimes known as strategic outsourcing.

Unbundling does not mean that scale economy is no longer important. On the contrary, it becomes more important than ever before in many activities, and many of the unbundled activities can grow rapidly in size. This has prompted scholars to suggest the need to unbundle the unbundled.[14] This issue will be discussed in detail later in the book.

When Is Virtual Virtuous?

It should be pointed out that cost, however important, is only one of the factors that organizations consider when making strategic decisions on organizational boundaries and strategic focuses, and under certain circumstances virtual organization is the wrong organizational form to adopt and the potential danger and pitfalls of going virtual should not be ignored.[15] Since not all the smart people work for an organization, the market gives the organization access to them. However, what we should not forget is that virtual organizations have advantages but so do large integrated organizations.

The benefits of virtual organizations have been well rehearsed, but the potential problems are often overlooked. The success of virtual organizations requires all partners to work towards a common goal, but it is not uncommon for each party to act in its own self-interest at the expense of others. Friendly partnerships can go sour, and unlike vertically integrated organizations, virtual organizations tend to pursue short-term goals at the expense of long-term objectives; and the pursuit of high rewards sometimes leads to excessive risk taking by some partners, exposing the entire network to higher levels of risk. Furthermore, by squeezing efficiency out of every stage of the value chain, very little organizational slack is left in the system for absorbing potential fluctuations and disruption.

Vertically integrated organizations discourage excessive risk taking. When problems occur between different departments or business units, there are well-established procedures for resolving conflicts and coordinating activities. Compared with virtual organizations, vertically integrated organizations are more suited to tackling long-term objectives, and it is relatively easy – or less difficult – for some part of the organization to sacrifice some short-term gains for the long-term well-being of the organization as a whole.

It is therefore very important to be clear about the circumstances under which the virtual organization is more suitable than vertical integration, and vice versa. One important factor to consider is the nature of the activities. There are two kinds of innovation. For autonomous innovations, innovations that can be pursued independently and supplied to multiple buyers, virtual, decentralized organizational designs work well. However, for systemic innovations where benefits depend on related innovations in different areas, virtual organizations may not be suitable, because the success of one partner depends on other partners over which the organization has no control. For such innovations, vertically integrated organizations tend to work better. Wrong organizational design can be extremely costly. More detailed discussions about the pros and cons of virtual organizations will be explored in more detail in the next section of the book when we discuss emerging strategies and business models.

General Implications

In this chapter, the links between the development of Internet and related technologies and changes in organizational boundaries and industrial structures were examined.

From the perspective of transaction cost economics, this chapter illustrated the changing cost structure in many industries as a result of the ongoing revolution in interactions associated with the rapid development of the Internet. The implications are very profound. All organizations need to consider alternative configurations of their structures and boundaries, and explore new business models, new organizational designs and new inter-organizational relations. In doing so they should also take into account changes in customer behaviours with the collapsing of interaction and information searching costs and the growing transparency of the market. The transaction cost analysis revealed the enormous cost pressure on all organizations to outsource an increasing range of activities, and to unbundle their core activities. However, it should also be noted that cost is only one of many factors an organization should consider when making strategic decisions, and there are circumstances when outsourcing and unbundling is exactly the wrong option even though such new business models and organizational designs could lead to reduced costs in many organizations and industries.

The business environment has indeed changed significantly in many aspects. One of the most significant changes is the rapid development and proliferation of ICTs in general and Internet and related technologies in particular, which is combined with the changing nature of the economy. This combination means that many old rules of the industrial economy are no longer appropriate, and many new rules are emerging. The changing business environment requires all organizations to re-evaluate their strategies, business models and organizational designs, amongst many other issues. It is in such a rapidly and radically changing context that e-Business has originated, emerged and evolved, and its profound effects are increasingly felt.

Discussion Questions

1   A McKinsey study concluded that the rapid development of the Internet and related technologies is leading to a 'Revolution in Interaction'. These developments are bringing about radical changes in organizational boundaries and industrial structures. From a transaction cost perspective, explain why the rapid development of the Internet and related technologies might lead to changes in organizational boundaries. Illustrate how organizations could be transformed from the developments. Where appropriate, support your views with examples.

2   Many concepts have been created to illustrate the emerging economy, including the information economy, the knowledge economy, the network economy, the new economy, the creative economy and the experience economy, as well as several other related concepts not explored in this book – such as the intangible economy and the post-industrial economy. In your view, what is the essence of the emerging economy? Is it simply a continuation from the past, or are there any step changes involved? From the perspective of e-Business, which concept captures the essence of the emerging economy most accurately? Explain why.

Assignments

1. Consultancy Report
   Choose one large company you are familiar with. Conduct some background research about its main activities and how it is structured and managed. Use the theories introduced in this chapter to illustrate how the 'Revolution in Interaction' brought about by the Internet and related technologies might enable this company to adopt alternative structures and organizational boundaries. Critically evaluate the potential benefits and problems with the changes. Write up your findings in the format of a consultancy report for the senior management of the company, with clear analysis and recommendations (3,000 words).

2. Case Study
   In the past few years, many large companies have restructured their divisions and the way their activities are organized and managed. Examples include General Motors, Ford, Sony, Microsoft, HP and many others; some of them were extensively reported in the *Financial Times* and many other online and offline media. Using the Internet and other sources, choose one suitable company and study the most recent restructuring and the rationales behind it. Write a report critically evaluating whether the restructuring can be justified from the perspective of shareholders and potential investors (3,000 words).

3. Academic Journal Paper
   In the format of an academic journal article, write a literature review systematically illustrating the main changes in the business environment and the evidence for and against such changes, discussing the implications for today's organizations and highlighting areas for future research. The paper should be around 5,000 words, including abstract and full bibliography.

NOTES

1 Coase, Ronald (1937) The nature of the firm. *Economica N. S.*, vol. 4, pp. 386–405.
2 Williamson, Oliver E. (1975) *Markets and Hierarchies: Analysis and antitrust implications*, Free Press, New York; Williamson, Oliver E. (1985) *The Economic Institutions of Capitalism*, Free Press, New York; Williamson, Oliver E. (1991) Comparative economic organization: the analysis of discrete structural alternatives, *Administrative Science Quarterly*, 36(2), pp. 269–296.
3 Chandler, A. (1962) *Strategy and Structure*. MIT Press, Cambridge, Massachusetts.
4 Channon, D. (1973) *The Strategy and Structure of British Enterprise*, Macmillan, London; Pooley-Dyas, G. (1972) Strategy and structure of French enterprise, PhD Thesis, Harvard Business School, Cambridge, Massachusetts; Suzuki, Y. (1980) The strategy and structure of top 100 Japanese industrial enterprises: 1950–1970, *Strategic Management Journal*, 1, 265–291.
5 Malone, Thomas W., Joanne Yates and Robert I. Benjamin (1987) Electronic markets and electronic hierarchies. *Communications of the ACM*, 30(6), pp. 484–497.
6 Burns, T. and G. Stalker (1961) *The Management of Innovation*, Tavistock Publications, London; Child, J. (1972) Organization structure, environment and the performance: the role of strategic choice, *Sociology*, 6, 1–22; Child, J. (1974) Managerial and organizational

factors associated with company performance (Part I), *Journal of Management Studies*, October, 175–189; Child, J. (1975) Managerial and organizational factors associated with company performance (Part II) – a contingency analysis, *Journal of Management Studies*, February, 12–27; Child, J. (1984a) *Organizations*, Paul Chapman, London; Child, J. (1984b) New technology and development in management organization, *Omega*, 12(3), 211–223; Woodward, J. (1965) *Industrial Organization Theory: Theory and practices*, Oxford University Press, London.

7   Williamson (1985) op. cit., p. xii.
8   Butler, P., Ted W. Hall, A. M. Hanna, L. Mendonca, B. Auguste, J. Manyika and A. Sahay (1997) A revolution in interaction, *The McKinsey Quarterly*, no. 1, 4–23.
9   Ibid.
10   Evans, Philip, and Bob Wolf (2005) Collaboration rules. *Harvard Business Review*, July–August, 96–105.
11   Butler et al. (1997) op. cit.
12   Hagel III, John and Marc Singer (1999) *Net Worth: Shaping markets when customers make the rules*, Harvard Business School Press, Boston; Chesbrough, H. W. and D. J. Teece (1996) When is virtual virtuous? Organizing for innovation, *Harvard Business Review*, January–February, 65–73; Birch, D. and E. Burnett-Kant (2001) Unbundling the unbundled, *The McKinsey Quarterly*, pp. 103–111.
13   Hagel and Singer (1999), op. cit.
14   Birch and Burnett (2001) op. cit.
15   Chesbrough and Teece (1996) op. cit.

FURTHER READING

Birch, D. and E. Burnett-Kant, E. (2001) Unbundling the unbundled. *The McKinsey Quarterly*, pp. 103–111.

Butler, P., Ted W. Hall, A. M. Hanna, L. Mendonca, B. Auguste, J. Manyika and A. Sahay (1997) A revolution in interaction. *The McKinsey Quarterly*, no. 1, 4–23.

Chesbrough, H. W. and D. J. Teece (1996) When is virtual virtuous? Organizing for innovation. *Harvard Business Review*, January–February, 65–73.

Evans, Philip and Bob Wolf (2005) Collaboration rules. *Harvard Business Review*, July–August, 96–105.

Hagel III, John and Marc Singer (1999) *Net Worth: Shaping markets when customers make the rules*. Harvard Business School Press, Boston.

Schlenker, Lee and Alan Matcham (2005) *The Effective Organization: The nuts and bolts of business value*. John Wiley & Son, Chichester.

Part II

Emerging Strategies and Business Models in the Network Economy

Introduction

Since the business environment has changed in several important aspects as illustrated in the last part of the book, organizations have no choice but to adapt and evolve in order to achieve new 'fit', or 'alignment', with the environment – or they may face extinction. The new business environment requires organizations to adopt new strategies, business models and new organizational designs, develop new ways of doing business and manage disruptive innovations effectively. This part focuses on some emerging strategies and business models in the new business environment.

Chapter 6 will explore an important new strategy – the web strategy – which is profoundly influential in the network economy. This strategy is closely linked to some of the new rules of the network economy highlighted in chapter 4. Closely associated to this new strategy is a new trend identified in several sectors – the unbundling of integrated business models and processes. This has not only led to the emergence of virtual organizations, but also underpinned several contemporary business phenomena, such as outsourcing and offshoring. It also highlights the critical importance of standards to companies and industries, and why it is strategically important to control and facilitate the development of certain standards.

Chapter 7 examines disruptive strategic innovations in the context of the network economy. Although the concept of disruptive strategic innovation is not unique to the new economy, the rapid development of the Internet and related technologies has provided numerous new opportunities for such disruptive innovations to be introduced in different sectors. This theory can also explain why many successful companies have failed to sustain their success over time, not because their management and employees did a bad job, but exactly because they were particularly good at what they did. Possible responses to disruptive strategic innovations will also be discussed.

Chapter 8 investigates two recent strategic reorientations in the new business environment and their underlying reasons: the changing strategic focus from products and services to integrated business solutions, and more recently to the co-creation of unique experience with consumers. The critical role of the Internet and related technologies in enabling these strategic reorientations will be highlighted.

Chapter 9 discusses emerging e-Business models in different sectors. In addition to illustrating various specific e-Business models, the chapter will also introduce a comprehensive, multidimensional taxonomy and an ontological framework for e-Business models.

These emerging strategies and business models are increasingly reflected in the design of organizations which will be discussed in the third part of the book.

Chapter 6

New Strategies for the Network Economy: Web Strategy, Business Unbundling and Virtual Organizations

The changing business environment requires organizations old and new to develop new strategies and business models. One such strategy that has emerged in recent years is the so-called 'web strategy', which was conceptualized and made popular by McKinsey consultant John Hagel III and his colleagues.[1] The web here is not the World Wide Web (although the Internet plays a critical role in the emergence of this strategy in many industries). Rather, the web refers to 'clusters of companies that collaborate on a particular technology' (p. 71). The concept of the 'web' overlaps with another popular concept in the studies of innovation – 'clusters', but clusters usually have a strong geographical connotation which is not necessarily important for a web. In contrast, webs are primarily concerned with technological standards, or customer or market segments.

Hagel regards the web as a natural response to environmental uncertainty and risks, and webs create powerful new ways to think about strategy, risk, technological uncertainty and innovation. Different from traditional strategic alliances or supply chains, the web explains how independent companies cluster around particular technological standards or customer segments to deliver complex value propositions to the final consumers. This strategy requires business executives to re-evaluate their management focus, organizational structure, performance measurement, and information systems, and Hagel went even further to say that webs 'may even represent the opening salvo in the transition from industrial-age to information-age strategies' (p. 71).

The web strategy also highlights the profound significance of virtual organizations in the new economy. However, unlike the web strategy, the virtual organization illustrates situations where a cluster of independent companies actively collaborate with each other to execute a project traditionally only manageable by large, integrated organizations. The relationships between the partners of the virtual organization could be strategic alliances or other formal contracts. This allows independent organizations to collaborate and compete with larger, vertically integrated organizations.

An important process that links the web strategy and virtual organizations is the unbundling – or deconstruction – of integrated business processes and organizational models. Earlier in the book, we saw that the rapid development of ICTs and the widespread proliferation of the Internet and related technologies are leading to a revolution in interactions. This revolution redefines the cost structure of many industries, and from the perspective of transaction cost (or interaction cost) analysis, the new business environment requires organizations to unbundle their activities and integrated processes. Unbundling is an effective mechanism that enables the web to grow rapidly, and it is increasingly leading to the development of virtual organizations in many sectors.

This chapter first illustrates the web strategy developed by Hagel and colleagues, and explores its implications for today's organizations in the knowledge-based, network economy. Following this, the chapter examines the deconstruction of value chains and integrated business models and, in particular, how this might be done. Finally, the chapter discusses the virtues – and potential pitfalls – of the virtual organization. These are only some examples of emerging strategies and business models in the new business environment, and they are used to illustrate that the business environment is indeed very different from the past, and under some circumstances new strategies and business models are needed for organizations to compete effectively today. These new strategies and business models are closely linked to some of the new rules of the network economy discussed in chapter 4.

The Web Strategy

Hagel defined webs as clusters of companies collaborating around a particular technology. Examples of webs include the Microsoft Intel platform, Novell PC networking system, SAP integrated IT solutions, Netscape and the Sony PlayStation, to name but a few. The webs create conditions whereby each company within them mobilizes the support of other companies to achieve its own objectives. There are many different types of web, including the economic web, the technological web and the value web. Two other potential webs, the customer web and the market web, are also emerging in a number of sectors, such as financial services.

Classification of the web

The most significant web is perhaps the economic web, which is a cluster of companies that use a common architecture to deliver independent elements of an overall value proposition to final consumers. One example of an economic web is the Microsoft and Intel personal computer web – the Wintel web. Within the web, independent companies combine to deliver the overall value proposition of a Windows PC. The members of the web are independent companies, and very often they do not know – indeed, do not even need to know – most other members of the web; a participant in the web rarely needs to develop any formal relations with the majority of other participants. All companies in the web are wholly independent; they price, market and sell their products autonomously. It is the pursuit of economic self-interest that brings them into the web.

Other webs include the technology web, where a cluster of independent companies organize around a particular technological platform. The rapid development of the Internet and related technologies allows a growing number of industries to unbundle their vertically integrated business models to allow specialized, independent players to enter the market. One example is online services where a cluster of independent companies could provide virtually every element of an online service technology platform, from the design and operation of networks and servers to billing and network operating systems. Unbundling has created more than virtual organizations, because the providers of various services are independent and they provide their services to multiple buyers, and many of these buyers could be competitors. In doing so the technology web lowers the barrier of entry to allow new entrants to concentrate on what they are good at and obtain the rest from other participants in the web.

Another type of web is the value web, which operates within the technology web. The technology web focuses on maximizing value to the customer, whereas the value web focus on creating value for a specific group of companies that have adopted a common technology platform. Examples are the value webs in the desktop-computing technology web, Apple's Macintosh versus the PC by Microsoft and Intel.

Webs do not necessarily formulate around a particular technology. Two other types of web are emerging in a number of industries with the rapid development of the Internet: the customer web and the market web. The customer web focuses on managing the ownership of customer relationships and customer segments. By developing and maintaining deep relationships with a particular segment of customers, a company could then leverage this special relationship and deep understanding to serve a wide range of their needs by finding and delivering the most suitable products and services they need from the market and maximally satisfy each customer. Over time a web will develop around the needs of these customers.

Similarly, a market web focuses on a specific type of transaction by developing deep relationships for a particular need with all customers. For example, a portal for mortgages is the focal point of a market web, where information about all mortgage products is displayed and compared, and any customer could come and find the most appropriate mortgage. These webs are often formed when vertically integrated industries are unbundled, and related issues will be discussed later in this chapter. The list here is not exhaustive and there may be other types of web.[2]

Two conditions of an economic web: technological standards and increasing returns

Drawing on the work of Arthur W. Brian, Hagel illustrated two conditions that must be present before an economic web can form: a technological standard and increasing returns.[3] When competing technology standards exist in a market, a company often has to take huge risks when selecting which standard to follow; and once the decision is made, it is often irreversible. So following the wrong standard could be costly and strategically damaging to the company. A common standard reduces risks by allowing companies to make irreversible investment decisions in the face of technological uncertainty. This issue was discussed in detail earlier in the book when exploring new rules of the network economy, and it provides the basis for 'increasing returns' and several other new rules illustrated by Kevin Kelly.[4] A technological standard is the *de facto* collective agreement which provides the stability and safety net for firms to make dedicated investments; and those who own or control the standard can often extract disproportionate reward from it. This to some extent explains why so many software companies give away their core technologies and products to boost widespread adoption by users; and when a sufficient number of users have been locked in, more developers will develop related products using the same standard, eventually making the standard the *de facto* standard for the industry.

The second condition of an economic web is increasing returns, which creates a mutual dependence that strengthens the web by drawing in more and more customers and producers. This is closely linked to the first condition, because before a common standard is formed, firms – and consumers – must decide which early protocol to support. Withdrawing later from – or staying with – the wrong standards can be extremely costly. Only when the initial parameters and conventions freeze into unalterable standards can firms – and customers – have the confidence to make irreversible investments. This creates a virtuous, a positive feedback loop, drawing in ever more companies and consumers and increasing the size of the whole market exponentially. The result is increasing returns for everyone within the web – the more people join the web, the more valuable it is to stay in the web, which draws in even more people.[5]

These conditions perhaps can be extended to other types of web. The standard can be extended beyond technology to include other common protocols. For example, in a market web, the vast number of different products or services (e.g. different types of mortgages) needs to be compared along multiple dimensions, and those dimensions will over time become 'standards' for both providers and consumers when designing and selecting products and services, which further reinforces the importance of these (as compared to other) dimensions.

Characteristics of the web

The web has several key characteristics. Webs are not alliances, because very often there is no formal relationship between the majority of participants. Each company in a web is largely independent and their behaviours are driven by the pursuit of economic self-interest. At least in theory, they operate autonomously in the market, including setting prices, marketing and selling their products and services. Many of the companies complete fiercely with one another.

Webs are natural responses to risk and uncertainty in turbulent environments, according to Hagel. The safety net of the web allows a firm to focus exclusively on activities where it can offer distinctive value, and the common standards ensure that the products and services offered by one company can work together with those from other companies in the web. The increasing returns serve to attract more and more companies and customers into the web, thereby enabling continued growth. The web reduces the overall investment requirements by a company to enter the market, and it allows the company to focus investments on areas most likely to succeed. The web also attracts multiple suppliers to provide bottleneck components, or to address the weakest links in the web, because those are the areas that are most likely to succeed.

Roles for different players in a web: shapers and adapters

A company can perform one of two roles in a web: a shaper or an adapter. Each role can potentially create substantial value but the strategies they need to pursue and the tactics they have to adopt differ significantly. For shapers, the central task is to define, mould and influence the environment in order to enhance their ability to create value. In contrast, adapters focus on staying ahead of competition by anticipating and responding to environmental changes quickly. To illustrate the differences we can examine the strategies and tactics of Microsoft and Dell in the desktop computing web.

Shaper versus Adapter: The Example of Microsoft and Dell

As a leading shaper of this web, Microsoft has concentrated on controlling and developing key technologies and relationships in the computer arena and using these positions to shape the web. Either accidentally or deliberately, Microsoft managed to establish MS-DOS, and then Windows, as the *de facto* operating system for PCs around the world. Its strategic alliance with Intel further strengthened its architectural leadership and facilitated standard adoption. For Microsoft, its huge profit and market value have been derived from the overall architecture rather than features and attributes of individual products. As a result, Microsoft's technology focus has always straddled product and architecture, and its long-term investment strategy is to strengthen the architecture and the web.

In contrast, Dell's desktop business has followed a very different strategy. Its focus is to use its low-cost business model to offer customized products at a low price and high quality. Unlike Microsoft, Dell's success depends on its ability to exploit near-term product opportunities in the Microsoft/Intel value web. Its marketing has focused on product excellence and customization, low cost and comprehensive service, rather than trying to define new standards or create a new architecture to rival Microsoft's Windows.

As illustrated by these examples, the conditions required for a shaper and an adapter to succeed are very different. For a shaper, the ownership of a key platform technology is essential, which shapes the broader architecture and provides long-term lock-in of other participants in the web. The shapers also need to deliberately unbundle their businesses to release profitable opportunities for other web participants so as to attract companies to enter the web and create conditions of increasing returns. For the shaper, owning a smaller slice of a large and rapidly expanding web is often far more profitable

– and financially more viable – than controlling a large slice of a small and stagnated web. As such the shaper needs to actively incentivize other companies to join and promote the web, and actively manage the increasing returns dynamic to accelerate web growth. Its strategic focus needs to go far beyond the organization's own boundary because its success depends not only on how efficient or innovative it is internally, but also, more importantly, on how successful the web is. By speeding up the adoption of core technologies and expanding the range of web participants, shapers set in motion a dynamic of increasing returns that raises barriers to entry for competing shapers and switching costs for web participants. These conditions are clearly reflected in the battles between Microsoft and Apple and with companies promoting open source standards and operating systems (e.g. Redhat) and alternative office packages (e.g. Open Office, Star Office), as well as in the games market with Nintendo's Cube and Sony's PlayStation through its X-Box.

In contrast, for an adapter to be successful, early participation in the winning value web is essential for establishing pre-emptive positions in attractive markets. The adapter must pursue market shares in the value web through aggressive competition, and strengthen relationships with the key shapers for information on the latest developments. Strategically they could either link their own strategies with key shapers or straddle several competing webs, although the latter can be expensive and often requires large scales. For example, a games company could develop games for multiple platforms, but there are serious cost and skill implications.

The implications of the web strategy

The implications of the web strategy are very profound, and it creates powerful new ways to think about strategy, risk, technological uncertainty and innovation, and allows companies to manage risk and generate innovation in today's complex, rapidly changing environment. It enables companies to reduce risks by focusing on what they are genuinely good at; and it also increases flexibility and reduces the overall investment required by each company and lowers the barriers of entry. This mechanism encourages multiple entries in bottleneck areas or in areas occupied by companies without distinctive capabilities, because they provide opportunities for innovative companies to succeed. It also encourages competition and reduces risks for all participants in the web because if one company fails multiple companies will take its place.

The web also encourages innovation because information is distributed far more widely and comprehensively than in a conventional marketplace. This serves to boost functionality, service and customer adoption. It enables participants to unbundle their business so they can focus on distinctive competence whilst outsourcing undifferentiated business activities. It requires participants, especially the shapers, to broaden their strategic focus, from maximizing value to themselves to maximizing the value of the web as well.

The web strategy has profound implications for management, and it requires a new mindset and a new way of thinking about strategy, industry structure, relationships between companies and value creation. Traditionally a firm forms its own strategy and then negotiates alliances in the market to advance its strategy. Within a web, management first needs to decide which web to enter and what role it should play, and then formulates strategy for the firm. Moreover, the performance measurement of business executives in shapers needs to place as much emphasis on firm performance as on the performance of the web. More recently, business unbundling and outsourcing has gone beyond undifferentiated business activities, and through the so-called 'transformational outsourcing' or 'strategic outsourcing' some firms are increasingly outsourcing carefully selected strategic activities from reliable, competent suppliers.[6] For product designs, not only does the firm need to satisfy the final customers, but also the designs need to appeal to providers of complementary products and services. The information system of the firm often needs to extend beyond its own boundary to enhance communications and information share along the entire supply chain. The Internet makes the establishment of direct links between organizations and between organizations and individuals easy and affordable.

Many issues remain unanswered. The web strategy requires organizations to adopt a flexible organizational design and to outsource non-strategic activities and, increasingly, some strategic activities it is not good at. It also gives rise to the emergence of virtual organizations and new inter-organizational relations. However, it remains unclear how unbundling can take place, and under what conditions a virtual organization should be adopted instead of vertical integration.

Unbundling the Integrated Business Models

As explained in chapter 5, the Internet and related technologies are leading to a revolution in interaction. These technologies are enabling companies to communicate and exchange information far more quickly and cheaply than ever before, which is leading to radical changes in industrial structures and organizational boundaries. Indeed, many basic assumptions about corporate organization need to be re-evaluated. Although the outsourcing of undifferentiated activities is not new, more recently many companies are also increasingly outsourcing activities that they have traditionally believed to be central to their business. Many new, specialized suppliers can provide those services faster, better and more efficiently. Examples include the outsourcing of IT functions by leading companies: J. P. Morgan signed a contract to allow IBM to take over most of the bank's computing operations for US$5 billion over 7 years; Ford's spin-off company Visteon also signed a computing-on-demand deal with IBM for US$2 billion over 10 years; and in Europe, Telecom Italia signed a contract with Hewlett-Packard (HP) to provide IT management services worth €225 million (about US$243 million at the time) over 5 years. So what activities should be outsourced? What should be kept in-house? Answers to such questions are strategically important to all companies.

In their attempt to make sense of the radical changes, McKinsey consultants John Hagel and Marc Singer asked business executives a basic question about their companies: what business are you really in?[7] They believe that answers to this simple question will determine the fate of these companies in the network economy.

What does your company actually do?

Whenever I ask senior business executives and MBA students this simple question, the answers are always very specific, be they an investment bank, a large retailer, a telecommunications company or a car manufacturer. However, stepping back from the sectoral details of these businesses, the nature of the activities that all organizations do is much simpler. As has been briefly outlined earlier in the book, Hagel and Singer believe that most of today's companies are made up of three businesses:

- the customer relationship business;
- the product innovation and commercialization business;
- the infrastructure management business.

In other words, most organizations' activities can be assigned to one of the three categories listed above, although the make-up of some organizations tends to lean more heavily towards some of these activities than others. Such an organizational composition is a major problem for many organizations in today's business environment, because these three businesses have very different characteristics and each of them requires very different strategies, business models and organizational structure and processes to function efficiently and effectively. Historically, when transaction costs were high companies chose to reduce transaction costs by bringing all three groups of activities under the same management using vertically integrated organizational models and processes. Even though this is an unnatural bundle and everything can operate only at sub-optimal levels, the choice is justified, or tolerated, because of the gains in higher levels of efficiency and better control and coordination of these activities. Today, the revolution in interaction, brought about by the Internet and related technologies, requires organizations to re-evaluate this situation.

The customer relations business is driven by economies of scope, that is, each customer should be treated as an individual and the offerings to each customer should be – as far as possible – tailor-made to maximally satisfy their needs. A customer-service-oriented culture is essential, and the organization must devote its efforts in customization to developing relationships with customers and understanding their individual needs. The company should offer as many choices as possible to maximize selection for customers. The objective is to offer tailored bundles of products and services in order to capture a large share of customers' spending.

In contrast, the product innovation and commercialization business is driven by speed – the faster an organization can innovate and commercialize new products and services the better. This requires the organization to use all possible distribution channels to reach potential customers. The organizational culture needs to be geared towards attracting and retaining creative talents, and operations need to be tailored to serve the needs of these creative talents for breakthrough innovations. In other words, the product innovation and commercialization business requires very different strategies, organizational culture and operational systems from the customer relations business.

The infrastructure management business is significantly different in its requirements from either customer relations management or product innovation and commercialization. It is driven by economies of scale, and the organization should use the infrastructure to deliver as many products as possible, as fast as possible, and at the lowest costs. The strategic focus is on the full utilization of facilities and low-cost operations, which require an organization to be oriented towards cost reduction and standardization.

Owing to the radically different characteristics of these three groups of activities, each of them will require very different strategies, business models and organizational structure and processes – and most of all, different organizational cultures – to function efficiently and effectively. Managing them within one organization means that a compromise has to be reached, and despite various other potential benefits, none of them can operate optimally.

Unbundling the unnaturally bundled corporations

The different characteristics of the three businesses unnaturally bundled together within the same organization can create serious problems for each of them. To illustrate this example, let us look at the following example.

The Organizational Constraints of Integrated Businesses

In the UK, a high street retail bank today provides a whole range of products to customers. It is common knowledge that no bank could possibly provide 'best products' in all categories. Almost all banks use certain 'best in class' products (e.g. high savings rates) to attract customers and then cross-sell less attractive products (e.g. insurance or mortgage) to make a profit. This creates a dilemma for the financial advisers in the bank branches. The customer service policies in most banks claim that they will maximally satisfy the needs of their customers by providing what is best for them, but organizationally this is an impossible proposition. Even when the financial advisers know that the bank's savings products are excellent but its mortgage products are very expensive, they are obliged to try to cross-sell a mortgage when a customer comes to buy a savings product. In the unlikely event that the adviser did what they were supposed to do and advised the customer to buy the savings product but go to a competing provider for a mortgage, the adviser would probably be sacked.

The moral of the story is that even if the customer relations management staff (the financial advisers) want to do a good job (that is, providing what is best for the customer), they cannot do so as long as they are part of an integrated bank. By organizational design, they are obliged to sell all products from their own bank even though some of the products are not the best options for the customer. In contrast, a specialized customer service company could search the entire market and find the best-in-class products from multiple suppliers in each of the categories, and then bundle them together to maximally satisfy the needs of a customer. So for customer services, the integrated company cannot possibly compete with a specialist provider.

The same is true for product innovation and commercialization. For an integrated company, once they have invested in producing a product, the company will need to recover the investment over a certain period of time and extract as much profit from it as possible. If halfway through an investment cycle a newer and better product is invented, it may well be in the company's interest not to commercialize the new product too quickly, in case it cannibalizes the existing product and the investment already made in the existing product cannot be recovered. In comparison, for an independent product innovation and commercialization company, the considerations will be very different and they will explore different routes to market and commercialize the product as quickly as possible.

For infrastructure management businesses, the driving force is scale economies and the more products that can be pumped through the infrastructure the more quickly the organization can recover its investment and make a profit. However, being part of an integrated business will restrict what can and cannot be delivered through the infrastructure.

The Cash Machine Networks (ATMs) and the Royal Mail

For example, the cash machine networks (automated teller machines (ATMs)) in the UK require huge investment to develop and maintain, and for most banks it is a service they have to provide to customers and often it is not a profitable activity. However, if the network can be detached from banks, the infrastructure can be used to deliver more than cash and it can also be used to provide a range of other services – for example, selling theatre or football tickets, providing local information and so on, thereby generating additional revenues for its providers. This may enable the ATM network to become a stand-alone, profitable business.

Another example is the Royal Mail in the UK. At the moment, the Royal Mail is simply an infrastructure to deliver letters to every household and business in the UK and the gateway for such services to the rest of the world. An alternative way to look at the business is as an infrastructure business, and the products it can deliver can be extended from letters to – depending on how far you wish stretch the boundary – pizzas and everything else that needs to be delivered to businesses and households. The nature of the post office branches could also be reoriented in a similar fashion – it is the only organization that has a presence in every community within the country! However, just delivering letters is increasingly insufficient to sustain the network profitably. Perhaps the long-term survival of the Royal Mail depends on such a reorientation?

The implications are very profound. Since the 1990s, large companies have spent considerable energy and resources re-engineering and redesigning their core processes. They have used the latest ICTs to eliminate human intervention, cut waiting time and reduce errors. For many companies, streamlining core processes has yielded impressive gains, saving money and time and providing customers with more valuable products and services. However, there are limits to such gains. The principles governing the three core processes conflict with one another. Bundling them into a single corporation inevitably forces management to compromise the performance of each process in ways that no amount of re-engineering can overcome.

In the past when transaction costs were high, and sometimes for other strategic reasons (which is still the case for many organizations today), these activities were bundled together under the same organizational roof and managed via vertically integrated business models and organizational designs. However, the conditions today have changed and it often makes more sense to unbundle them and run each of the three activities as stand-alone businesses. Examining the fundamental nature of the businesses provides one way to deconstruct the vertically integrated business model and processes. From a transaction cost perspective, there is also enormous cost pressure for organizations to do so, even though for other strategic reasons some organizations may choose not to unbundle – or deconstruct.

It should be pointed out that unbundling does not mean that scale economies are no longer important. On the contrary, some of the unbundled businesses can grow to massive scales but the nature of the businesses is more homogeneous and the activities within the organizational boundary require similar strategy, organizational culture and management styles. Hagel and Singer believed that only product innovation is likely to be dominated by a large number of small companies because of the need for creativity, which favours smaller companies. The other two businesses – customer relations management and infrastructure management – are likely to consolidate quickly and be dominated by a small number of large companies.

For many organizations, unbundling should not be treated as a one-off activity and, over time, the unbundled and more specialized businesses will evolve and develop other activities within the organization's boundary. For example, an infrastructure management business unbundled from customer relations management and product innovation and commercialization businesses will need to develop these two latter activities over time, albeit at smaller scales and focusing on different customers and product innovations. The infrastructure management business will need to be supported by personnel specializing in dealing with customers requiring the infrastructure; and it will also need to devote resources and effort to developing, identifying or introducing innovations in relevant technologies or new products for the infrastructure. As the new businesses evolve, the same logic that is leading to the unbundling of integrated business models today may apply to each of the unbundled, specialized businesses. This is in fact already happening in some industries.

Unbundling the unbundled: the second wave

According to Birch and Burnett, a second wave of unbundling is transforming the way asset-intensive companies work.[8] They refer to this process as 'unbundling the unbundled'. Before deregulation in the 1980s in the USA and other developed countries such as the UK and Japan, most basic capital-intensive services were heavily regulated and/or owned by the state. Such services were mostly delivered by monopolies (single supplier); examples include gas, electricity, water, telecommunications, railways and other utilities. Since deregulation, most of these services have been privatized, and the previously vertically integrated service delivery models have been unbundled into discrete businesses, each focusing on a segment or an aspect of the previous integrated processes. For example, the electricity business was unbundled into electricity generation, high-voltage distribution, low-voltage distribution and retailing. Similar unbundling also happened in other industries such as gas, water, railways and telecommunications.

The unbundling of the integrated business model in utilities and other industries stimulated innovation and led to significant improvements in efficiency. This was largely achieved by introducing competition into those stages of the value chain that are not natural monopolies. However, more recently, a second wave of unbundling is taking place within the unbundled businesses – this time to separate asset ownership, asset management and service delivery. An example of this is the gas business, where the ownership of the pipeline is separated from the business of pipeline operation, maintenance and upgrading, and the business of day-to-day work. These activities may first become separate divisions of an integrated company but eventually may divest into separate stand-alone businesses. Similar ideas have been implemented in the railway industry in the UK, albeit with mixed results. More research is needed in this area.

The Emergence of Virtual Organizations

The implementation of the web strategy and the unbundling of the integrated business model in a series of industries, combined with rapid growth of simple and strategic outsourcing, are leading to the emergence of virtual, network organizations. According to McKinsey, collaborative networks of suppliers, distributors, subcontractors and customers have created far more value than their industry peers since the mid-1990s and held up more robustly during the market downturn.[9] Because manufacturing, product innovation and customer care require different talents and make conflicting claims on organizations, it would probably be wise to unbundle these activities under many circumstances. This is achievable because today, with the Internet, computer networks can be easily and cheaply established between organizations for the exchange of information about inventory, production, demand and so forth, through common software platforms and protocols. Such changes are happening in a variety of industries, from transportation to passenger airlines to car manufacturing.

The ideas on which such forms of organization have been built go back several decades. Back in 1969 Peter Drucker began writing about knowledge workers and their preference for purposefully focused organizations. Then Charles Handy noted the existence of shamrock organizations, made up of a core of essential executives and workers supported by outside contractors and part-time help, which was also referred to as the 'flexible firm' by some researchers.[10] Virtual organizations, or network organizations, have not simply emerged to meet the needs of the unbundled corporation. Rather they have emerged to exploit declining interaction costs, tightly linked supply chains, and Internet-based ordering platforms. These developments allow interactions to take place between themselves, their business partners and their customers which promote collective learning in the organization, especially in terms of how to coordinate diverse production skills and integrate multiple streams of technologies. This allows each company to leverage the resources and core competences of their partners to earn higher margins with less capital than do their industry peers. Remo Hacki and Julian Leighton went even further to say that this business model may forever change the way companies compete.[11]

'When is virtual virtuous?'[12]

Since the turn of the 1990s, there has been copious praise for the virtual organization.[13] According to Chesbrough and Teece, the logic behind this enthusiasm is that managers and academics alike are increasingly convinced that bureaucracy is bad and flexibility is good. Virtual organizations require less investment and are far more responsive to market changes than integrated companies, and therefore are more suited for today's volatile business environment. Despite repeated warnings about the potential pitfalls of the virtual organization since the mid-1990s, managers are still urged to subcontract everything possible today, through downsizing, decentralization, alliances and, more recently, strategic and operational outsourcing.

Back in 1996, Chesbrough and Teece famously pointed out that despite the fact that many large, integrated companies had been outperformed by smaller networked, virtual organizations, there were perhaps even more failures of virtual organizations that did not make the headlines.[14] They went on to investigate the circumstances under which the virtual organization has advantages, and circumstances that are more suited for large integrated companies. Virtual organizations have many advantages but so have large integrated organizations.

According to Chesbrough and Teece, the keys to the success of virtual organizations are incentives and responsiveness. Rather than relying on administrative measures of the hierarchy to deploy resources and set priorities, virtual organizations use market mechanisms to bring free agents together to buy and sell goods and services. In particular, not even the largest companies can claim that all the smartest people in the world work for them, so the market gives organizations access to such talents when required. Virtual networks of free agents can often harness the competence of one another to develop, manufacture, market, distribute and support integrated solutions for the final consumers in ways integrated companies could not. In particular, many of the free agents will work harder and take greater risks in order to reap greater financial rewards. In other words, by stimulating innovation and encouraging risk taking, such networks can be more sensitive, innovative and responsive to market changes than integrated companies.

The problem is that the greater incentives could lead to excessive risk taking by some of the free agents, and when some of them fail, there is the risk of the entire network being pulled down with them. Also, because each of the free agents is independent, each party in the network tends to act in its own self-interest, often at the expense of others. Furthermore, the transient nature of many such arrangements means that most partners will take a short-term view, and there is also the risk of friendly partnerships going sour. Market mechanisms are not as effective in resolving conflicts as integrated companies. Also, the responsiveness of the virtual organization is often oversold: unlike some integrated companies, virtual organizations often squeeze every little inefficiency out of the system with the result that very little organizational slack is left in the system to absorb potential disruptions and market fluctuations. When the market changes direction suddenly, the whole network often collapses.

In contrast, integrated companies rely on internal administrative measures to coordinate activities, control resources and set priorities. Despite their various shortcomings, integrated organizations discourage excessive risk taking. Within such organizations it is possible for some sections to make local sacrifices for the benefit of the whole organization. There are also well-established procedures for resolving conflicts and coordinating activities. Unlike virtual organizations, integrated organizations are better suited to tackling long-term objectives by forgoing some short-term gains. Even the inefficiency inherent in integrated companies can be beneficial, because such organizational slack can be deployed to absorb sudden increases in demand, for example, which increases the reliability and resilience of the organization in the market over the long term.

Chesbrough and Teece regarded the virtual organization and the integrated company as two extremes of a continuum; in the middle are various alliances. The key is to strike an appropriate balance between incentive and control, which depends on the nature of the innovation the organization is pursuing.

Autonomous versus systemic innovations

There are two types of innovation. On the one hand there are innovations that can be pursued independently. An example of such an innovation is a turbo charger for cars which can be developed independently but fitted to all models from different manufacturers. In contrast, another type of innovation must be pursued collaboratively in a systemic fashion, and one cannot function without the other. An example is instant photography which depends on a perfect marriage of camera technologies with film technologies.

When innovations are autonomous, virtual organizations can manage the development and commercialization of the innovation very well, as illustrated earlier in this chapter when discussing the need to unbundle integrated corporations. In contrast, when the innovation is systemic, integrated organizational designs are often more appropriate because the organization does not need to rely on other independent partners over whom they have no control. The wrong organizational designs can be extremely costly.

It should also be noted that all innovations depend critically on information flows. Codified information can travel relatively easily between organizations, but tacit knowledge is deeply embedded in an organization and does not travel across organizational boundaries easily. The information needed to integrate an autonomous innovation with existing technologies is usually well understood and sometimes such information is codified in industry standards. In contrast, systemic innovations often require information that is largely tacit in nature, and it is often easier and safer to coordinate the

exchange of such information within the boundary of an organization. This is particularly the case when industry standards do not exist. When multiple standards exist in
a market, a large integrated company can choose to advance one particular standard
by investing in a particular technology and using its influence to persuade customers
and other companies to support the standard. Once a standard is firmly established,
however, virtual organizations can often use their flexibility to develop further innovations within the safety net of the established standards more effectively than large
integrated companies can. Some of the related issues have been explored in detail
when discussing the web strategy.

Going Virtual? The Rise and Fall of IBM

The success and failure of virtual organizations were clearly illustrated by the
rise and fall of IBM since the 1980s. Under threat from aggressive advances
by Apple, IBM launched its first PC in 1981. Rather than developing its own
technologies, IBM chose to outsource all major components from the market:
microprocessors were purchased from Intel and the operating system licensed
from Microsoft. The PC was based on a standard and components that were
widely available on the market, and this enabled hundreds of third-party developers of software and hardware to join the fray. IBM also relied on third parties
to distribute its products. In doing so IBM greatly reduced the time and investment required and was able to bring the product to market in 15 months. This
approach brought clear early success to IBM, and by 1984, IBM replaced Apple
as the number one supplier of PCs with a market share of 26 per cent, which
further grew to 41 per cent.

However, the early success was soon eroded because IBM lost control of the
PC architecture it created. Competitors were able to buy the same components,
license the same operating system and application software, and use the same
distribution channels, leaving IBM with little to establish competitive advantages. When IBM tried to regain control of the architecture by launching its own
OS/2 operating system, Microsoft introduced a competing system, Windows,
which was backward compatible with the old operating system, DOS. Windows
offered a more attractive option to third-party developers and customers who
invested in the original operating system, making switching to OS/2 far less
attractive. Compaq was also able to work with Intel to launch the first 386
PC before IBM. By 1995, IBM's PC market share had been reduced to a mere
7.3 per cent, against Compaq's 10.5 per cent – and in 2005 the IBM PC was sold
to China's Lenova. However, IBM did help create some super-rich companies in
the industry – from Intel and Microsoft to Hewlett-Packard and Dell.

Main lessons

The moral of the story is that a company should not outsource everything, because
companies need to choose, nurture and guard their internal capabilities to underpin

their long-term competitive advantages. Without core competences and strong internal strength, strategic positions in virtual networks are often short-lived. This important lesson was further illustrated by Chesbrough and Teece with a series of other examples.[15]

Many other lessons can also be learnt. The virtual organization is not a panacea and it is only effective under particular circumstances. For most organizations, especially large organizations, striking the right balance between a mixture of internal development capabilities, licences, partnerships and alliances, as well as new technologies purchased from other companies, is essential to their long-term competitiveness and survival. Without control over key technologies and relationships, backed by strong internal capability, market-led virtual networks often do not work. Internal capability is particularly crucial for a firm to shape the market.

A further lesson is that organizations need to evaluate a new strategy and business model over different time scales and the right balance between long-term opportunities and short-term gains is very important. Too short a time horizon in evaluating new strategies and business models is dangerous; equally dangerous – and irresponsible – is the decentralization and outsourcing of key activities and technologies without strategic leverage and central coordination and control over the relationships or the providers.

The potential pitfalls of the virtual organization do not imply that this phenomenon is not significant. On the contrary, the concept of the virtual organization is essential to understanding how many of the new businesses actually work. Tom Peters, in his usual provocative style, vividly illustrated how a tiny band of Internet-savvy fundamentalists humbled the world's only superpower on 11 September 2001, through passionate focus, coordinated communication and a few $3.19 box cutters.[16] He argued that in an era when terrorists use satellite phone and encrypted e-mails, the US gatekeepers – the police, CIA and FBI, amongst others – stand armed against them with pencils and paperwork, and computer systems that do not even talk to each other. To a certain extent, Peters regarded this as the failure of organizations invented for another era, which was brilliant for fighting the Soviet Union but a lousy structure for dealing with al Qaeda. This was an expensive lesson that perhaps we should have learnt from the business world: Sears was brilliantly equipped for dealing with Montgomery Ward, but totally unprepared for Wal-Mart. IBM was effective in developing mainframe computers and competing with Control Data, but ill-equipped to compete with Microsoft. Merrill Lynch was fully equipped to compete with J. P. Morgan but unprepared for Charles Schwab. Virtual organizations have many advantages over integrated companies, under certain circumstances and if implemented properly. The critical issue is to identify the right circumstances and the activities and processes to unbundle or outsource from the market, and execute the strategy effectively.

Summary

In the context of the changing business environment and the new rules of the networked, knowledge-based economy, this chapter illustrated one set of emerging strategies and business models. The web strategy represents a powerful new way to think about strategy, risk, technological uncertainty and innovation, and it encourages business executives to re-evaluate their management focus, organizational structure, performance measurement, and information systems.

The web strategy highlights the critical importance of standards in today's business environment; and once standards are established, it requires organizations to unbundle integrated business models and processes in order to unleash opportunities for other companies and grow the market rapidly. This is leading to the unbundling of many corporations and facilitating the emergence of virtual, network organizations.

However, virtual organizations are not panaceas for today's organizational problems, and they pose new challenges to business executives. Under specific circumstances the virtual organization is very effective in harnessing the resources and competence of independent companies in the market to deliver integrated solutions to customers, and it is indeed more responsive and flexible than many of the vertically integrated companies in responding to market changes. At the same time it should be noted that under some circumstances, vertically integrated organizations still have many advantages and can effectively deal with many strategic and operational issues in ways far superior to virtual networks of independent organizations. The conditions for each of these organizational models were illustrated in detail in the chapter.

Before turning to the next chapter, it should also be emphasized that these are only some examples of emerging strategies and business models in the new business environment, and some other new theories will be discussed in the following chapters. Even if you do not fully accept some aspects of these theories and the changes they imply, this chapter has clearly demonstrated that changes in the business environment are increasingly reflected in emerging strategies and business models. All organizations at least need to re-examine the suitability of their existing strategies and business models in the context of the new business environment.

Discussion Questions

1 The changing business environment means that organizations need to adopt new strategies and business models. One such strategy is the so-called 'web strategy'. What is the web strategy? Critically evaluate its relevance to today's organizations.

2 Outsourcing – and offshoring – has been a major business phenomenon in recent years, and the activities being outsourced and offshored have also been extended from routine, peripheral activities to more complex and strategically important ones (strategic or transformational outsourcing). Using the theories covered in this chapter and any other theories you feel appropriate, systematically map out the benefits and potential problems of outsourcing and offshoring. Support your points with examples where appropriate.

3 Explain what a virtual organization is. Discuss the main rationales for going virtual, and explain under what conditions virtual organizations are the wrong organizational design to adopt and why.

4 Standards are extremely important in many industries – ranging from computer games (the competition between the Sony PlayStation, Nintendo Cube and the

Xbox) to information systems (Microsoft versus open source) and business processes. Explain why standards are so important in the network economy. Highlight the implications for today's organizations.

Assignment: Case Study

Webs do not necessarily form around a particular technology. The customer web focuses on managing the ownership of customer relationships and customer segments; and a market web focuses on a specific type of transaction by developing deep relationships for a particular need with all customers. Using the Internet as your main source of information to identify a customer or market web, study how it is formed, who the main players are, where revenues come from, and the role played by Internet and related technologies in the web, and make recommendations to the main companies involved. Write up your main findings as an essay. The target audience is students in your class (3,000 words).

NOTES

1   Hagel III, John (1996) Spider versus spider, *The McKinsey Quarterly*, no. 1, 4–19. Some of the ideas were further explored in two subsequent books – *Net Gain* and *Net Worth*.
2   Sviokla, John and Anthony Paoni (2005) Every product's a platform. *Harvard Business Review*, October, 17–18.
3   Arthur, W. Brian (1994a) *Increasing Returns and Path Dependence in the Economy*, University of Michigan Press, Ann Arbor; and Arthur, W. Brian (1994b) Positive feedbacks in the economy, *The McKinsey Quarterly*, no. 1, 81–95; Hagel (1997) op. cit.
4   Kelly, Kevin (1997) New rules for the new economy: Twelve dependable principles for thriving in the turbulent world, *Wired*, September, 140–197, http://www.wired.com/wired/archive/5.09/newrules.html.
5   Ibid.
6   Linder, Jane C. (2004) Transformational outsourcing. *Sloan Management Review*, 45(2), 52–58.
7   Hagel III, John and Marc Singer (1999) *Net Worth: Shaping markets when customers make the rules*, Harvard Business School Press, Boston; Hagel III, John and Marc Singer (1999) Unbundling the corporation, *Harvard Business Review*, March–April, 77(2), 133–141.
8   Birch, D. and E. Burnett-Kant (2001) Unbundling the unbundled. *The McKinsey Quarterly*, no. 1, 4–23.
9   Singer, Marc (2001) A new business model may forever change the way companies compete. *The McKinsey Quarterly*, no. 3, 1–3.
10 Atkinson, J. and N. Meager (1986) *Changing Working Patterns*. NEDO, London.
11 Hacki, Remo and Julian Leighton (2001) The future of the networked company. *The McKinsey Quarterly*, no. 3, 26–39.
12 Chesbrough, H. W. and Teece, D. J. (1996) When virtual is virtuous? Organizing for innovation. *Harvard Business Review*, January–February, 65–73.
13 Ibid; Barnett, Christopher (1995) Office space, cyberspace and virtual organization, *Journal of General Management*, 20(4), 78–91.
14 Chesbrough and Teece (1996), op. cit.
15 Ibid.

16   Peters, Tom (2003) *Re-imagine! Business excellence in a disruptive age.* Dorling Kindersley, London.

FURTHER READING

Birch, D. and E. Burnett-Kant (2001) Unbundling the unbundled. *The McKinsey Quarterly,* no. 1, 4–23.

Chesbrough, H. W. and Teece, D. J. (1996) When virtual is virtuous? Organizing for innovation. *Harvard Business Review,* January–February, 65–73.

Hagel III, John (1996) Spider versus spider. *The McKinsey Quarterly,* no. 1, 04–19.

Hagel III, John and Marc Singer (1999) *Net Worth: Shaping markets when customers make the rules.* Harvard Business School Press, Boston.

Hagel III, John and Marc Singer (1999) Unbundling the corporation. *Harvard Business Review,* March–April, 77(2), 133–141.

Linder, Jane C. (2004) Transformational outsourcing. *Sloan Management Review,* 45(2), 52–58.

Sviokla, John and Anthony Paoni (2005) Every product's a platform. *Harvard Business Review,* October, 17–18.

Chapter 7

Managing Disruptive Strategic Innovations in the New Economy

Since the late 1990s, a very influential strategic innovation has been the theory of disruptive strategic innovations – also known as the strategy of disruption. This theory was first developed and made popular by Professor Clayton Christensen of Harvard Business School in his bestseller *The Innovator's Dilemma* in 1997.[1] In this book he explained how industry leaders that focused on high-end products for their most profitable customers can be 'blindsided' by disruptive innovations from new competitors. Two books followed a few years later, one in 2003, *The Innovator's Solution: Creating and sustaining successful growth*, co-authored with Michael Raynor.[2] This book showed established companies how to create disruptive innovations rather than being destroyed by them, and how to turn innovative ideas into new disruptive products that can lead to long-term profitable growth. Then in 2004, another book was jointly written with Eric Roth and Scott Anthony: *Seeing What Next: Using theories of innovation to predict industry change*, which summarized and further developed the theory of disruptive strategic innovations and supported it with new evidence and more detailed explanations.[3] Several other authors also contributed to the debate; amongst them are Constantinos Charitou and Constantinos Markides of London Business School,[4] and Clark Gilbert of Harvard Business School.[5] Other research, such as the work on radical product and process innovations, also contributed to our understanding of relevant issues.[6]

The strategy of disruption is one of the most influential theories in recent years and it provides a powerful framework for executives to identify emerging opportunities and challenges in the market and develop appropriate strategic responses. In particular, it provides an insightful explanation to a question that has been puzzling academics, consultants and business executives for decades: why do successful companies fail to sustain profitable growth for more than a few years? According to this theory, these companies fail not because the executives and workers are doing a bad job. Ironically many of them fail exactly because they have been doing an excellent job in what they are supposed to be doing – improving products rapidly and continuously and focusing on the needs of the high-end, most profitable customers.

The theory of disruptive innovation is not specific – or unique – to the knowledge-based, network economy. Many disruptive innovations were introduced in different sectors several decades ago – perhaps throughout a large part of the history of indus-trialization in some sectors. However, disruptive strategic innovations are particularly influential – and disruptive – in today's business environment, mainly because of the extremely rapid development and widespread proliferation of ICTs and the network effects associated with the Internet and related technologies. Despite the dot.com bust in 2000 and 2001, we need only look at examples such eBay, Google, Amazon.com, Yahoo, Charles Schwab, Expedia, Travelocity and so on to see how these new entrants have radically disrupted a wide range of industries, from auctions, directories and search, stock-brokering and book retailing to holidays, travel and hotel booking. Equally, many of the failed dot.com companies have also indicated the resilience of established incumbents in the competitive fight against new entrants through what Christensen called sustaining innovations. In either case, different industries have been significantly shaken up by disruptions from new entrants, or through the defensive measures by incumbents against new entrants by using the Internet to sustain their existing services and business models. To date, the Internet Revolution has unleashed numerous disruptive and sustaining opportunities in many sectors, and the effects will continue to be felt in the days to come.

The Strategy of Disruption: From Innovator's Dilemmas to Innovator's Solutions

Christensen pointed out that roughly only one company in every ten is able to sustain the kind of growth that translates into above-average increases in shareholder returns over more than a few years. Once a company's core business has matured, the pursuit of new platforms for growth entails significant risk and, in fact, most companies simply do not know how to grow. Worse still, pursuing growth the wrong way can be worse than no growth at all.[7]

Managers have long sought ways to predict the outcome of competition based around innovation, but it has become increasingly difficult to do so in recent years. It is no longer simply a matter of large companies using their resources to crush smaller competitors or to bring about incremental changes and innovations that enable them to outperform the competition. It is the 'circumstances' of innovations that often determine whether incumbent industry leaders or upstart companies win a competi-tive battle. New entrants are more likely to overtake entrenched leaders in disruptive circumstances, when the challenge is to commercialize a simpler, more convenient product that sells for less money and appeals to new customers. Established compan-ies, conversely, can capture disruptive growth, rather than be defeated by it, if they are aware of the circumstances of disruptive innovations and are able to leverage them for their own benefit.

Two types of innovation: sustaining versus disruptive innovation

Different from the classification of innovations into autonomous innovations and systemic innovations when examining the suitability of different organizational models and designs in the last chapter, Christensen classified innovations into two categories along a different dimension: sustaining innovations and disruptive innovations. The nature of the innovation determines whether established companies or new entrants eventually win the competitive battle in the market.

In every industry, there is a rate of improvement in products that customers can fully utilize or absorb. However, in most industries, the pace of technological progress almost always outstrips the ability of customers in any given tier of the market to use it, partly because companies keep trying to make better products that they can sell for higher profit margins to their most demanding, high-end customers. This overshoot creates a serious problem for established companies making such products, because at some point the features of their latest products will not be fully utilized – or even required – by more and more customers, first by customers at the lower end of the market but eventually even by the most demanding customers at the top end. This creates opportunities for new entrants to enter the market with products with fewer features and lower specifications, first selling them to customers at the lower end of the market (i.e. the least attractive customers to established companies), but eventually moving upwards to include the more profitable customers for the established companies as well (figure 7.1).

The materialization of such a scenario depends critically on the nature of the innovation in question. There are two types of innovation. A sustaining innovation targets

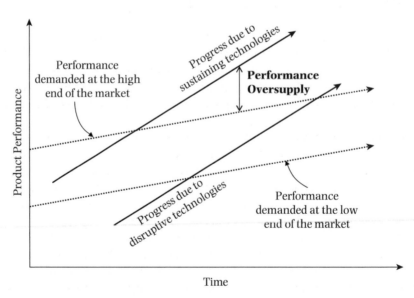

Figure 7.1 The impact of sustaining and disruptive technological change
Source: Adapted from Christensen (1997)

those demanding, high-end customers with better performance than previously available, whether that performance is an incremental improvement or a breakthrough improvement. In contrast, disruptive innovations do not attempt to bring better products to established customers in existing markets. Instead, they introduce products and services that are not as good as existing products, but which are simpler, more convenient, and less expensive than existing ones. As these simpler products continue to improve, new entrants soon get a foothold in the market and gradually squeeze out the established incumbent suppliers. The history of the computing industry in the past few decades provides an example of this scenario.

Disruption often paralyses industry-leading companies, which are more accustomed to bringing about sustaining innovations. In other words, established companies are motivated to focus on pursuing innovations to meet the needs of their high-end, most profitable customers. This leaves the door open for new entrants to target the low-end customers. Eventually, because the rate of technological progress often outstrips the rate of new improvements that customers can absorb, the new entrants can gradually disrupt the market of established companies from the bottom up and eventually attract the latter's most profitable, high-end customers as well.

Worse still, constitutionally industry leaders often cannot respond to such disruptions effectively. The resource allocation process and performance measurement are designed and perfected to support sustaining innovations, and they are always motivated to go up-market, rather than defend the low-end or new markets where the disruptions are being targeted, because the profit margins in the latter tend to be less attractive. By the time the new entrants enter the core markets of the established players, it is often too late for the incumbents to defend their positions.

Two types of disruption: low-end disruption and new market disruption

To identify where disruptions can take place, an important concept used by Christensen is the value network. Christensen defined the value network as a plane of competition and consumption in which the application and customers reside. In other words, a value network is 'the context within which a firm establishes a cost structure and operating processes and works with suppliers and channel partners in order to respond profitably to the common needs of a class of customers' (pp. 103–104).[8] He went on further to argue that within a value network, a firm's strategy, especially its cost structure and choices of markets and customers to serve, determines its perceptions of the economic value of an innovation. These perceptions in turn shape the rewards and threats that firms expect to experience through disruptive and sustaining innovations.[9]

Building on the original two-dimensional model in *The Innovator's Dilemma* (performance and time), Christensen and Raynor added a third dimension to the disruptive innovation model in *The Innovator's Solutions* by extending into new contexts of consumption and competition, i.e. new value networks. The new value networks constitute new customers who previously lacked the money or skills to buy and use the product, or different situations in which a product can be used. These were made possible by improvements in simplicity, portability and costs.

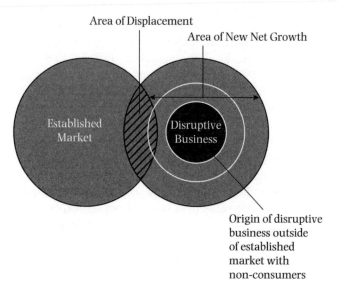

Figure 7.2 The process of new market disruption
Source: http://www.insightcentre.com/disruptbackground.htm. Adapted from Christensen and Raynor (2003)

Within the original value network of established companies, disruptions can happen by attracting low-end customers and moving upwards over time as the technologies improve, which is called low-end disruption. Disruptions that take root at the low end of the original, mainstream value network do not create new markets, but simply use low-cost models that pick off an established firm's least attractive customers. In contrast, new-market disruptions take place in different value networks, by competing with non-consumption, i.e. by converting previous non-customers into active customers and creating a new market. As improvements are made in new-market disruptions, the companies that foster them are able to pull customers out of old, mainstream value networks and into new ones (figure 7.2).

Circumstances: what products do customers want to buy?

Christensen criticized the fact that marketers often segment markets by product type, price, or demographics of the individuals or companies that comprise their customer base. This segmentation is often defined by the attributes of products or customers, which reveals correlations between those attributes and outcomes. It does not, however, offer plausible causality: what features, functions and positioning will cause customers to buy a product. To address this problem, Christensen introduced the concept of 'circumstances' and offered a more plausible way of segmenting the market. He argued that in essence, customers 'hire' products to do specific 'jobs', and managers must segment their markets to mirror the way their customers experience life. Successful products must target the circumstances in which customers find themselves, rather than the customers themselves.

Using the example of a simple product – a milkshake – during different times of day, and the different 'jobs' the same customer is hiring the product to do in the USA, Christensen vividly illustrated the flaws of existing approaches in segmenting the market by most companies, and highlighted the importance of understanding the circumstances under which a customer buys a product. Knowing what job a product gets hired to do, and knowing what jobs out there are not getting done very well, can give innovators a much clearer road map for improving their products to beat the true competition from the customer's perspective. This segmentation can then be used to gain a disruptive foothold – the initial product or service that is the point of entry for a new-market disruption. While it may never be possible to get every dimension of a product introduction in a new-market disruption right straight away, using the jobs-to-be-done lens can help innovators come to market with an initial product that is much closer to what customers ultimately value.

The best customers for your products: low-end and new-market customers

The low-end disruptor's marketing task is to extend the low-cost business model up towards products that do the jobs that the more profitable customers are trying to get done. New-market disruptions require the innovators to invent the upward path, because no one has been up that trajectory before. It is relatively straightforward to identify ideal customers for a low-end disruption – the current customers of the mainstream product who are uninterested in high-performance products. However, identifying new-market customers is a complex task, because there are different reasons for non-consumption that the new entrant tries to attract.

When only a fraction of a population is using a product, some of the non-consumption may simply reflect the fact that there is not a job that needs to be done in the lives of non-consumers. Thus, a product that aims to help non-consumers do something that they had not already prioritized in their lives is unlikely to succeed. Another kind of non-consumption occurs when people try to get a job done but find themselves unable to accomplish it, because the available products are too expensive or too complicated for them. Hence, they put up with getting it done in an inconvenient, expensive or unsatisfying way, or simply do not do it at all. This type of non-consumption is a growth opportunity awaiting a new-market disruption that enables these consumers to begin buying and using a product that helps them do the job.

Organizational responses to disruptive innovations: core competence versus outsourcing

Decisions about what activities to handle in-house and what to procure from suppliers and partners have a huge impact on a new venture's chances of success. Most companies follow the core competency rule – if something fits a company's core competence, the company should do it in-house; if it is not a core competence and another firm can do it better, then it should be outsourced from that firm.

This issue was discussed in detail in the last chapter when exploring the circumstances when virtual organizations are superior to vertically integrated organizations, and vice versa. The problem with this approach is that what seems to be a peripheral activity today might become an absolutely crucial competence to have in the future.

Core Competence versus Outsourcing: IBM

IBM's decision to outsource the microprocessor for its PC business from Intel and its operating system from Microsoft is a good example. As discussed in the last chapter, when IBM made these decisions in the early 1980s, it did so in order to focus on what it did best, that is, designing, assembling and selling computers. This also enabled IBM to keep development costs and time to the bare minimum. However, in the process of outsourcing what was not its core or its competence, IBM helped grow two companies that eventually captured most of the profit in the industry. The moral of the story is that instead of asking what their company does best today, managers should determine what they need to master today and in the future in order to excel on the trajectory of improvement that customers will define as important.

From the job-to-be-done perspective, customers will not buy your product unless it solves a problem for them. What comprises a solution, however, differs across two circumstances: whether products are not good enough, or more than good enough. The advantage goes to integration when products are not good enough, and to outsourcing when products are more than good enough. Interestingly, this is linked to the conclusions in the last chapter that such a decision should be based on the nature of the innovation in question: if it is systemic innovation, vertical integration is superior to virtual organization; and when the innovation is autonomous and can be pursued independently, virtual organization is superior to vertical integration.

When product functionality and reliability are not yet good enough to address the needs of customers in a given tier of the market, companies must compete by making the best possible products. Firms that build their products around proprietary, interdependent architectures (i.e. one part cannot be created or used independently of another part) enjoy important competitive advantage over competitors whose product architectures are modular (in which the fit and function of all elements are so connected that it does not matter who makes the separate components). Companies that compete with proprietary, interdependent architectures must be integrated and they must control the design and manufacture of every critical component of the system.

Once customers' requirements for functionality and reliability have been met, they redefine what is not good enough, which changes the basis of competition in that market. The pressure of competing along this new trajectory of improvement forces a gradual evolution in product architecture, away from the proprietary and interdependent, towards more modular designs in a period of 'too good' performance. Modular architectures enable companies to introduce new products faster because they can upgrade individual pieces of a product without having to create a brand-new design. Modularity enables independent, non-integrated organizations to sell, buy and assemble components and subsystems. This scenario clearly favours outsourcing and virtual organizational designs. So in parallel with the nature of innovation (systematic versus autonomous innovation), another important dimension to consider when choosing appropriate organizational designs (integrated versus virtual organization) is the stage of development from the customers' job-to-be-done perspective.

Organizational structures and disruptive innovations

Organizations have different cost structures, and this structure often determines if an innovation is worth pursuing. If, for example, the structure of a company's overhead costs requires it to achieve gross profit margins of 50 per cent, most ideas that promise gross margins below 50 per cent are likely to be killed off. Such an organization would be incapable of succeeding in low-margin businesses. In contrast, a different organization with a different cost structure might accord a high priority to a similar project. If a new product has the potential to generate $10 million revenue, it might not be attractive to Microsoft at all, but it would be extremely attractive to many other companies with lower cost structures and smaller sizes. These differences create the asymmetries of motivation that exist between disruptors and those that are disrupted.

Incumbent leaders in an industry almost always emerge victorious in sustaining technology battles, whereas historically they have almost always lost battles of disruption. Industry leaders develop and introduce sustaining technologies over and over again, and this enables them to develop a capability for sustaining innovation that resides in their processes. Sustaining technology investments also fit the values of the leading companies, because they promise improved profit margins from better or cost-reduced products. In contrast, no company has an established process for handling disruptive innovations. Disruptive products typically promise lower profit margins and cannot be used by the best customers, making disruptions inconsistent with many companies' values. Leading companies have the resources required to succeed, but their processes and values are not designed to pursue disruptive innovation. Smaller, disruptive companies are different: they might lack resources, but their values can embrace small markets and their cost structures can accommodate lower margins. These advantages can add up to enormous opportunity for them to beat industry leaders through disruptive strategic innovations.

Top-Down Disruptions

Most authors of strategic disruption have focused on bottom-up or new-market disruptions. A disruptive product or service usually underperforms established products or services in the mainstream markets. These disruptive products and services are usually sold for less money than the current mainstream offering, to the least profitable customers of established players at low margins. As the performance of the product or service improves steadily, they redefine the entire market and displace the

incumbents in the process. This model can convincingly explain why many big, successful companies fail to defend their market positions against low-end new entrants.

However, Nicholas Carr highlighted another type of disruptive innovation – top-
down disruptions.[10] He used the examples of Federal Express and Wang Labs' word
processing system to illustrate how these companies started at the top end of the
market and rapidly moved downwards to disrupt established markets. In contrast to
bottom-up disruptions, top-down disruptions outperform existing products when they
are introduced, selling at a premium price rather than a discount. These products
and services are initially purchased by the most demanding and least price-sensitive
customers, and they move steadily downwards to disrupt the entire market. Such disruptions also give the incumbents a better chance of surviving. He also used a number
of other examples such as the Apple iPod and Satellite Radios to illustrate this point.

However, the potential danger of the top-down strategy was not emphasized in his
paper, even though Carr briefly mentioned how Wang Labs itself was quickly disrupted
from the bottom up. In recent years, many premium brands moved downwards from
the top-end, premium market niches to the mainstream market. Such a move often
increases revenue and profit very rapidly for a few years, but the long-term viability of
this strategy is less certain. It may damage – or cheapen – the brand and disfranchise
their most profitable customers at the top end in the long term. There are times when
'selling the family silver' is the only option, but it depends on the specific circumstance
and it must be carefully managed. More research is clearly needed to evaluate the
long-term viability of top-down disruptions. Examples that are worth researching and
monitoring are perhaps Marks & Spencer in the UK and BMW of Germany.

Disruptive Strategic Innovations in Action in the Network Economy: Some Examples

Although the strategy of disruptive innovations is not unique or specific to the
knowledge-based, network economy, rapid development of the Internet and related
technologies has led to disruptions in many industries in recent years. In some sectors,
the incumbents managed to fight back and further secured their dominant positions,
but in others, newcomers have made a significant impact. This theory can provide
significant insights into the rise and fall of Internet start-ups of the late 1990s. It
also provides valuable strategic guidance to established companies on how to exploit
the strategic value of the Internet and fend off the advances of new entrants.

The dot.com disruptors

Many Internet start-ups of the late 1990s attempted to use the Internet as a sustaining
innovation relative to the business models of established companies, which contributed to the spectacular dot.com bust in March 2000. However, amongst the exceptions
is eBay, which effectively pursued new market disruptions, by enabling owners of
unwanted items to sell them off cheaply and conveniently. In fact, almost all the dot.com
survivors have disrupted established and/or new markets in some way – very often
profoundly.

The Dot.Com Disruptors: eBay, Amazon.com, Charles Schwab and Google

At the beginning, rather than competing head-on with established auction houses, eBay focused on items that were not suitable for conventional auctions. As eBay became more established, it gradually attracted some of the customers in the core markets of established auction companies and caused major disruptions in several markets. Today, eBay remains one of the most successful – and profitable – dot.com companies in the world, with enormous future potential. The low-cost and pervasive Internet enables eBay to make full use of this new channel to develop a unique model and pursue the strategy of disruption.

Another successful example is Amazon.com. Unlike eBay which pursued a new market disruption strategy, Amazon.com initially pursued a low-end disruption strategy through its low cost structure, simple, convenient processes and extensive collection of books. As it became more established, Amazon.com also extended to new markets to sell non-book items, first DVDs and CDs, and then electronic goods and other household items. Established players, such as Barnes and Noble, simply could not compete with the low-end disruption, because of the constitution of their resources, processes and values. Even the heavy investments in barnesandnoble.com could not fend off the advance of Amazon.com.

A further successful example of the strategy of disruption occurred in stock broking, by Charles Schwab. As a discount broker started in 1975, Charles Schwab successfully created a separate online trading business in the late 1990s to pursue low-end disruptions to established stock-broking companies. The new organization was so successful that it even took the original Charles Schwab within the new organization. It forced most established investment banks to make significant changes in order to protect their core market and keep their most profitable customers. It should be pointed out that online trading of equities is a sustaining innovation relative to the business models of discount brokers such as Ameritrade, but disruptive innovation to full service brokers such as Merrill Lynch. The disruptions by some companies and the defensive reactions by the established leading players have radically shaken up the industry.

Other examples include Google, which successfully disrupted Yellow Pages and many other directory businesses from the low end. Today, the competition in searching is fiercely fought between a handful of established, powerful companies, including Google, Yahoo and MSN amongst others, mainly through sustaining innovations (e.g. new techniques such as clustering). However, opportunities perhaps still exist for new-market disruptions, for example through the so-called 'webifying' of everything as search moves off the web into other things.[11]

Online travel agencies, including Expedia, Travelocity and, in the UK, Lastminute.com, have so significantly disrupted full service brick-and-mortar travel agencies that the travel industry perhaps has been changed forever.

Disrupting the PC market: Dell

Another interesting example is Dell. Through its direct sales model and fast through-put, combined with its ability to allow customers to configure the products to their own requirements at no extra cost, Dell is able to disrupt established key players in the personal computer market – Compaq, IBM, Hewlett-Packard and a series of others.

Disrupting the PC Market: Dell

Prior to the advent of the Internet, Dell sold computers directly to customers by mail or telephone. For Dell, the Internet is a sustaining innovation, because it made Dell's core business process work better, and it helped Dell to make more profit in the way it was structured to make money. However, the same strategy of selling directly to customers over the Internet was a disruptive innovation relative to the business models of Compaq and IBM, because their cost structure and business processes were set up for in-store retail distribution. Who came out the winner today is therefore not surprising. Christensen and Raynor went even further to say that if Dell had not existed, many start-up Internet-based computer retailers might have succeeded: because the Internet was a sustaining innovation to the established Dell, new entrants could not have won the battle.[12]

Internet banking and insurance

Internet banking, which has generated considerable discussion and debate since the late 1990s, is another interesting example. As new entrants aggressively entered the market, either from established companies in other sectors (such as retailers or utility companies) or as Internet-only new banks, almost all established banks were forced to react quickly, either by introducing the Internet as a new channel to complement other channels or by setting up separate Internet-only units to compete with the new entrants, and in some cases, both (e.g. Halifax, which introduced the Internet channel but also set up the successful Internet-only unit, Intelligent Finance – IF.com). Today, the established banks seem to have successfully fended off the aggressive advances from the new entrants; some new entrants from other sectors have quietly folded their banking operations, and almost all stand-alone Internet-only banks have been acquired or are owned by established banks.[13]

Christensen and Raynor believed that disruptions using the Internet are not possible in retail banking.[14] The reasons they listed include the fact that there is not a large population of people who have been unable to open and maintain a bank account because they lacked the money or skill. Existing banks' penetration of this market is very high, which rules out a new-market disruption strategy for Internet banking. They also raised the question of whether current bank customers at the low end would be happy to accept a bank account with fewer privileges and features in order to get the services at a lower price. They also argued that it is difficult to develop a low-cost business model that would allow a new entrant to attract such customers while delivering attractive profit. Many Internet banks have been seeking answers to the low-cost business model question but so far no one has managed to succeed, largely because the cost of money is similar for all banks; also, the cost structure of even Internet-only banks has not been as low as expected, and many cost savings from the Internet have to be passed back to customers in order to retain them and attract new ones – and to compensate them for their efforts in self-service in using Internet banking. Furthermore, many established banks are prepared to forgo profit in basic services in order to retain customers and extract value from high-margin services – almost all current accounts in established banks are subsidized anyway, and they are also effectively using the Internet as an additional channel to sustain their business model.

However, my own research has indicated that this is not yet the end of the story. Some new entrants, by focusing on a limited number of products (e.g. savings), or by adopting low-cost business models, made significant inroads in taking away customers from established banks. In the UK, examples include the banks set up by leading supermarkets such as Tesco and Sainsbury's, and Internet-only banks such as Egg.com (created by the life assurance company Prudential, but there were several attempts to sell it to an established bank) and ING.com (high-interest savings only in the UK for the time being). Some of the online-only units owned by established banks, such as IF.com, Smile.com and Cahoot.com, to name but a few, have also managed to attract a large number of customers, including customers from their own parent companies, within a short period of time. In the meantime, some incumbent banks have effectively integrated the Internet channel into their existing business model as a sustaining innovation; examples include Royal Bank of Scotland and HSBC. The first round of the competitive battle in Internet banking is perhaps over, with the incumbents winning the battle by introducing the Internet as a sustaining innovation, by setting up their own Internet-only business units or by acquiring some of the Internet-only new entrants. Despite the fact that no new entrants have managed to successfully disrupt the industry and gain a strong foothold in the market, the industry itself has been radically transformed over the past ten years. As other new technological innovations are being developed, and in particular as mobile communications continue to develop rapidly, the situation may still change in the years to come, and I for one am eagerly waiting for round two of the battle to commence.

The Insurance Market: From Directline to Esure

Esure, an insurance broker set up in February 2000 by Halifax (a building society turned retail bank in the UK) and Peter Wood (the founder of the highly successful Direct Line, the first and most successful telephone-based insurance broker in the UK), managed to attract 900,000 customers in little more than five years during a period of turmoil for dot.com companies. With a total investment of £125 million, Esure already turned a £11 million loss in 2003 into a £4 million profit in 2004. This was the fastest growth ever for a new UK motor insurance business. However, due to the sustaining nature of the Internet to some telephone-based insurance brokers in the UK, Esure has so far failed to cause too much disruption in the market.[15]

Summary of the section

There are many other interesting examples of new entrants successfully using the Internet to disrupt established incumbents either through low-cost disruptions or new-market disruptions. Many established companies reacted quickly either by using the Internet to sustain their core business model and protect their core markets, or by setting up a separate unit to compete with the new entrants. Some incumbents went even further to acquire the new entrants while sustaining their existing business models and services. As the Internet continues to grow more versatile and proliferate rapidly, as people get more comfortable with using the Internet for different activities, as the broadband infrastructure and services continue to penetrate into our homes, and as mobile networks and handsets become more advanced, it is possible to develop new business models that are radically different from the existing ones in a wide range of industries, and new products and services that could turn non-consumers into profitable customers.

The Strategy of Disruption: Threats, Opportunities and Possible Responses

Disruptive technologies and business models have toppled many established industry leaders, and owing to the enormous negative implications of disruptive innovations for established companies, the potential threats from low-end or new-market disruptive innovations are well understood today. However, research has also shown that disruption always creates new markets and new net growth, which provides new opportunities for old and new companies alike.[16] In particular, for the established incumbents under attack from low-end or new market entrants, they could go on the offensive by seeking new customers different from those of their established businesses.

According to Gilbert, disruption is not an all-at-once phenomenon, and it develops over three distinct phases. During the initial phase, the innovation creates a new market independent of the established business of the incumbents. As the new market expands, it gradually slows the growth of the established businesses. Then in the third phase, having improved significantly over time, it drastically reduces the size of the old market.[17] This applies to both the low-end disruptions and new-market disruptions outlined by Christensen and Raynor.[18] Using the computing industry as an example and how PCs and microcomputers gradually disrupted the mainframe market, Gilbert argued that a disruption may not completely destroy the established business, although it usually takes away all the growth. This is good news for established incumbents as there is time for them to identify new markets before their established old markets stagnate and eventually decline. However, in order to do so they often need to adopt new business models different from those used for the established markets.[19]

Charitou and Markides argued that disruptive strategic innovations are not necessarily superior to traditional ways of competing, and nor are they always destined to conquer the market.[20] Based on the experience of a wide range of industries that have

been under threat from disruptive strategic innovations in recent years, they came up
with five possible responses and explored 'when to do what' for the established industry leaders.

The challenges from disruptive innovations for established industry leaders are
real and significant, and in a whole range of industries, once formidable companies
were attacked by relatively unknown firms employing radically different strategies –
and some of the new strategies are in conflict with the strategies of the industry
leaders. The dilemma is that the established incumbents could not compete with the
new entrants with their existing strategies and business models, but if they adopt the
strategies of the new competitors they run the risk of damaging their existing business and undermining their existing strategies which have brought them success in
the past.

Charitou and Markides regarded strategic innovation as a fundamentally different
way of competing in an existing business. Disruptive strategic innovation is only one
specific type of strategic innovation, a way of playing the game that is 'both different
from and *in conflict* with the traditional way' (p. 56) of doing business.[21] They used
Internet banking, low-cost airlines (through Internet-based booking and a low-cost,
no-frill strategy), direct insurance, online brokerage, online distribution of news and
online supermarkets as examples to illustrate how these companies have managed
to disrupt their respective industries. These new entrants usually emphasize different
product or service attributes from the established industry leaders, and all of them
started out as small, low-margin businesses, targeting customers that established
players find unattractive. Over time, these new entrants can compete with established incumbents by delivering performance that is good enough in the old attributes
that established companies emphasize but superior in the new attributes. This usually
enables them to capture a large share of the established market very quickly.

The most common responses by the established companies are either to ignore the
new entrants and stick to its core strategy, or embrace the disruption by setting up a
separate unit or company. However, the research by Charitou and Markides revealed
at least five viable responses:

1. Focus on and invest in the traditional business – the new entrants will usually
   capture only 10–20 per cent of the market and the established companies do not
   necessarily have to embrace the new innovation.
2. Ignore the innovation because it is not your business – embracing strategic innovations often requires different value propositions, skills and competences, targeting new customers, and often means diversifying in an unrelated market, which
   if not managed properly can lead to disaster.
3. Fight back by disrupting the disruption – new entrants often compete with established players by being good enough in old attributes of products and services
   but emphasizing certain new attributes. Rather than playing the new game,
   established players can often emphasize and compete with even newer attributes
   to disrupt the disruptions.
4. Adopt the innovation by playing both games simultaneously – this is usually done
   by creating a separate business unit, with high levels of autonomy, often using a

different name from the parent company, with its own new CEO. However, many of these new units share back-office activities with the parent company.

5. Embrace the new innovation completely and scale it up – this means abandoning existing ways of doing things and embracing the disruptive strategic innovation as the new business model.

This may not be an exhaustive list of potential options but they provide significant options for established companies to consider when faced with disruptive innovations. Charitou and Markides went on to develop a two-dimensional model to help companies determine how to respond to disruptive strategic innovations: the motivation to respond and the company's ability to respond effectively. If both motivation and ability to respond to a new strategic innovation are low, then the best option for the established company is to focus on its core business. At the other end of the spectrum, when both are high, the established company should consider the different responses outlined above.

Summary

The theory of disruptive strategic innovation is one of the most influential theories since the late 1990s. It provides valuable insights to some of the spectacular competitive battles between industry leaders, with unassailable strategic positions on the one hand, and relatively unknown new entrants employing new strategies and business models on the other. In industry after industry, new entrants have managed to disrupt the core markets of the established players and quickly establish themselves as a force to be reckoned with, and some established incumbents have even been squeezed out of the market. This theory is not specific to the knowledge-based, network economy, but since the mid-1990s, the rapid development and proliferation of the Internet and related technologies have provided numerous opportunities for new entrants to develop low-cost models and compete with industry leaders in ways impossible in the past. Even when the new entrants do not win the battle, the industries themselves are often seriously disrupted and many industries have already been changed beyond recognition within a short period of time. Despite the various flaws and criticisms of the work by Christensen, the significance of this theory is widely accepted today.

As the technology and infrastructure continue to develop extremely rapidly and penetrate into every corner of our society and economy, and most of all as people get more and more used to doing things through the Internet and mobile communications, more disruptive strategic innovations will no doubt be developed and introduced in many industries. This provides both opportunities and challenges for old and new players alike. To survive and thrive in the network economy, all companies must understand the situation and make proper strategic responses.

Discussion Questions

1 What is low-end disruption? What is new-market disruption? And what is top-down disruption? Could you think of any other forms of strategic disruption?

Identify some real-life examples for each of these disruptions. Critically evaluate their implications for contemporary organizations and highlight the main lessons that can be learnt.

2   Charitou and Markides suggested several possible responses to strategic disruptions, but Christensen and Raynor argued that any responses from established players will not work in the long run. What is your view? Explain why.

3   Do you agree with Nicholas Carr's idea of top-down disruption? Why? Support your views with examples where appropriate.

Assignment: Presentation for an Executive Development Workshop

You are an expert delivering an executive workshop to senior executives from a particular industry about the theory of strategic disruptions. Prepare a 30-minute presentation using PowerPoint, clearly explaining the theory and the key issues involved, and discuss its implications for today's organizations.

NOTES

1   Christensen, Clayton M. (1997) *The Innovator's Dilemma*. Harvard Business School Press, Boston.

2   Christensen, Clayton M. and Michael Raynor (2003) *The Innovator's Solution: Creating and sustaining successful growth*. Harvard Business School Press, Boston.

3   Christensen, Clayton M., Eric A. Roth and Scott D. Anthony (2005) *Seeing What Next: Using theories of innovation to predict industry change*. Harvard Business School Press, Boston.

4   Charitou, Constantinos and Constantinos Markides (2003) Responses to disruptive strategic innovation. *Sloan Management Review*, 44(2), 55–63

5   Gilbert, Clark (2003) The disruption opportunities. *Sloan Management Review*, 44(4), 27–32.

6   Bessant, John and David Francis (2004) *Developing Parallel Routines for Radical Product Innovation*, AIM Research Working Paper Series, 10 August; Phillips, Wendy, Hannah Noke, John Bessant and Richard Lamming (2004) *Beyond The Steady State: Managing discontinuous product and process innovation*, AIM Research Working Paper Series, 9 August.

7   Christensen and Raynor (2003) op. cit.

8   Christensen and Raynor (2003) op. cit. pp. 43–44.

9   Ibid.; Christensen (1997).

10   Carr, Nicholas (2005) Top-down disruption. *Strategy + Business*, Issue 39, Summer. http://www.strategy-business.com/magazine.

11   LeClaire, Jennifer (2005) Experts predict where search will go in 2005. *E-Commerce Times*, 3 September, http://www.ecommercetimes.com/story/41141.html.

12   Ibid.

13   Li, Feng (2002) Internet banking: from new distribution channel to new business models, *International Journal of Business Performance Management*, 4(2/3/4), 134–160; Li, Feng (2001) The Internet and the de-construction of the integrated banking model, *British Journal of Management*, 12, 307–322.

14   Christensen and Raynor (2003) op. cit.

15   Crost, Jane and Andrea Felsted (2005) Pru eager to see when Egg will get cracking. *Financial Times*, Tuesday 8 March, p. 4.

16 Gilbert (2003) op. cit.
17 Ibid.
18 Christensen and Raynor (2003) op. cit.
19 Gilbert (2003) op. cit.
20 Charitou and Markides (2003) op. cit.
21 Ibid, p. 56.

FURTHER READING

Carr, Nicholas (2005) Top-down disruption. *Strategy + Business*, Issue 39, Summer. http://www.strategy-business.com/magazine.
Charitou, Constantinos and Constantinos Markides (2003) Responses to disruptive strategic innovation. *Sloan Management Review*, 44(2), 55–63.
Christensen, Clayton M. (1997) *The Innovator's Dilemma*. Harvard Business School Press, Boston.
Christensen, Clayton M. and Michael Raynor (2003) *The Innovator's Solution: Creating and sustaining successful growth*. Harvard Business School Press, Boston.
Christensen, Clayton M., Eric A. Roth and Scott D. Anthony (2005) *Seeing What Next: Using theories of innovation to predict industry change*. Harvard Business School Press, Boston.
Gilbert, Clark (2003) The disruption opportunities. *Sloan Management Review*, 44(4), 27–32.

Chapter 8

Strategic Reorientations in the Network Economy: From Products and Services to Solutions and Experiences

Since the 1990s, there have been two profound strategic reorientations in leading organizations. The first began in the early 1990s when the strategic focus of many companies was increasingly shifted from providing excellent products and services to offering customers integrated solutions. This reorientation was sometimes also seen as an attempt by product companies to create new revenue growth through services.[1] The second reorientation began at the turn of the new millennium, when the focus increasingly shifted from integrated solutions or services to customer experiences. There are some overlaps between these two reorientations, and both of them are underpinned by the development of electronic communication platforms that effectively integrate different stages of the value chain and a network of companies and consumer communities, which together enable companies to provide integrated solutions for various problems and to co-create unique value and experience with consumers.

Several studies have been published in recent years to illustrate these developments. One of the most comprehensive was by Joseph Pine II and James Gilmore in 1999: *The Experience Economy: Work is theatre and every business a stage.* Many related ideas have been explored both in popular business books and in more serious research, including the paper by Prahalad and Ramaswamy on 'The new frontier of experience innovation' in 2003, and by Sawhney, Balasubramanian and Krishnan on 'Creating growth with services' in 2004, both published in the *Sloan Management Review.*[2] This chapter will explore some of the key issues involved in these strategic reorientations in the context of the knowledge-based, network economy.

The Context for Strategic Reorientations: The Changing Business Environment

These strategic reorientations reflect fundamental changes in the business environment. One such change is the increasing 'sameness' in the products and services we receive from almost all providers despite the rapid increase in product variety. These strategic reorientations reflect the strong need for organizations to constantly search for differentiation in the new economy. In their best seller, *Funky Business*, Jonas Ridderstrale and Kjelle Nordstrom argued:

> [t]he world is alive with knowledge, with products and services, with information. But more often simply means more of the same. The surplus society has a surplus of similar companies, employing similar people, with similar educational backgrounds, working in similar jobs, coming up with similar ideas, producing similar things, with similar prices, warranties, and qualities. (p. 97)[3]

They went on to use the car as an example to illustrate this problem. Today there are no bad cars any longer because they are all good. 'The new competitive battlefield is not the engine or the air conditioner – it is the design, the warranty, the service deal, the image and the finance package. Intelligence and intangibles. And of course, people' (p. 43). A similar point was made by Tom Peters who quoted Jesper Kunde that '[c]ompanies have defined so much best practice that they are now more or less identical'; or as Paul Goldberger put it: 'while everything may be better, it is also increasingly the same' (p. 87).[4]

Underneath the increasing sameness in the products and services offered to us and the search for differentiation by companies, the strategic reorientations perhaps reflect an even more fundamental change that is taking place in our society and economy. As illustrated briefly earlier in this book, Shoshana Zuboff and James Maxmin argued that the enterprise logic known as managerial capitalism has outlived its usefulness.[5] This system was invented for the production and distribution of things. It has been uncomfortably adapted to the delivery of services. 'But neither goods nor services adequately fulfil the needs of today's market' (p. 4). They believe that people have changed much more than the commercial organizations upon which they depend. Corporations today continue to operate according to a logic invented a century ago, and today a new business logic is needed. The chasm between individuals and commercial organizations cannot be bridged within the context of today's business models, and the unsatisfied demands of individuals are harbouring a new support economy based on what Zuboff and Maxin call 'distributed capitalism'.

This process reflects a fundamental transformation that is taking place in the nature and purpose of business, and more importantly in the underlying logic of capitalism itself. New enterprises will emerge as they learn to obey the new logic and support new individuals in their pursuit of new consumption experiences. The authors went on to argue that the chasm between individuals and institutions is not limited to the business world. It is also evident between citizens and their public institutions, and worshipers and their religious institutions, for example, implying that wide social changes are needed in our society. The rapid development and proliferation of electronic communications networks (ICTs) have made what they called distributed capitalism possible.

From a different angle, C. K. Prahalad and Venkat Ramaswamy highlighted the shift in the balance of influence between the individual and the institution.[6] This shifting balance is partly the result of the rapid development of the Internet and related technologies and the emergence of new forms of organization in the post dot.com era. Like Zuboff and Maxmin, they believe the change is not cosmetic or limited to the commercial world. It is happening in our legal systems, hospitals and universities as well as in corporations. Although they stopped short of suggesting a revolution, they identified significant departures from traditional ways of 'sensing, thinking and doing'.

Prahalad and Ramaswamy argued that the traditional 'firm-centric' view of the economy is no longer effective in today's business environment. Instead, the joint efforts of the consumer and the firm, through their extended networks and the consumer communities, are challenging the traditional notions of value and its creation and 'are co-creating value through personalized experiences that are unique to each individual consumer' (p. x). This requires individuals to be actively involved in the process by which these institutions generate value, and the consumer and the firm are 'intimately involved in jointly creating value that is unique to the individual consumer and sustainable to the firm' (p. x).[7] Also, like Zuboff and Maxmin, they believe that this proposition challenges the fundamental assumptions about our industrial system, including assumptions about value itself, the value creation process and the nature of the relationship between the firm and the consumer. In doing so a new paradigm is emerging where value is co-created by the firm and the consumer at points of interaction, rather than by the firm thinking and acting unilaterally.

Prahalad and Ramaswamy also echoed the views of many others that product variety has not necessarily resulted in higher levels of consumer satisfaction or better consumer experiences. Today, consumers have more choices that deliver less satisfaction, and management have more strategic options that create less value. To resolve this paradox requires us to shift from the traditional system of company-centric value creation to a new system of value co-creation between the firm and the consumer. At the heart of the emerging new reality are complex interactions between and amongst firms and consumer communities. The electronic communications technology and infrastructure provide the essential links for communities of firms and consumers to co-create value bundles that are appropriate for each of the connected, informed and active consumers.[8]

These studies clearly illustrate some radical changes in the business environment, including the shift of business logic from a company-centric view of innovation and value creation to a new system where consumers are an integral part of the value creation process. In the 1990s, we experienced the strategic reorientation from delivering better products to delivering integrated solutions; and since the turn of the new millennium the strategic focus is further shifting towards jointly creating unique experiences for consumers. These strategic reorientations are facilitated, and enabled, by the rapid development of the Internet and related technologies, but they reflect deeper and more fundamental changes in our society and the economy. The changes have profound implications not only for organizations, managers and business leaders, but also for consumers, employees, citizens and indeed for everyone.

From Products to Solutions: Creating Growth with Services

In his book *Re-imagine*, Tom Peters used many examples to argue forcefully for 'the solutions imperative' in today's organizations.[9] The dramatic turnaround of Big Blue (IBM) since the 1990s has been well documented. By the time Lou Gerstner retired after nine years at the helm of IBM in 2002, the company grew by $20 billion in sales. Interestingly, much of this growth was not generated from selling more computers and systems, but from IBM Global Services which generated a staggering $35 billion in revenue. The strategy underpinning this reorientation was to make IBM the 'systems integrator of choice', particularly by providing e-Business solutions – rather than by selling more computer hardware and software to customers. Today, offering excellent products and services is not enough, because this is simply the 'price of entry'. All products – even excellent products – are quickly commoditized. In such a new business environment, companies must focus on providing sophisticated 'turnkey solutions' to customers. This view was also a recurring theme in Ridderstrale and Nordstrom's book *Funky Business*.[10]

The solutions imperative was also illustrated by Peters with many other examples, including the failed $18 billion bid for the consulting business of PricewaterhouseCoopers (PwC) by Hewlett-Packard (HP) in 2000, with PwC Consulting eventually purchased by IBM for a mere $3.5 billion in 2001 after the dot.com crash. Several other companies, such as Sun Microsystems, also showed strong interests in PwC Consulting. These interests reflected the underlying strategic reorientation of many leading computing companies, from offering customers excellent hardware and/or software, to offering them consulting services that would solve problems and provide solutions to them, which involve using computing and communications hardware and software. This strategic reorientation has certainly paid off for IBM, and today more than half its revenue is generated from services, although it remains one of the most advanced technological companies in the world. Many other companies are making similar strategic reorientations. AT&T shifted its focus from selling telecommunications capacity between places to offering bundles of corporate communications services, which involved lucrative consulting services to large global corporations. Ericsson, the Swedish mobile phone manufacturer, has increasingly outsourced its production and R&D activities to others and focused on services for revenue generation and future growth. Similar reorientations have been identified in GE Power Systems and Industrial Systems, Siemens, UPS and Home Depot, to name but a few.

In 2004, Sawhney, Balasubramanian and Krishnan published their research in the *Sloan Management Review* to illustrate the need for organizations today to create new growth opportunities through services. They argued that in a world of commoditized products, many companies have turned to services for new growth. They used examples similar to those offered by other authors mentioned earlier, such as General

Electric, IBM, Siemens and HP, to illustrate how these companies have managed to maintain revenue growth even when some of them experienced declines in their traditional core product markets. Examples of failed attempts, such as Intel's $250 million data centre for web hosting and Boeing's attempt to break into financial services, were also used to illustrate the enormous challenges involved in making such a strategic reorientation.[11] They went on to develop a systematic approach to creating service-led growth, which can provide useful guidance for business leaders when embarking on such ventures. Although their focus was on product companies, this approach is equally applicable to companies in the services sectors.

Back in 1973, Peter Drucker famously pointed out: 'What the customer buys and considers value is never a product. It is always utility – that is, what a product does for him.'[12] In a more blunt fashion, Jonas Ridderstrale and Kjelle Nordstrom asked business leaders to look beyond the physical elements of products. They argued that what companies sell and what their customers buy are two different things. When a woman buys a lipstick, she is not buying a lump of coloured fat in a plastic container. Rather she is buying hope, the hope that this product will make her more beautiful.[13] Sushi is another example they used, which I will not repeat here. In today's business environment, companies must redefine their markets in terms of customer activities and customer outcomes, instead of products and services.

Sawhney, Balasubramanian and Krishnan argued that '[c]ustomers seek particular outcomes, and they engage in activities to achieve them' (p. 34).[14] They developed the concepts of the customer-activity chain and the service–opportunity matrix to help business leaders systematically explore new service opportunities. The customer-activity chain maps the activities that customers engage in to achieve particular outcomes. It contains an end-to-end sequence of logically related activities, which together can lead to defined customer outcomes. A customer-activity chain is unique to specific segments of customers, and it often involves activities that cut across industry and product-market boundaries.

When identifying new service opportunities, an organization can use a two-dimensional service–opportunity matrix to explore the focuses and types of growth: where growth occurs and how. By adding or reconfiguring customer activities along a primary activity chain or an adjacent one, four types of new opportunities for growth can be identified. The first type of growth comes from services that add new activities to the primary activity chain. The authors used Eastman Kodak as an example to illustrate how the company added many new services that enhance its interactions with customers. By adding new services before, during and after the sale of core products to help the customer 'manage and share memories', the company managed to exploit new growth opportunities while its core product market declined. The new services are enabled by the Internet and related technologies. Between the traditional customer activities of taking photos and ordering prints, customers now can undertake many other activities such as edit photos, share photos with friends and families, create electronic photo albums, archive photos and order merchandise with photos, amongst others.

The second type of growth involves introducing new services in closely linked, adjacent activity chains. Unlike the first type of growth which deepens relations with customers, this type of growth broadens relations. The authors used the example of General Motors to illustrate how the company leveraged its core business to offer new services in adjacent activity chains. In addition to expanding services in its primary activity chain (new automotive services such as auto-financing, auto-insurance and roadside assistance, which is the first type of growth), it also actively expanded into telematics services through its OnStar platform to help customers with related tasks, including emergency services, mobile voice and data services, vehicle monitoring and travel services. Furthermore, leveraging its relations with customers, the company also expanded into home services to offer mortgages, home insurance, home monitoring, satellite TV and several other services for the home. The key to this type of expansion is to exploit the company's relations with customers developed through its core products to create new service opportunities in adjacent markets. Many of these services are enabled and integrated by advanced ICT infrastructure and services.

The third type of growth involves the company taking on additional activities along its primary customer activity chain – activities that used to be handled by the customers themselves. UPS used to focus on a limited range of activities of picking up, shipping, tracking and dropping off packages, but it has now expanded into a much broader range of activities in logistic services, including warehousing and inventory management, inbound and outbound logistics management, service-part logistics management, customer support management, and assembly, testing and repairs. These activities used to be performed by customers themselves, but UPS can perform them in an integrated fashion. By leveraging its expertise in its core business, UPS has explored new growth opportunities by performing activities that are central to its own business but peripheral to those of its customers. ICTs once again play a fundamental role in enabling the integration and reconfiguration of activities along the primary customer activity chain.

The fourth type of growth involves a company in a customer's primary activity chain taking charge in an adjacent chain. An example of this type of expansion is Nike's branding of US Sports Camps. The Nike brand is used to position and promote the Camps, and the Camps in return reinforce the brand and enhance the loyalty of participants to Nike products.

Many other examples were also used to illustrate different opportunities in expanding new services both in the primary customer activity chain and adjacent activity chains. In most cases, the expansion was underpinned – and enabled – by the new capabilities afforded by information and communications systems. However, the authors also emphasized that the reorientation from products to services involves considerable risks which need to be understood and carefully managed. Typical risks include capability risks (can you execute the new services?), market risks (would the customers adopt the new services?) and financial risks (could you grow profitable revenue?). However, for many product companies, expanding into services, particularly by providing customers with integrated solutions, is perhaps the only opportunity for them to survive and grow when their core markets stagnate and decline and core products are commoditized.

The Services Revolution: The Industrialization of Services

Alongside the rapid expansion of product companies into services, a contrasting trend is the rapid industrialization of services, which is underpinning the outsourcing and offshoring of many highly paid, white-collar jobs from developed countries to developing countries. As Uday Karmarkar argued: 'We are now riding a tide wave of change that we can think of as the industrialization of services. Global competition is on the rise, and some service markets are being invaded by foreign firms and new entrants. Automation is also transforming the services sector. New hardware and software systems that take care of back-room and front-office tasks such as counter operations, security, billing, and order taking are allowing firms to dispense with clerical, accounting, and other staff positions. And self-service is having a major impact: why use a travel agent when you can book your own flight, reserve a hotel room, and rent a car online?' (pp. 101–102).[15]

Although there will still be people who will use a travel agent to book flights and hotels, more and more people are making their own bookings, which significantly affects the business volume of traditional travel agencies. Karmarkar believed that the service revolution is similar to the transformation of manufacturing in the past fifty years, when the share of manufacturing jobs in the USA reduced from 34 per cent in 1950 to a mere 12 per cent in 2003. Between 2000 and 2003, over 2 million US manufacturing jobs were lost either through offshore outsourcing or through global competition. Today a similar process is happening with service jobs. According to Karmarkar, the primary change driver behind the service revolution is technology: advanced ICT infrastructure and services are creating 'an information assembly line'. Just like manufacturing, information can also be 'standardized, built to order, assembled from components, picked, packed, stored, and shipped, all using processes resembling manufacturing's [assembly lines]' (p. 102). He went on to argue that industrialized information will become more efficient, less expensive and highly automated. The costs of logistics and storage are minimal so only labour and intellectual property will matter.[16] One result of the service revolution is the radical reconfiguration of core information processes.

Reconfiguration of Core Information Processes

Karmarkar used the example of the diagnostic imaging industry to illustrate the reconfiguration of the information process. In the past, and to some extent still the case today in many countries, this industry involved multiple discrete processes and people, typically co-located in a large hospital. A technician usually performs a scan using a CAT scanner, X-ray machine or ultrasound scanner. The image is then examined by a radiologist to identify any potential problems. The report is then sent to the physician. However, with advanced communications networks today, the entire process can be reconfigured. The patient can be scanned at a convenient location rather than in the main hospital (perhaps even be in a mobile trailer). The image can then be sent electronically to a diagnostic radiologist who could be located miles away. Voice recognition software can transcribe the diagnosis or the transcription can be performed offshore. Intelligent software can even assist the radiologist with diagnosis. The reconfigured process enables much greater flexibility in terms of who does what where, when and how, and the way the process is reconfigured determines clear winners and losers, with profound implications for all stakeholders involved.

In the past few decades, ICTs have already fundamentally changed some services such as simple data entry and credit card processing. Today, more interactive and complex business and administrative services are being affected by the same process – IT, market research, content management, accounting, data management, billing and some customer services. As information services are turned into industrialized components in an assembly line, radical restructuring of many services industries and the service functions of manufacturing industries is inevitable, with profound implications for the balance of power and the distribution of profit in many industries.

To survive the service revolution, Karmarkar believes that all organizations need to realign their strategies and redesign their processes. Most of all, organizations need to be built around the restructured information and value chain. The front office takes responsibilities for the customer experience, the back office handles internal processes invisible to customers, and a third organization needs to take responsibility for dealing with partnerships with suppliers and co-producers. 'In the end, the survivors of the service revolution will be those who understand that opportunities lie in removing and supplanting links of the information chain and also in understanding how the chain is being restructured. Once they understand their own information chains from end to end, companies must begin reorganizing strategies, processes, and people for the challenges ahead' (p. 107).[17]

From Solutions and Services to Experiences: The E(motional)-Business

Despite the significance of the strategic reorientation from products and services to solutions, however, Prahalad and Ramaswamy believe that this is not enough in today's business environment. Solution-based innovations go beyond the features and functions embedded in products, and the company offering solutions to customers needs to effectively combine knowledge and skills in products with new domain knowledge of the customers. However, they questioned the basic conception of value and the processes that lead to its creation and argued that neither value nor innovation can be successfully generated through company-centric, product- and service-focused approaches. To survive, companies must enable individual customers to co-create unique experiences for themselves through a network of companies and consumer communities.[18]

E(motional)-business

Since Joseph Pine II and James Gilmore published their book in 1999 on *The Experience Economy: Work is Theatre and Every Business a Stage*, several influential authors have called for such a radical shift of business focus under different guises.[19] Back in 2000, Ridderstrale and Nordstrom argued for the need to deliver emotional satisfaction to customers. This requires organizations to shift their focus from internal functional efficiency and product and service excellence to the extended experience of customers. 'In an excess economy, success comes from attracting the emotional customer and colleague – not the rational one' (p. 260). This requires an organization to appeal to the feelings and fantasies of their customers. They went on to call for the development of the 'Emotional Enterprise'.[20]

Tom Peters also argued for the need to go beyond solutions and provide memorable experiences for customers.[21] The 'integrated solutions' idea is important but not enough, and to move up the value chain, companies need to explore the soft attributes of their products, services and solutions and deliver a full-fledged experience for customers. Different from a solution or a service, which is a transaction, Peters believes that an experience is an event which is more holistic, total, encompassing, emotional and transformational. More importantly, this is not just a play of words, because billions of dollars of value-added comes from the quality of experience. However, this reorientation requires companies to radically rethink their value focus, the propositions of their offerings, performance measurement, and many other issues.

The Lifestyle Business

Rather than seeing themselves as manufacturers of motorcycles and sportswear, companies such as Harley-Davidson and Nike have long promoted the image of being in the 'lifestyle' business. Peters quoted a senior executive of Harley-Davidson: 'What we sell is the ability for a 43-year-old accountant to dress in black leather, ride through small towns, and have people be afraid of him' (p. 116). Being in the lifestyle business – rather than manufacturing – has added billions of dollars of stock market capitalization to these companies. It also means that Harley-Davidson is not simply competing with Honda or BMW for the quality and technical performance of their motorcycles.

Many other companies have also successfully made the shift. Examples include Starbuck as the 'third place' which is neither work nor home – rather than a simple café; Guinness as a brand bringing a community of people together and sharing stories, rather than a drink; and Club Med as a means of rediscovering oneself or inventing an entirely new self, rather than a mere resort. Other masters of experience include Nokia, Lego and Virgin. Tom Peters went even further to argue that experience is the 'essence of life in the new economy' (p. 123).

Co-creating unique experience with customers

The strategic reorientation from products and solutions to experience is hailed as the 'next practices' of innovation by Prahalad and Ramaswamy.[22] The experience environment is supported by a network of companies and consumer communities, which enable them to co-create unique value for individual consumers. Until recently, features and functionality were embedded in products, but digitization has enabled the combination of features and functions of traditional industries and products in new ways. However, major discontinuities in the business environment such as deregulation, ubiquitous connectivity and globalization are resulting in the rapid erosion of the distinctive identities of products, services, channels, industries and companies. This means that the traditional strategy of increasing product variety is not necessarily leading to better consumer experiences but often creating confusion and difficult choices for customers.

Drawing on the early experimentation in companies such as General Motors, Lego and Medtronic, Prahalad and Ramaswamy argued that the locus of value creation will inevitably shift from products and services to what they referred to as the experience environment. The purpose is not to improve a product or service, but to enable the co-creation of an environment in which personalized, evolvable experiences can be delivered. They used the cardiac pacemaker as an example to vividly illustrate this strategic reorientation.

A Cardiac Pacemaker Experience Network

In the USA alone there are around five million adults who suffer cardiac problems. Many of them have pacemakers implanted which monitor and manage their heart rhythm and performance. A desirable service is to have professionals remotely monitor the pacemakers continuously and alert the patient and doctor to any deviations. Remedial actions can then be decided if necessary by the doctor in consultation with the patient. If the patient is travelling, the local hospital will need to gain quick access to the patient's medical history and coordinate diagnosis and treatment with the primary doctor. The family members of the patient may also need to be notified. Such a scenario depends on the support of an ICT system and a community of stakeholders including doctors, hospitals, the patient, the patient's family, and many others. However, the value of such a scenario is not derived from any single component of a complex network of people, products, communications networks, organizations or technologies. Rather, the value is in the co-creation experience derived from the patient's interaction with all the elements involved. Moreover, value creation is determined by the experience of a specific customer, at a specific point in time and location, in the context of a specific event. In other words, value is determined by personal and other circumstances.

The example indicated that the co-creation experience is not company- or product-centric, and nor is it customer-centric. '[T]the network, not owned by a single company, multiplies the value of the product to the patient, his family and his doctor. The patient is an active stakeholder in defining the interaction, the context of the event and what is meaningful to him. In other words, the individual and his inter-actions define both the experience and the value derived from it' (p. 14).[23]

Similar experiences were identified in the examples of OnStar launched by General Motors and Mindstorms launched by Lego. They went on to argue that although products, services and solutions are all embedded in an experience-based approach, the reorientation is nothing short of a quantum leap when managerial attention must shift from products and services to the experience network. The movement towards experience innovation is believed by the authors to be inevitable. Convergences of technologies, industries, consumers and company roles are transforming the meaning and process of innovation.

The changing role of consumers plays a key role in the emergence of the experience economy. Today, consumers are connected, informed and active. The Internet gives consumers unprecedented access to all kinds of information, making them more know-ledgeable than ever before, and as a result, they are increasingly challenging or questioning the service providers. For example, patients are today using the Internet to learn about diseases and treatments, as well as tracking the records of doctors and hospitals, and clinical drug trials and new treatment procedures, so they are able to participate actively in their own treatments. Geographical limitations on informa-tion are increasingly eroded, so consumers increasingly have access to information about organizations, products, technologies, performances, prices and consumer reac-tions from around the world. The rapid development of electronic communities linked together by the Internet enables consumers to share information with each other more easily. The growing influence of blogs (web logs) also significantly affects the perception by consumers of companies and their products. The result is that compan-ies can no longer act autonomously, and consumers can seek influence in every part of the business system – and influence they do. The emerging reality is that interaction becomes the basis for co-creation of value and experience, with profound implications for value creation and innovation as well as the strategies, organizational structures and processes, and inter-organizational relations of today's and tomorrow's businesses.[24]

Products, Services, Solutions and Experiences: The Exponential Expansion of Business Value

The strategic reorientations from products and services to solutions and experience are extremely significant, with enormous implications for innovation and value crea-tion, and for the operational strategies and business models, organizational structures and processes, inter-organizational relations and customer relations management as well as the way that business leaders and employees think and work. With each reorientation there are lucrative opportunities for new value creation. Tom Peters quoted Tim Sanders of Yahoo! to illustrate the value-added that can be derived from strategic reorientations. They used a birthday cake as an example to illustrate the four steps in the value-added experience ladder highlighted by Pine and Gilmore: from raw materials, via goods and services to experiences. The story might be simplistic but it illustrates that transitions up the value-added ladder bring exponential growth in business value!

From the Raw Material to the Experience Economy

In a raw material economy, Grandma would spend about $1 to buy all the ingredients separately in order to bake a cake for the grandchild's birthday. Then in the goods economy, Mum would buy a package of pre-prepared ingredients to bake a cake which would probably cost $2. In the service economy, rather than buying a package of ingredients Mum could simply buy a cake for $10. In the experience economy, rather than buying a cake, Dad would spend $100 to book a birthday party at a special venue for the child and friends.

This example to some extent explains why IBM is increasingly shifting its focus from computing hardware and software to services and integrated solutions, despite the fact that it remains one of the most advanced computing companies in the world. It also explains how companies like Nike could focus on marketing and design and capture the lion's share of the huge value its products generate. It also explains why Harley-Davidson could effectively compete with products with far better technical performance. It also explains the success of many other companies from Starbuck to Nokia. These reorientations are still evolving rapidly and more research is clearly needed to monitor their developments and understand the critical issues.

Organizational Implications and the Role of the Internet and Related Technologies

In this chapter, two strategic reorientations from products and services to solutions and experiences were illustrated, supported by some early evidence identified in leading organizations. The strategic reorientations have profound organizational implications, requiring companies to radically re-examine their value chains and business focuses, and reconfigure their structures and core processes and inter-firm relations. In particular, business leaders need to understand changes in terms of where value is created and how it is distributed amongst stakeholders, and then position themselves strategically to ensure they are not marginalized in the process. New structures, processes and inter-organizational relations as well as new ways of thinking and working need to be implemented in their organizations.

Although in some cases strategic reorientations may or may not depend directly on advanced ICT systems, in most cases the new capabilities afforded by new technologies are essential in enabling organizations to make strategic reorientations – especially by enabling new structures and processes and new forms of inter-organizational relations. Indeed, some of the strategic and organizational changes are direct responses to changes in the market and in consumer behaviours that are brought about by the rapid development of the Internet and related technologies. Providing integrated solutions to customers often requires improved communications between the provider and the customer, and ICTs often play the essential role of enabling information sharing and service delivery amongst all stakeholders. To co-create unique consumer experience, it is essential to use the Internet and other communications technologies to link together companies and user communities – as most experience innovations are underpinned by a strong brand, an ICT platform and a community of users and suppliers. Some scholars believe that the transitions are inevitable, so the question for business leaders is how to compete effectively in the new business environment and maximize the benefits that can be derived from these strategic reorientations.

Discussion Questions

1 Describe the strategic reorientations from product, to services, solutions and further to experience. What is your view of these transitions? Why? Critically evaluate the implications of these reorientations for contemporary organizations.

2 Using a sector you are familiar with, discuss what the strategic reorientations from product to services, solutions and experience could mean. Highlight the potential opportunities and challenges.

Assignment: Case Study

Conduct some research on the Internet and identify one company that has successfully managed some of the strategic reorientations discussed in this chapter. Write it up as a case study for students in your class. The case study should clearly illustrate the strategic reorientations and highlight the opportunities and challenges involved (3,000 words).

NOTES

1 The shift from products to services is not limited to companies making physical products. It also includes 'service' companies selling standard 'products' making the shift towards solving problems for customers by extending their activities horizontally to related markets and/or vertically to adjacent stages of the value chain and then flexibly bundling these services together.

2 B. Joseph Pine II and James Gilmore (1999) *The Experience Economy: Work is theatre and every business a stage*, Harvard Business School Press, Boston; the book was an extension of their paper, B. Joseph Pine II and James Gilmore (1998) Welcome to the experiences economy, *Harvard Business Review*, 76(July–August), 97–105; Sawhney, M., S. Balasubramanian and V. Krishnan (2004) Creating growth with services, *Sloan Management Review*, Winter, 34–43; Prahalad, C. K. and V. Ramaswamy (2003) The new frontier of experience innovation, *Sloan Management Review*, Summer, 12–18.

3 Ridderstrale, Jonas and Kjelle Nordstrom (2000) *Funky Business*. FT Prentice Hall, London.

4 Peters, Tom (2003) *Re-imagine! Business excellence in a disruptive age*. Dorling Kindersley, London.

5   Zuboff, Shoshana and James Maxin (2004) *The Support Economy: Why corporations are failing individuals and the next episode of capitalism.* Allen Lane, London.
6   Prahalad, C. K. and Venkat Ramaswamy (2004) *The Future of Competition: Co-creating unique value with customers.* Harvard Business School Press, Boston.
7   Ibid.
8   Ibid.
9   Ibid.
10 Ridderstrale and Nordstrom (2000) op. cit.
11 Sawhney, Balasubramanian and Krishnan (2004) op. cit.
12 Drucker, Peter (1973) *Management: Tasks, responsibilities and practices.* Harper & Row, New York.
13 Ridderstrale and Nordstrom (2000) op. cit.
14 Sawhney, Balasubramanian and Krishnan (2004) op. cit.
15 Karmarkar, Uday (2004) Will you survive the Services Revolution? *Harvard Business Review,* June, 101–107.
16 Ibid.
17 Ibid.
18 Prahalad and Ramaswamy (2003, 2004), op. cit.
19 Pine and Gilmore (1999) op. cit.
20 Ridderstrale and Nordstrom (2000) op. cit.
21 Peters (2003) op. cit.
22 Prahalad and Ramaswamy (2003, 2004), op. cit.
23 Prahalad and Ramaswamy (2003), op. cit
24 Prahalad and Ramaswamy (2004), op. cit.

FURTHER READING

Allmendinger, Glen and Ralph Lombreglia (2005) Four strategies for the age of smart services. *Harvard Business Review,* October, 131–145.

Peters, Tom (2003) *Re-imagine! Business excellence in a disruptive age.* Dorling Kindersley, London.

Pine, B. Joseph II and James Gilmore (1999) *The Experience Economy: Work is theatre and every business a stage.* Harvard Business School Press, Boston.

Prahalad, C. K. and V. Ramaswamy (2003) The new frontier of experience innovation. *Sloan Management Review,* Summer, 12–18.

Prahalad, C. K. and V. Ramaswamy (2004) *The Future of Competition: Co-creating unique value with customers.* Harvard Business School Press, Boston.

Ridderstrale, Jonas and Kjelle Nordstrom (2000) *Funky Business.* FT Prentice Hall, London.

Sawhney, M., S. Balasubramanian and V. Krishnan (2004) Creating growth with services. *Sloan Management Review,* Winter, 34–43.

Chapter 9

Emerging E-Business Models in the Network Economy

The rapid development of the Internet and related technologies, combined with the changing nature of the economy and other changes in the business environment, has facilitated the emergence of new business strategies. Some of the new strategies have been discussed in the last three chapters. One of the main aims of a good strategy is to lead to circumstances in the long term that are favourable to profit generation.[1] However, strategies do not automatically translate into profit. Instead profit is earned through the day-to-day operation of the company. Structural profit potential, as derived from the ability to create value for customers and make a unique contribution, is specified systematically by what is known as the business model.[2] In other words, to implement new strategies and to translate them into new structures, processes and day-to-day activities, the missing link that needs to be explored is the business model.

The Internet Revolution has enabled the emergence of many e-Business models, which are sometimes referred to as Internet business models or web-based business models, amongst others. Since the mid-1990s, numerous studies have been undertaken to identify, describe and conceptualize them. This chapter will highlight some of the key research findings in recent years.

What Is a Business Model?

Before discussing what an e-Business model is, the concept of a business model itself needs to be defined. Definitions of the concept vary but a common description is about how a business works and the logic that creates its value.

Timmers defined a business model as the organization, or architecture, of product, service and information flows, and the sources of revenue and benefits for suppliers and customers.[3] Similarly, Afuah and Tucci defined the business model as the method by which a firm builds and uses its resources to offer its customers better value than its competitors and to make money in doing so. In particular, a business model details how a firm makes money now and in the future, and it enables a firm to have sustainable competitive advantages over its competitors.[4] To understand a business model we need to explore its components, linkages between the components, and dynamics.

Amongst the numerous definitions of business models, most scholars tend to focus on one or two key aspects of the concept, either how a firm generates revenue, manages the relationships of different stakeholders and the linkages between them, or how the firm engages with the market. Ethiraj and colleagues, for example, used business model to refer to the sources of revenue,[5] whilst other researchers have defined it as the core strength of the business (Rayport), or the business method (Rappa).[6] Fox described a business model as the unique configuration of elements consisting of the organization's goals, strategies, processes, technologies and structures that is conceived to create value for customers and thus enable the firm to compete successfully in a particular market.[7]

Revenue generation is clearly an important aspect of the business model, but it should be noted that the connotation of the concept is much broader. As Porter argued: 'The definition of business model is murky at best. Most often it seems to refer to a loose conception of how company does business and generates revenue. Yet . . . generating revenue is a far cry from creating an economic value . . .' (p. 73).[8] Similarly, Amit and Zott also argued that some analysts misapprehend the business model as the revenue model, which is the specific way in which a business model enables revenue generation. They describe a business model as the way in which a firm enables transactions that create value for all participants, including partners, suppliers and customers. As such, a business model can be defined as the architectural configuration of the components of transactions designed to exploit business opportunities.[9] Many other definitions of business model have been described by various authors. Vassilopoulou and colleagues compiled a useful table, which demonstrated the variations within relevant literatures. The table has been expanded to take account of subsequent work in this area (table 9.1).[10] These definitions illustrate the multi-dimensional nature of the concept.

What Is an E-Business Model?

E-Business models generally describe emerging business models that exploit the new capabilities of the Internet and related technologies. Since the dot.com boom of the late 1990s, many studies have been carried out. Early studies have mainly focused on identifying and describing various e-Business models and classifying them into different categories. Examples include the seminal work by Paul Timmers and the online resources by Michael Rippa,[11] as well as several popular e-Commerce and e-Business textbooks, which have been regularly updated.[12] Other authors have focused on developing a taxonomy of generic e-Business models to illustrate how the Internet can be used in business in a systematic fashion, often through a synthesis of previous, more descriptive work.[13] Furthermore, based on a systematic review of previous studies, Alexander Osterwalder developed an e-Business model ontology in order to provide a shared and common understanding of the phenomenon so as to

Table 9.1 Business model definitions

Authors	Definition
Magretta (2002)	A story that explains how an enterprise works.
Petrovic et al. (2001); Auer and Follack (2002)	A description of the logic of a 'business system' for creating value that lies behind the actual processes.
Jutla, Bodorik et al. (1999)	The business model determines processes and transactions.
Applegate (2001)	A description of a complex business that enables study of its structure, the relationships among structural elements, and how it will respond to the real world.
Timmers (1998)	An architecture for the product, service and information flows, including a description of the various business actors and their roles; a description of the potential benefits for the various business actors; and descriptions of sources of revenues.
Osterwalder and Pigneur (2002)	A description of the value a company offers to one or several segments of customers and the architecture of the firm and its network of partners for creating, marketing and delivering this value and relationship capital, in order to generate profitable and sustainable revenue streams.
Weill and Vitale (2001)	A description of the roles and relationships among a firm's consumers, customers, allies and suppliers that identifies the major flows of product, information and money, and the major benefits to participants.
Hawkins (2001)	A description of the commercial relationship between a business enterprise and the products and/or services it provides in the market. More specifically, it is a way of structuring various cost and revenue streams such that a business becomes viable, usually in the sense of being able to sustain itself on the basis of the income it generates.
Tapscott et al. (2000)	A business model is about the invention of new value propositions that transform the rules of competition, and mobilize people and resources to unprecedented levels of performance.
Yip (2004)	A business model embraces the target customer, the nature of the business and how revenues (and hopefully profits) are generated.
Rappa (2004)	A business model is the method of doing business by which a company can sustain itself – that is; generate revenue. The business model spells out how a company makes money by specifying where it is positioned in the value chain.
Mansfield and Fourie (2004)	A business model most commonly describes the linkage between a firm's resources and functions and its environment. It is a contingency model that finds an optimal mode of operation for a specific situation in a specific market.

Source: Adapted from Vassilopoulou et al. (2003).

enable communications between people from heterogeneous backgrounds in a diverse range of applications.[14]

Like the concept of the business model, e-Business model is also a multidimensional concept. Many authors have attempted to conceptualize e-Business models in a systematic fashion. For example, based on a comprehensive review of literature, Yousept classified previous studies of e-Business models into three main categories:[15]

- e-Business model building blocks – e.g. Dubosson-Torbay, Osterwalder and Pigneur (2002); Alt and Zimmermann (2001); Weil and Vitale (2001); Afuah and Tucci (2000); Hamel (2000);
- e-Business model content and evaluation – Amit and Zott (2001); Gordijn and Akkermans (2001); Petrovic, Kittl, and Teksten (2001);
- e-Business model taxonomy – e.g. Applegate and Collura (2000); Rappa (2000); Tapscott, Lowi and Ticoll (2000); Timmers (1998).[16]

Those defining e-Business models from the perspective of building blocks outlined the main components and building blocks that make up the architectural configuration of e-Business. E-Business model content framework focuses on what is and should be the essence of a good e-Business model (viability, value creation and capture potential); whilst e-Business model evaluation provides tools and frameworks to systematically assess the viability of the e-Business model. E-Business model taxonomy focuses on the classifications of various models.

Current E-Business Models: Paul Timmers

In his seminal book, Timmers made a first attempt to classify different ways of doing business on the Internet and provided some preliminary categorizations of the phenomenon.[17] He started with a systematic approach of identifying architectures for business models, and based on the idea of value chain deconstruction and reconstruction and identifying possible ways of integrating information along the chain between the different components, he illustrated eleven e-Business models that can be observed in the real world. He then explored two dimensions of each of the business models – the extent of innovation of the business model, and the extent of integration of information and functions along the value chain (figure 9.1).

Timmers defined a business model as an architecture for product, service and information flows, including a description of the various business actors and their roles, a description of the potential benefits for the various business actors, and a description of the sources of revenue. Based on this definition he illustrated, with examples, eleven e-Business models, which have been widely referred to in other studies of e-Business models. Most of these models are self-explanatory.

1. e-Shops – Web marketing by an organization or an online shop;
2. e-Procurement – the electronic tendering and procurement of goods and services;

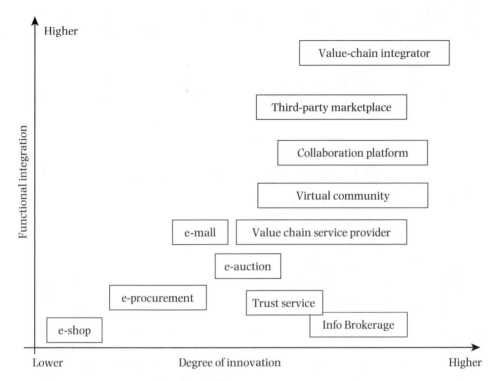

Figure 9.1   E-Business models identified by Timmers
Source: Timmers, Paul (1999) *Electronic Commerce: Strategies and Models for Business-to-Business Trading*, Chicester: John Wiley & Sons Ltd. Copyright John Wiley & Sons Ltd, reproduced with permission

3. e-Malls – a collection of e-Shops enhanced by a common umbrella;
4. e-Auctions – electronic implementation of bidding mechanisms;
5. virtual communities – online communities of members with common interests;
6. collaboration platforms – the provision of tools and information environment for collaboration between enterprises;
7. third-party marketplaces – using a third party to provide web marketing or online shop;
8. value-chain integrators – integrating multiple steps of the value chain, with the potential to exploit the information flows between those steps as further added value;
9. value-chain service providers – companies specializing in a specific part of the value chain (e.g. e-Logistics, e-Payments);
10. information brokerage – new information services such as information search, customer profiling and business opportunity brokerage;
11. trust and other services – trust services by certification authorities or others. Other services include the provision of business information and consultancy services.

The list is not exhaustive and many other categories (e.g. e-Betting and e-Syndication) have since also been identified. However, this study remains important today because it kick-started many other studies of e-Business models. By mapping these business models onto a two-dimensional framework – the level of innovation and the extent of integration – Timmers identified two opposite trends for the future evolution of e-Business models. One is the move towards increased integration of information flows, and the other is the development of specialized, highly innovative services.

Taxonomy of E-Business Models: Michael Rappa, Allan Afuah and Christopher Tucci

Rappa identified and conceptualized a series of e-Business models primarily from the perspective of revenue generation, and published his results on the Internet. The main categories are summarized in table 9.2.

Drawing on the work of Timmers, Rappa and many others, Afuah and Tucci moved beyond the identification of individual categories of e-Business models to developing a taxonomy.[18] Although Afuah and Tucci believe that the business model is a very broad concept, which encompasses many elements and dimensions, they have specifically emphasized the importance of revenue generation in their taxonomy of e-Business models. The key components the authors identified as part of the e-Business model include:

- the value that a firm offers its customers;
- the segment of customers it targets to whom it will offer the value;
- the scope of products and services it offers to each segment of customers;
- the profit site it chooses;
- its sources of revenue;
- the prices it puts on the value offered to its customers;
- the activities it must perform in offering that value;
- the capabilities these activities rest on;
- what a firm must do to sustain any advantages it has;
- how well it can implement all these different elements.

The authors then argued that these components must work in a system, and how well the system works depends not only on the key components but also on the relationships between and amongst them. Furthermore, the relationship between the business model and its environment is also very important, and a good business model needs to be capable of taking advantage of any new opportunities and containing the effects of emerging threats and challenges.

Afuah and Tucci regarded the e-Business model as the method by which a firm plans to make money long term using the Internet. It is the system that takes advantage of the properties of the Internet to make money. They identified seven possible revenue models to in their classification of e-Business models:

Table 9.2 E-Business models by Rappa

E-Business model	Meaning	Sub-models
Brokerage	Market-makers, bringing buyers and sellers together and facilitating transactions. It makes its money by charging a fee for each transaction it enables	Marketplace exchange, buy/sell fulfilment, demand collection system, auction broker, transaction broker, distributor, search agent, virtual marketplace
Advertising	An extension of the traditional media-broadcasting model. The website provides some kind of information (usually for free), and services (e.g. e-mail, chat, e-forums) mixed with advertising messages, usually in the form of banner ads	Portal, classified, user registration, query-based paid placement, contextual advertising/behavioural marketing, content-target advertising
Infomediary	Helping consumers both protect and enrich themselves by capturing their own customer information and then selling it to the many companies that are now getting that information for free (Hagel and Singer, 1999)	Advertising networks, audience measurement service, incentive marketing, metamediary
Merchant	The classic wholesalers and retailers of goods and services (e-tailers)	Virtual merchant, catalogue merchant, click-and-mortar and bit vendor
Manufacturer	Based on the power of the web, in this model manufacturers reach buyers directly and thereby compress the distribution channel. It can be based on efficiency, improved customer service, and a better understanding of customer preferences	Purchase, lease, license, brand integrated content
Affiliate	It provides purchase opportunities wherever people may be surfing by offering financial incentives (in the form of percentage of revenue) to affiliated partner sites. It provides purchase-point through to merchants	Banner exchange, pay-per-click and revenue sharing
Community	Initially a group of people with common interests and needs who come together online. This could potentially end up as a cluster of people with a critical mass purchasing power, as communities allow members to exchange product quality and price information. Revenue comes from advertising, infomediary, specialized portal opportunities or subscription fees	Open source, public broadcasting and knowledge networks
Subscription	Charging users for access to the site	
Utility	Metered usage or pay-as-you-go approach	

Source: Adapted from Rappa (2000). http://digitalenterprise.org/models/models.html

- commission – fees levied on transactions based on the size of the transaction;
- advertising – revenue generated by charging for advertising rather than by charging the end users for using the website;
- mark-up – the primary source of revenue from mark-up on the products it sells via the Internet;
- production – which Rappa called the manufacturing model, where the manufacturer sells to the customers directly via the Internet;
- referral-based – firms rely on fees for steering visitors to another company's site;
- subscription-based – the company charges users a flat rate on a periodic basis for certain services;
- fee-for-service based – activities are metered and the users pay for what they consume, which Rappa calls the utility model.

The authors recognized that their taxonomy was based on the dominant revenue model, but the revenue model is only one of at least four dimensions that determine the classification of business models. By analysing and comparing previous studies of business models along four dimensions – profit site, revenue model, commerce strategy and pricing model, they are able to describe the typology of e-Business models in a systematic fashion.

They identified eleven profit sites within the Internet infrastructure, which are summarized as e-Commerce, content aggregators, brokers/agents, market-maker, service providers, backbone operators, ISPs, last mile, content creators, software suppliers and hardware suppliers. Along the dimension of commerce strategy, they identified five main categories, namely, B2B (business to business), B2C (business to consumer), P2P (person to person or peer to peer, also known as consumer to consumer – C2C), C2B (consumer to business), and B2E (business to employee). In terms of pricing models, the authors identified five separate categories – fixed pricing, one-to-one bargaining, auctions, reverse auctions and barter. By overlaying these four dimensions, the authors believe that most e-Business models can be characterized. This remains one of the most comprehensive taxonomies of e-Business models today.

An E-Business Model Ontology: Alexander Osterwalder

Osterwalder[19] believed that despite the significant progress made by previous studies of e-Business models, most previous studies dealt with only some aspects of the concept while neglecting or downplaying others. He defined a business model as the logic of a business system for creating value that lies behind the actual processes. A business model needs to address the revenue and product aspects, the business actor and network aspects, and the marketing aspects of a business. In order to provide an appropriate foundation for tools that would allow the effective and consistent understanding, sharing and communicating, changing, measuring and simulating of the e-Business models, an ontology of e-Business models is necessary.

An ontology is a rigorously defined framework that provides a shared and common understanding of a domain that can be communicated between people and

Table 9.3 The business model ontology: pillars and building blocks by Osterwalder

Pillars	Building blocks of business model	Description
Product innovation	Value proposition	A value proposition is an overall view of a company's bundle of products and services that are of value to the customer
Customer interface	Target customer	The target customer is a segment of customers to whom a company wants to offer value
	Distribution channel	A distribution channel is a means of getting in touch with the customer
	Relationship	The relationship describes the kind of link a company establishes between itself and the customer
Infrastructure management	Value configuration	The value configuration describes the arrangement of activities and resources that are necessary to create value for customers
	Capability	A capability is the ability to execute a repeatable pattern of actions that is necessary in order to create value for customers
	Partnership	A partnership is a voluntarily initiated cooperative agreement between two or more companies in order to create value for customers
Financial aspects	Cost structure	The cost structure is the representation in money of all the means employed in the business model
	Revenue model	The revenue model describes the way a company makes money through a variety of revenue flows

Source: Adapted from Osterwalder (2004) by Yousept (2006).

heterogeneous and widespread application systems. Given the current confusion about e-Business models, such an approach would be very significant both theoretically and practically.

Olsterwalder uses 'business model' to describe the value a company offers to one or several segments of customers and the architecture of the firm and its network of partners for creating, marketing and delivering this relationship capital, in order to generate profitable and sustainable revenue streams. The ontological framework of the e-Business model is based on four main pillars: product innovation, customer relationship, infrastructure management and financials (table 9.3). This framework is very similar to the conceptual framework that Hagel and Singer used when exploring the deconstruction of integrated business models.[20] The origin of this framework can be traced back at least to the framework by Abell in 1980.[21]

Product innovation describes what business the company is in, while customer relationship illustrates who the company's target customers are. Infrastructure management describes how the company efficiently deals with the logistical issue, and the financials deal with the revenue model. Previous studies have explored some of these aspects but few studies have so far investigated these aspects simultaneously. This framework illustrates the relationships between the four key pillars and the key elements of each of the components, as shown in figure 9.2.

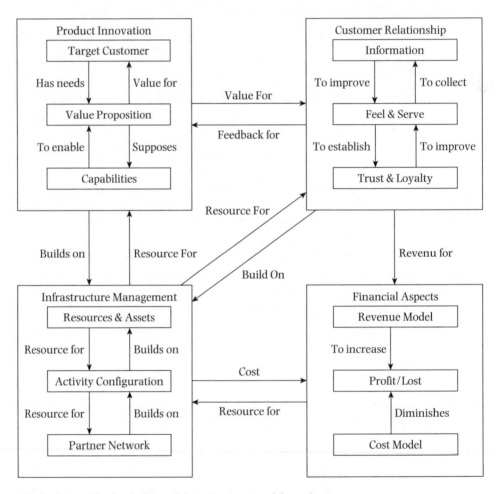

Figure 9.2 The four pillars of the e-Business model ontology
Source: Osterwalder and Pigneur (2002). Reproduced with kind permission of Alex Osterwalder and Yves Pigneur

The ontology of the e-Business model is the conceptualization and formalization into elements, relationships, vocabulary and semantics of the essential subjects in the e-Business model domain. It can be structured into several levels of decomposition with increasing depth and complexity. It provides a valuable toolkit that would enable business leaders to define, assess and change their business models, and enable information system developers to undertake information system requirement engineering.

General Implications: Linking Emerging Strategies with Organizational Innovations

In this chapter, previous studies of e-Business models were discussed, and in particular, the work of Timmers, Rappa, Afuah and Tucci, and Olsterwalder was illustrated in detail. Business models provide the essential link between business strategies and organizational innovations. A systematic understanding of this concept is essential for translating new opportunities and new business thinking into specific activities and revenue streams.

The rapidly changing business environment has put enormous pressure on all organizations to explore new strategies and business models. Many of these new strategies and business models have already been implemented in different sectors and industries (e.g. banking, telecommunications), and new ones are continuously being invented.[22] It is important that we continue this effort to identify, investigate and conceptualize emerging strategies and business models within different contexts. Such studies will provide valuable guidance for business leaders to capture emerging opportunities effectively and contain potential threats and challenges, by actively exploiting the new capabilities afforded to them by the Internet and related technologies.

To translate the new strategies and business models discussed in this part of the book into real business benefits, it is essential that organizations redesign their structures, processes and inter-organizational relations to reflect these changes and capitalize on emerging opportunities. These issues are the focus of the next part.

Discussion Questions

1 What is an e-Business model? How do you define it? In what ways is it useful to contemporary organizations?

2 Conduct some background research on five e-Businesses you are familiar with, and illustrate their business models to your class, highlighting the main dimensions and elements. Discuss possible ways these business models could be improved.

Assignments

1. Developing a New Conceptual Framework of E-Business Models
    Based on a comprehensive, critical literature review, develop your own framework of e-Business models. Write up your findings in the form of a short article for

a business magazine (such as *The Economist* or *Business Week*). The article should be around 3,000 words.

2. Developing a Wikipedia of E-Business Models

This assignment is for the whole class. Use Wiki to develop a comprehensive *Wikipedia* on e-Business models for current and future students on your course (http://www.mediawiki.org/wiki/MediaWiki). An example of Wikipedia is available at http://en.wikipedia.org/wiki/Main_Page. The tasks should be evenly divided amongst the students in the class (for example, each student could be asked to be responsible for a particular type of e-Business model). To encourage collaboration and learning from one another, each student is not only required to undertake research and write up his/her assigned section of the Wikipedia, but also edit and contribute to other people's sections. Each student's own section will account for only 60 per cent of the total mark; 20 per cent will be based on the student's contributions to other sections of the Wikipedia. The remaining 20 per cent will be based on the quality of the entire Wikipedia on e-Business models by the class. This assignment could also be used as an exercise to prepare the students for the main Assignment 3 illustrated at the end of this book.

NOTES

1 Cropper, S., Eden, C., Gunn, L., and van der Heidjen, K. (1995) *General Strategic Management: Business policy.* Strathclyde Graduate School of Business, University of Strathclyde, Glasgow, UK.

2 van der Heidjen, Kees (1996) *Scenarios.* John Wiley & Son, Chichester.

3 Timmers, P. (1998) Business models for the electronic markets, *Electronic Markets*, 8(2), 3–8; Timmers, P. (1999) *Electronic Commerce: Strategies and models for business-to-business trading*, John Wiley & Son, Chichester.

4 Afuah, A. and C. L. Tucci (2000, 2003) *Internet Business Models and Strategies: Text and cases.* McGraw-Hill, Boston.

5 Ethiraj, S., Guler, I., and Singh, H. (2000) The impact of Internet and electronic technologies on firms and its implications for competitive advantage. *Knowledge at Wharton.* Available from: http://knowledge.wharton.upenn.edu.

6 Rayport, J. F. (1999) The truth about Internet business models. *Strategy + Business*, Third Quarter, no. 16; Rappa, M. (2000) *Business Models on the Web*, http://ecommerce.ncsu.edu/business_models.html.

7 Fox, C. (2000) *E-Commerce Business Models.* http://www.chrisfoxinc.com/eCommerceBusinessModels.html.

8 Porter, M. E. (2001) Strategy and the Internet. *Harvard Business Review*, March, 63–78.

9 Amit, R. and Zott, C. (2000) Value Drivers of e-Commerce Business Models. *Knowledge at Wharton.* http://knowledge.wharton.upenn.edu.

10 Vassilopoulou, K., X. Ziouvelou, A. Patell, and A. Pouloudi (2003) Examining e-business models: applying a holistic approach in the mobile environment. In Ciborra, C. et al. (eds), *New Paradigms in Organizations, Markets and Society. Proceedings of the 11th European Conference on Information Systems (ECIS 2003)*, 16–21 June. This table was extended by my researcher Joanna Berry at Newcastle University. Applegate, L. M. (2001) E-business models: making sense of the Internet business landscape, in G. Dickson, W. Gary, and G. DeSanctis (eds), *Information Technology and the Future Enterprise: New models for managers,*

Prentice Hall, Upper Saddle River, NJ; Auer, C. and M. Follack (2002) Using action research for gaining competitive advantage out of the Internet's impact on existing business models, in *Proceedings of the 15th Bled Electronic Commerce Conference – eReality: Constructing the eEconomy*, Bled, Slovenia, 17–19 June, pp. 767–784; Hawkins, R. (2001) *The 'business model' as a research problem in electronic commerce*, STAR (Socio-economic Trends Assessment for the digital Revolution) IST Project, Issue Report No. 4, July, SPRU – Science and Technology Policy Research; Jutla, D. N., P. Bodorik and Y. Wang (1999) WebEC: A benchmark for the cybermediary business model in e-commerce, *IMSA 1999*, 388–392; Mansfield, G. M. and L. C. H. Fourie (2004) Strategy and business models – strange bedfellows? A case for convergence and its evolution into strategic architecture, *South African Journal of Business Management*, March, 35(1), 35–44 (AN 12952944); Margretta, Joan (2002) Why business models matter, *Harvard Business Review*, May, 80(5), 86–92; Osterwalder, Alexander and Tves Pigneur (2002) *An E-Business Model Ontology for Modelling E-Business*. 15th Bled Electronic Commerce Conference – E-Reality: Constructing the E-Economy, Bled, Slovenia, 17–19 June; Petrovic, O., C. Kittl and D. Teksten (2001) *Developing Business Models for eBusiness*, Paper presented at the International Conference of Electronic Commerce, Vienna, Austria, 31 October – 4 November; Rappa, M. (2004), *Business Models on the Web*. http://digitalenterprise.org/models/models.html; Tapscott, D., D. Ticoll and A. Lowy (2000) *Digital Capital: Harnessing the power of business webs*, Nicholas Brealey Publishing, London.; Timmers (1998) op. cit.; Weill, P. and M. R. Vitale (2001) *Place to Space; Migrating to eBusiness models*, Harvard Business School Press, Boston, MA; Yip, G. S. (2004) Using strategy to change your business model. *Business Strategy Review*, 15(2), 17–24.

11 Timmers (1998, 1999) op. cit.; Rappa (2000) op. cit.
12 E.g. Turban, Efraim, David King, Jae Lee and Dennis Viehland (2004) *Electronic Commerce: A managerial perspective*, Pearson Prentice Hall, New Jersey; Laudon, Kenneth C. and Carol Guercio Traver (2003) *E-Commerce: Business, technology and society*, 2nd edn. Pearson Addison Wesley, Boston.
13 E.g. Afuah and Tucci (2000, 2003) op. cit.
14 Osterwalder, A. (2004) *The Business Model Ontology: A proposition in a design science approach*, PhD Thesis, Ecole Des Hautes Etudes Commerciales, University of Lausanne, Lausanne; Osterwalder and Pigneur (2002) op. cit.
15 Yousept, Irene (2006) *Internet and Emerging E-Business Models: Developing an integrated analytical framework for UK Internet banking and online grocery shopping*. PhD Thesis, University of Newcastle upon Tyne, Newcastle upon Tyne, UK.
16 Afuah and Tucci (2000) op. cit.; Alt, R. and H. Zimmermann (2001) Introduction to special section – business models, *Electronic Markets*, 11(1), 3–9; Amit, R. and C. Zott (2001) Value creation in e-business, *Strategic Management Journal*, 22, 493–520; Applegate, L. and M. Collura (2000) *Overview of E-Business Models*, HBS Note (Vol. 9-801-172, pp. 1–18), Harvard Business School, Boston, MA; Dubosson-Torbay, M., A. Osterwalder and Y. Pigneur (2002) E-Business model design, classification, and measurements, *Thunderbird International Business Review*, 44(1), 5–23; Gordijn, J., H. Akkermans, H. V. Vliet and E. Paalvast (2000) *Electronic Commerce and Web Technologies*, Lecture Notes in Computer Science, Vol. 1875, Springer-Verlag, Berlin, pp. 48–62; Hamel, G. (2000) *Leading the Revolution*, Harvard Business School Press, Boston; Petrovic et al. (2001) op. cit.; Rapa (2000) op. cit.; Tapscott et al. (2000) op. cit.; Timmers (1998) op. cit.; Weill and Vitale (2001) op. cit.
17 Timmers (1999, 2000) op. cit.
18 Afuah and Tucci (2000, 2003) op. cit.

19   Osterwalder and Pigneur (2002) op. cit.; Osterwalder (2004) op. cit.
20   Hagel III, John and Marc Singer (1999) *Net Worth: Shaping markets when customers make the rules.* Harvard Business School Press, Boston.
21   Abell, D. F. (1980) *Defining the Business: The starting point of strategic planning.* New Jersey: Prentice Hall, Inc.
22   E.g. Li, Feng (2001) The Internet and the deconstruction of the integrated banking model, *British Journal of Management*, 12, 307–322; Li, Feng (2002) Internet banking in the UK: From new distribution channel to new business models, *Journal of Financial Transformation*, http://www.capco.com/pdf/j06art10.pdf; Li, Feng and Jason Whalley (2002) Deconstruction of the telecommunications industry: from value chains to value networks. *Telecommunications Policy*, 26, 451–472.

FURTHER READING

Afuah, A. and C. L. Tucci (2000, 2003) *Internet Business Models and Strategies: Text and cases.* McGraw-Hill, Boston.
Li, Feng (2001) The Internet and the deconstruction of the integrated banking model. *British Journal of Management*, 12, 307–322.
Rappa, M. (2005) *Business Models on the Web.* http://ecommerce.ncsu.edu/business_models.html.
Timmers, P. (1999) *Electronic Commerce: Strategies and models for business-to-business trading.* John Wiley & Son, Chichester.

Part III

Organizational Innovations through Information and Communications Technologies (ICTs)

Introduction

The business environment has changed, and many new strategies and business models have been developed to capitalize on emerging opportunities in the new business environment and to contain potential threats and challenges, through innovative exploitation of the new capabilities afforded to us by ICTs in general and the Internet and related technologies in particular. However, the potential of these emerging strategies and business models can only be realized if they are effectively implemented in organizations: they need to be deeply embedded in the fabrics of the organizations and translated into day-to-day activities.

This means that organizations need to review the way they do business at all levels, and in particular, how different activities are structured, linked and coordinated. They need to innovate in the way they are structured, how the processes are designed and the way they relate to their suppliers and customers – often along the entire supply chain. At a more micro-level, organizations also need to re-examine the way individuals and groups work and how they relate to one another, especially in terms of who does what, where, when and how. One of the main sources of organizational innovations is the rapidly developing ICTs in a context where information has become the most critical strategic resource for all organizations across different sectors of the economy.

In this section, some of the most significant organizational innovations – in structures, processes, work organization and inter-organizational relations – will be discussed. Most organizational innovations reflect the new strategies and business models that have emerged in the new business environment, and they are enabled by rapid developments in ICTs.

In chapter 10, some recent changes in the structure of organizations – structural innovations – will be discussed, and these changes are leading to significant changes in the shape and form of organizations. Following that, chapter 11 investigates organizational transformation from the perspective of business processes – that is, how the organization does its business. Both incremental and radical process innovations will be explored. Chapter 12 examines organizational innovations at a more micro-level. Some new ways of working – both individually and in groups – will be discussed. Finally, chapter 13 goes beyond the organization's boundary to look at changes in inter-organizational relations and the opportunities and challenges involved. Through these organizational innovations, many organizations have been transformed into new forms that are more suited for the new business environment.

Chapter 10

Structural Innovations and Emerging Forms of Organization

Over the past few decades numerous studies have been conducted on ICTs and changes in the structures of organizations. On 25 May 2005, the *Financial Times* published a comment by Columbia University Professor Eli Noam on how a company's tools can define its structure. Noam argued that a company can be without any production activities but not without information activity. 'Companies come to look like their information systems. [Change the IT and the company changes its structure.'] He regarded the company as a kind of information processing apparatus and then illustrated the changing structures of organizations from the pre-industrial companies with their simple structure, via the machine model of the industrial age, the post-war mainframe model with centralized, mainframe-based information processing tools, to the network model of the mid-1980s when hierarchy declined and flexibility increased with the growing use of networked microcomputers. More recently, with the rapid proliferation of ubiquitous computing, human-to-machine communications, sensor networks, automated information processing and semantic networks, '[m]any companies then become coordinators and integrators; employees become increasingly independent free-agents; a myriad of highly specialized suppliers vie for their services; and customers seek customized products'. He referred to this as the market model of the company; and to paraphrase Marshall McLuhan, 'The [IT] medium is the company'.

Noam's vision is nothing new, and like other similar utopian visions, it is overly simplistic, technological deterministic, misleading and conceals many hidden risks. Other people who promoted such visions in recent years include Larry Downes and Chunka Mui, who argued that a truly frictionless economy does not need permanent firms.[2] Business guru Don Tapscott has also been arguing for the death of the stand-alone company as the fundamental unit of commerce.[3] They often quote Nobel laureate Ronald Coase to justify such views, but the flaws of such misuse of transaction cost economics have been discussed by many authors previously, and also discussed in chapter 5 of this book.

There is no doubt that the increasing use of ICTs has enabled organizations large and small to adopt new structures (amongst other things) significantly different from, and often far superior to, traditional forms of organizations that have served us well in the past but have become increasingly unable to cope with the uncertainty and increased volatility of today's business environment. However, the relationship between ICTs and changes in organizational structures is a sophisticated one, and this has been repeatedly demonstrated by comprehensive research and practice in the past few decades. For example, one of the main conclusions of the eight-year, £8 million research Programme on Information and Communications Technologies (PICT) funded by the Economic and Social Research Council (ESRC) in the UK was that the role of ICTs can only be fully appreciated in the socio-economic contexts in which these technologies are embedded. Many other research programmes have reached similar conclusions – such as the $5 million MIT study in the USA[4] and numerous projects within the Framework Programmes funded by the EU. It is ironic that even after so many years of comprehensive research, the temptation to adopt simplistic, technological deterministic views is still hard to resist today.

In understanding the role of ICTs in organizations, we should not confuse business with information processing. Organizations are much more than computers and information systems, and those physical and human characteristics of organizations that cannot be digitized cannot and should not be neglected or downplayed even in the information age.[5] This chapter will explore the nature of the relationship between ICTs on the one hand and changes in the structures of organizations on the other. The relationship is a sophisticated one, and it is through a complex interactive process that both the technology and the organizational structure evolve over time under various circumstances: they both shape, and are shaped by, the other through an interactive process.

Structural Innovations: What Are They and Why?

Pick up any business newspapers or magazines and you are likely to find discussions about empowerment, de-layering, downsizing, right-sizing, networking, restructuring, reorganization, flattening the corporate hierarchy, and functional integration and disintegration. The list can go on and there has also been considerable talk about new forms of organization, including the network or cellular organization, the federal organization, the flexible firm, the horizontal or process-based organization, knowledge-based organizations, learning organizations, team or project-based organizations, adaptive organizations and the virtual organization. This is not an exhaustive list and new terminologies are continuously being invented. Many such terminologies are illustrating changes in the shape – especially the structure – of organizations. In this chapter, structural innovations are used to illustrate the development of new organizational structures aimed at improving the performance of the organization, be it more efficient or less costly, more flexible or more responsive to external changes.

There have been considerable changes in the structures of organizations in the past few decades but the views people hold differ significantly. ICTs played a key role in many of these structure changes. Some researchers have argued that the increasing use of computers and their networks has led to the centralization of control, whilst others have argued that the opposite is the case and the increasing use of ICTs has led to the decentralization of control and the dispersion of various activities; and employees at the frontline are increasingly empowered and their job contents enriched. There is ample empirical evidence to support either view. Furthermore, it has been argued that the need to be entrepreneurial and responsive to markets favours agile and focused companies, but what we are observing in the commercial world have been unprecedented corporate mergers and acquisitions around the world, which is a powerful testimony to the benefits of scale and scope economy.[6] The truth is that corporations today are increasingly unwilling to sacrifice size and breadth for market responsiveness or vice versa. The real challenge is to change the way businesses are organized in order to realize the benefits of both. Advanced ICTs have been regarded as the main source of innovation that would enable organizations to adopt new structures and achieve both the benefits of scale and scope economies of large organizations, and the flexibility and responsiveness of small organizations, simultaneously.   *ASP's*

The need for corporate restructuring has been well rehearsed in academic and business literature. A simplified version of the argument is that bureaucracy is bad, and flexibility is good. Traditional hierarchies have outlived their usefulness and new organizational models are needed. Since the 1980s, the prime targets of major organizational reforms have been rigid hierarchies and swollen middle management ranks. Since then, many other measures have also been introduced to transform organizations into less hierarchical and more flexible forms, and the search for new forms of organization continues today.

For many years, one fundamental problem facing almost all organizations has been the internal contradictions, or compromises, inherent in most organizational designs. If an organization wishes to improve local autonomy through decentralization, it will lose some central control and coordination, and vice versa. In addition to centralization versus decentralization, other compromises inherent in existing organizational designs include globalization versus localization, scale versus scope economies, efficiency versus effectiveness, control versus flexibility, rigidity versus responsiveness, and spatial separation versus functional integration. The list is not exhaustive. Within such a context, many organizational reforms promoted by business consultants and practised by private and public sector organizations have often been aimed at changing the balance of such compromises. The gains in one aspect happen at the expense of the other. The challenge is whether we can develop new organizational forms that would deliver benefits in both directions along multiple dimensions; in particular, how to develop an organizational structure that would enable large organizations to survive in volatile business environments.

The Search for Ideal Forms of Organization: Organizational Species in the Business Environment

For many years, we have been talking about the new 'business environment' and what organizations can and should do to 'survive' in the new business environment, from classrooms to boardrooms, as if organizations are some kind of living organism in a natural environment. Despite the limitations of such a metaphor, the benefits of this approach are widely accepted.[7] Within this context, researchers have been proposing ideal organizational forms most suited to particular business environments, which are then used to prescribe how to design an organization to achieve optimal alignment, or fit, both within the organization and between the organization and its environment.

The organizational design challenges discussed in this chapter are not new. At the beginning of the last century, the bureaucratic hierarchy and the entrepreneurial forms of organizations were already well defined. The difficulties of balancing the flexibility and responsiveness of entrepreneurial organizations and the efficiency, scope and control of the large bureaucracy were debated extensively during the 1950s and 1960s. Many 'new' organizational forms were proposed and experimented with – such as the matrix organization, which is still being promoted and implemented in some organizations today.

One widely used framework of ideal forms of organization was developed by Mintzberg.[8] He conceptualized five configurations of ideal organizational forms and discussed in detail each of their main environmental and organizational characteristics:

- the machine bureaucracy;
- the divisional form;
- the simple structure;
- the professional bureaucracy;
- the adhocracy.

Building on the work of Mintzberg, several other organizational forms were proposed to address various problems with these five traditional organizational forms. One such new organizational form is the matrix structure, which was heralded as an obvious organizational solution to managing environmental complexity. It was designed to provide a formal mechanism to understand and manage the diverse and conflicting needs across functions, products and geography. Despite all the good intentions, the matrix organization never lived up to expectations in practice, because rather than combining the benefits of the bureaucratic hierarchy and the simple structure, it created power struggles and turf battles which led to confusion, conflict and indecision. Even though some organizations claim to have successfully introduced matrix structures, many of them are simply traditional hierarchies re-sketched as matrixes.

Matrix Organization: A Hierarchy in Disguise?

A certain business school (which should remain anonymous) claimed to have successfully adopted the matrix structure. Traditionally, the school was organized as eight departments such as accounting and finance, human resource management, operations management and information systems, with each head of department reporting directly to the dean. When a new dean was appointed, he decided to restructure the school into twelve divisions (cognitive areas).

Instead of managing them through traditional departments, the activities of the business school were managed under three vice-deans: research, teaching, and commercial activities. The vice-deans and their teams sourced human resources from the twelve cognitive divisions for various teaching programmes, research projects and commercial consultancies and executive training. A matrix was formed between three vice-deans occupying the horizontal dimension and the twelve divisions populating the vertical dimension, which was heralded as a major success – and a living example of the matrix organization.

However, upon closer examination of the new structure, it became plainly obvious that the main reason it succeeded was because this was not a real matrix. The heads of the divisions were effectively under the management of the vice-deans. So the new structure simply introduced a new layer of management and extended the number of heads at the departmental (division) level within a traditional hierarchy, with more centralized decision making. Furthermore, this new structure added over £1 million of extra annual costs for the salaries and operating costs of the vice-deans and their teams, and the additional heads of divisions. However, the new hierarchy did force some 'unwanted' – or less 'desirable' – employees to take early retirement or move to other institutions.

Today the search for hybrid forms of organization continues. The new organizational forms need to combine the advantages of bureaucratic and entrepreneurial organizational forms, and allow central control and coordination to coexist with high-level autonomy and empowerment. My research since the late 1980s, as well as many other studies during this period, has shown that despite all the changes, hierarchy remains the fundamental organizational form for all organizations. Most organizations continue to embody the fundamental characteristics of the hierarchical form. Almost all the reported or identified changes are in the number of levels and the span of control within the organization, but these structural changes do not modify the basic assumptions of the hierarchical model. After many years' search for new organizational forms, I have reluctantly concluded that hierarchy is alive and kicking today and is likely to remain so in the foreseeable future. If any reader has identified an organization that is not a hierarchy, please do get in touch with me.

The study by Andrew Pettigrew and his team also concluded that their comprehensive research across three regions in the 1990s did not reveal revolutionary changes in the form of organizations. They found that innovative forms of organizing were emerging but they were supplementing, not supplanting, existing forms. The new was emerging alongside or within the old, rather than replacing the old.[9] The study also concluded that organizations were not converging towards a single type of form.

Since the 1980s, a wide variety of measures have been implemented to transform the traditional hierarchy. One of the central objectives is to transform the organizational structure into less bureaucratic and more decentralized forms. Examples include the flattening of the organizational hierarchy; decentralization of decision making; the centralization of management control; the concentration of strategic activities; and increasing levels of hierarchical and functional integration. Furthermore, some organizational reforms are increasingly extended beyond the organization's own boundary to include more flexible relations with other companies. Networking is increasingly regarded as an intermediary or superior form to vertical integration, and there have been continuous searches for organizational forms lying in between the market and hierarchy. These reforms have led to considerable changes in organizational structures, and compared with before, most hierarchies today are characterized by blurring functional boundaries, wider spans of control and shorter chains of command. These changes have been backed by empirical evidence.[10]

Research has also revealed that even though the hierarchy remains the fundamental organizational form today, the increasing use of advanced information systems has enabled organizations to introduce some radical changes within the context of the hierarchy. In fact, many hierarchies today are significantly different from traditional hierarchies in the way they function, even though sketches of the organizational structures (the boxes and lines) remain similar. Before introducing some of these changes, it is first necessary to examine the different roles of ICTs in organizational changes.

Understanding the Role of ICTs in Organizational Changes

Numerous studies have been conducted on the role of ICTs in organizational changes, and most studies tended to emphasize one type of role the technologies play in a specific context. One of the most comprehensive and most widely used frameworks was developed by Venkatraman in 1994, and many subsequent studies have been based on this framework.[11] He believed that ICTs can play a significant role in five types of organizational change, and the benefits the organization can expect depend on how radical the organizational change is:

- business scope redefinition;
- business network redefinition;
- business process redesign;
- internal integration;
- localized exploitation.

Localized exploitation is the most basic use of ICTs in an organization, and it usually delivers improvements in individual productivity. For example, by replacing a typewriter with a personal computer, a secretary's productivity can be improved. Typing mistakes can be easily corrected on a computer; and rather than typing a standard letter from scratch, the secretary could save a template to create new letters more quickly.

The next level up is internal integration, and productivity gains in individuals can be shared between co-workers. For example, by using internal networks, one secretary could share the templates for standard letters with other secretaries, thereby extending the productivity gains by one secretary to others.

Business process redesign is the next level up where the use of computers and their networks enables the organization to redesign its business processes to achieve significant improvements in productivity and responsiveness. Most large organizations have implemented business process reengineering or redesign (BPR) since the 1990s, and this will be the focus of the next chapter of this book.

Business network redefinition extends productivity gains within the organization through computer networking and organizational changes to its close business partners – often across the entire supply chain.

Finally, at the highest level, the use of ICTs can facilitate radical changes in the nature of the business and the scope of its activities. Examples include how the online booking system Sabre (before the de-merger from American Airlines) generated more revenue for American Airlines than flying planes; and Otis, the elevator company, generated more revenue and profit from fixed-fee service contracts (some form of insurance) than making and installing new elevators.

Although the framework was first published more than a decade ago, it remains one of the most comprehensive and most widely used frameworks when exploring the role of ICTs in organizational transformation. From a different angle, my own research identified four generic types of relationship between the use of ICTs and changes in organizational structures:

• enhancing existing organizational designs;
• reacting to organizational changes;
• parallel changes;
• generating organizational change.

The first type refers to cases where ICTs are simply used to enhance existing ways of doing things. The second type refers to cases where organizational designs have been changed and ICTs are put in place to support new ways of doing things. The third type refers to cases where organizational changes are not possible without the support of new ICTs, but once the technologies are implemented they enable further changes in organizational designs, and the relationship between them is interactive. Finally, the use of ICTs often generates radical organizational changes that were not possible or not even conceivable in the past. For example, the use of hand-held terminal devices in many retailers was originally implemented as a cheap input device for small outlets of large retailers when personal computers were still too expensive for them, but such hand-held devices have enabled the development of entirely different logistics systems, which significantly reduced stock holdings in stores and at the same time improved stock availability.

Structural Innovations through ICTs: What Can Be Restructured and Where to?

In order to study the restructuring of organizations, it is necessary to systematically identify the key elements and dimensions involved: what can be restructured, and where to. For example, rather than talking about centralization and decentralization in general, it is necessary to identify what can be centralized and decentralized along the vertical dimension, and in which direction these elements are moved.

My research has identified at least three key elements of corporate restructuring: namely, power, responsibility and activity. Power refers to the capacity, or capability, of a person or a group of people at a certain level of the organizational hierarchy in performing management control, direction and inspection over people at lower levels of the hierarchy. Power is a capacity, and having power does not mean it has to be used constantly in an active way. In some ways it is like money: it does not matter if you own £5 million or £20 million, but it matters a great deal when you need £3 to buy a sandwich when you have only got £2.95. In other words, power matters most when one needs it but has not got enough.

Responsibility refers to the duties ascribed to a person or a group of people in looking after certain activities or people during the execution of certain activities or when pursuing certain objectives. So the person or the group of people is/are to blame if things go wrong and to be praised if things go well. Financial accountability is one of the most important responsibilities, for example.

Activity refers to the various low-level, non-strategic business functions, tasks and procedures in an organization, particularly the physical components and the people responsible for the operation and execution of these functions and procedures.

These elements can be restructured along four dimensions: vertically in terms of the centralization and decentralization of power, responsibilities and activities; horizontally in terms of the integration and disintegration of business functions and the associated reorganization of power and responsibilities; thirdly, incorporation of activities and responsibilities previously held by people into the design of the information systems, which affects the power structure of the organization. A further dimension is the informal coordination and cooperation between functions and organizational tiers which cannot be neglected if the new structure is to work. Using this framework, the rest of this chapter will explore some of the significant structural innovations that have been implemented in recent years by exploiting the capabilities of computers and their networks.

Structural Innovations: Resolving Compromises through Information Systems

Through innovative use of ICTs, some organizations have implemented significant structural changes in recent years within the parameters of the hierarchy. As illustrated earlier, most existing organizational designs are based on a series of compromises, for instance between central control and empowerment, scale and scope economies, and between spatial separation and process and functional integration. Conventional organizational reforms have tended to change the balance between them. However, rapid developments in ICTs, coupled with the informatization of corporate activities, have allowed firms to resolve, rather than to live with, some of these compromises, which offer new opportunities for radical organizational reform. Even though the restructured organizations remain hierarchies, the actual functioning of the new hierarchies can be profoundly different from traditional ones and radical changes can be implemented within the parameters of the hierarchy.

Resolving the compromise between centralization and decentralization

One major compromise inherent in the design of most organizations today is between centralization and decentralization, i.e. to what extent control should be centralized in order to monitor and coordinate activities throughout the organization, and to what extent people at lower levels should be empowered so that their knowledge and experience can be better used and the organization can be more responsive to market changes. Both centralization and decentralization are desirable, but in conventional organizational designs, one can only be improved at the expense of the other, so a compromise has to be reached. However, to some extent, ICTs can be innovatively used to resolve this compromise and enable the organization to enhance centralization and decentralization simultaneously.

Centralization is primarily concerned with to what extent people at higher levels of the firm are aware of what is going on at lower levels, and with the ability of people at higher levels to influence or overrule – if they choose – the actions of people at lower levels. An essential aspect of centralization is, therefore, the centralization of power, although very often it also entails the centralization of decision making and responsibilities. In contrast, decentralization is primarily concerned with the freedom that people at lower levels of the firm have in doing their job according to their own judgements within certain established rules and principles; in other words, what decisions can be made and actions taken without seeking approval from people at higher levels.

Until recently, most organizations relied heavily on middle management layers to communicate decisions and instructions from the top to the bottom, and operational information from the bottom to the top. Such communications can be time consuming and in the process information is often distorted. As a result, people at higher levels often know very little about what is going on beyond the immediate next level. Centralized decision making and tight control from one layer over the immediate lower level is essential for the organization to hold together. However, with the support of integrated information systems, the situation can be radically changed, because people at higher levels can easily find out what is going on at any lower level via the system. The increased transparency of the organization can significantly increase senior managers' knowledge and level of awareness of various activities throughout the organization, which improves their capacity in monitoring progress and maintaining control in the organization – in essence, increases the level of centralization of power.

What is special about this kind of centralization is that it is based not on the centralization of decision making but on improved information, which actually gives senior managers the confidence they never had before to decentralize decision making and delegate associated responsibilities to lower levels without worrying about losing central control. In doing so, the compromise between centralization and decentralization inherent in conventional organizational designs is to some extent resolved. Essential to this process are, first, improved information about the organization and its environment, which enables management at higher levels to monitor progress and to override decisions at lower levels when necessary; and second, the redistribution of responsibilities accompanying the decentralization of decision making, which can significantly affect the organizational form and influence people's behaviour.

Resolving the Compromise between Centralization and Decentralization in a Large Industrial Group

This tendency is clearly reflected in a large industrial group in the brewery, hotel and retailing business. Before the development of the group-wide corporate network, senior directors in the head office relied almost entirely on the director of each division for information about the performance of different activities in the group. The CEO knew very little about what happened at, for instance, the regional level. To overcome this problem, tight control was maintained throughout the group via the hierarchy (i.e. the CEO maintained tight control over divisional heads, and divisional heads over regional heads, and so forth).

After the development of an integrated information system in the group, the CEO was equipped with online access to a wide range of information about the group – not only historical and aggregate data, but also detailed, up-to-the-minute information about every level of the group. In fact, the CEO could even inspect items such as the occupancy rate of a particular hotel at any time, or use the information system to identify the five hotels with the worst performance record over a specified period, using a multiple criteria performance evaluation system. As such, the transparency of the group increased dramatically for the CEO, and his capacity to monitor and control activities throughout the group (i.e. his power) was significantly improved.

The divisional heads could access detailed information throughout their own division, but detailed information about other divisions was denied to them. For these directors, the transparency of their own division was significantly improved, although they were themselves under closer monitoring from the group head office. Employees at the lowest levels were under closer monitoring from all the layers above – sometimes on an individual basis.

It should be pointed out that having the capacity to monitor and control does not mean the CEO is going to spend all day long checking out the performance of employees at lower levels. It is a new capacity at the CEO's fingertips enabled by ICTs – he can do something if necessary or if he chooses to, but he does not have to. The information systems have various built-in controls to notify relevant directors and employees automatically if something is progressing beyond pre-set criteria. Also, knowing their performance can be monitored by people at higher levels also affects the behaviours of middle managers and employees at lower levels.

As a result of the centralization of power through improved information, a wide range of decision making and some associated responsibilities were increasingly pushed down to lower levels. In particular, the autonomy of each of the hotels, breweries and retail stores in the group was significantly improved, and their managers were given increased autonomy to run their business units in their own ways.

Whilst centralization of power has happened throughout the organization, the decentralization of decision making and associated responsibilities has happened mainly at two levels: from the head office to senior middle management layers (such as the divisional offices or regional offices); and from middle management levels to the bottom-level establishments (such as branch plants of manufacturing firms, retail branches of banks and building societies, and shops and stores of retail chains). Such changes are necessary in today's volatile business environment, as they speed up decision making and make the organization more responsive to external changes. Some selected middle management layers and most units at the bottom level of the firm thus acquired new responsibilities and activities, while other middle management layers experienced rapid downsizing and some were eliminated. The role of people at the frontline (e.g. shop assistants, front-office employees) was significantly enhanced, although their activities were more closely monitored by people at higher levels – often on an individual basis. In doing so, ICTs were used to resolve the compromise between centralization and decentralization inherent in conventional organizational designs. This change is reflected in a wide range of business phenomena, including the downsizing of head offices and the centralization of corporate control, the enhancement of some senior middle management layers and the de-layering of the corporate hierarchy, and the increased local autonomy for bottom-level establishments and the empowerment of frontline employees.

Overcoming the compromise between spatial separation and functional integration

Another major compromise inherent in conventional organizational designs was between spatial separation and functional or process integration. The spatial separation of activities (or different parts of an activity) can undermine the level of process integration, but it is often necessary to exploit various locational factors, which until recently has been a major compromise that most multi-locational organizations have to live with. However, with today's ICTs, this compromise can to a large extent be resolved for many activities, because spatially separated activities can be electronically reintegrated via computer networks. By doing so, the organization can gain enormous flexibility in locational choices and in the way activities are organized and conducted. The compromise between spatial separation and process integration is particularly significant at the operational level, although it also exists at other levels. The current wave of outsourcing and offshoring – including high-skilled or strategic activities – is made possible primarily by this new capability afforded by advanced ICTs, especially by the Internet and related technologies.

In service sectors, such as the retail branches of banks and building societies, many back-office activities have conventionally been co-located with front-office activities in the same premises to ensure the smooth operation of the daily business. However, in recent years, many back-office activities (data processing) have been increasingly separated from front-office activities (e.g. serving customers), and then the former are centralized and relocated to spatially separated, functionally specialized administration centres. Many such activities can now be efficiently operated in other countries such as India or China (offshoring), and performed by another company (outsourcing). Information systems are used to reintegrate these activities electronically over distance. This, on the one hand, reduces the amount of administrative work in retail branches and leaves these branches more space and time to serve customers; on the other hand, centralizing and specializing back-office activities from several retail branches (normally located in expensive population centres) and relocating them to specialized administration centres in low-cost areas can lead to scale economy and reduction of office overheads.

The situation in retailing is quite similar. In the past, many high street department stores maintained large, on-site warehouses, which occupied expensive shop floor space that could otherwise be used for serving customers. Today, integrated information systems – particularly the integrated logistics system underpinned by inter- and intra-organizational information systems – allow these stores to reduce on-site storage space dramatically. The time required from order to delivery – both within the organization from central warehouses to stores, and outside the organization from suppliers – can be greatly reduced, thereby reducing or eliminating the need for in-store storage while improving the availability of merchandise.

By resolving the compromise between spatial separation and process integration through innovative use of ICTs, some firms have gained enormous locational flexibility in organizing various activities. On the one hand, organizations can make radical changes in their structures within their existing corporate geography – by reorganizing the information flows linking different sites rather than by physically relocating facilities and people. On the other hand, organizations can disintegrate activities further – deliberately – and relocate them to different places to exploit geographical differentiation in cost factors while maintaining process integration. In both cases, the organizational form is changed.

The rapid development of call centres is another example where customer service functions are increasingly carried out via the telephone or the Internet in the back-office environment. The introduction of new tele-mediated services has resulted in new forms of organization in some sectors, as well as new ways of service delivery to customers at low cost. In most cases, this change involves the concentration of service supply from geographically dispersed locations in downtown areas to a few central locations in cheaper areas, often away from downtown, and increasingly in low-cost countries hundreds or even thousands of miles away. The links with customers conventionally maintained via face-to-face contact are maintained by telecommunications over distance.

Directline and Esure

Direct Line, the highly successful subsidiary of Royal Bank of Scotland, became the largest motor insurance service firm in the UK only a few years after it was launched, and its household insurance and mortgage businesses have also been growing rapidly. Instead of setting up numerous high street retail outlets, the firm is organized as six service centres in the UK, which are linked together by a corporate network. All businesses are conducted over the phone and supplemented by postal mail. In recent years the company has been increasingly encouraging its customers to use the Internet. The even more rapid growth of Esure.com in the UK – the Internet-only insurance broker – is another example. Similar examples have been identified in banking, airline reservation and many other industries. By resolving the compromise between spatial separation and process integration, and by exploiting the new geographical flexibility from ICTs, the nature of the workplace is being radically redefined and new forms of organization are emerging.

Incorporation through automation and the informal dimension

Significant structural innovations have also been introduced along a third dimension: instead of improving certain activities, ICTs can be used to eliminate them from the conventional business processes altogether, and in doing so a wide range of responsibilities previously held by people can be incorporated into the design of the information systems through the automation of associated activities. By bypassing the human interfaces in the business processes, the level of process integration is improved. For example, logistical managers used to have the responsibility of allocating tasks to the lorry drivers each day, but today this responsibility is largely incorporated into the logistics system where road conditions and multiple drop-off and pick-up can be built into the schedules for each driver to improve lorry capacity utilization and optimize the total mileage required. The growing standardization of business processes through the increasing adoption of ERP systems, and the rapid proliferation of offshoring and outsourcing of routine and strategic activities and functions, are further fuelling structural changes along this dimension.

The informal dimension

For new organizational structures to function efficiently and effectively, many informal changes are often also necessary, which should not be neglected. This is clearly reflected in the restructuring of a heavy engineering firm. The moral of the story below is that without corresponding changes in organizational culture and politics, simply installing ICTs and making organizational changes would rarely deliver the anticipated results.

The Informal Dimension

In a heavy engineering firm, design was traditionally carried out by engineers in the design department, and the finished designs were then redrawn and modified by technicians in the manufacturing department to make them more suitable for fast fabrication before they were handed over to the workers operating the machines. After the introduction of CAD/CAM (computer-aided design/

computer-aided manufacturing), the CEO decided that the two departments should merge as the new operations department, and an electronic data link should be installed between them so the finished designs could be fed into the computer-controlled machines directly. This restructuring, however, initially caused considerable problems because it would now require the workers in manufacturing to work much more closely and interactively with the engineers in design; the technicians who used to provide the links between the engineers and workers were eliminated from the process.

Owing to the differences in their professional backgrounds and social status amongst other things, it was not easy for these two groups of employees to communicate effectively. The power struggles between the two directors and their camps did not help the situation either. Measures such as knocking down the walls between their canteens did not seem to work because the employees from the two groups were still reluctant to socialize ('mingle during lunch and tea breaks'). Only after considerable deliberate efforts by the company, for example appointing a senior vice president to oversee the operations of the newly merged department and organizing football matches and social activities involving family members, were the social barriers between them gradually reduced.

Why Hierarchies Thrive: In Praise of Boundaries and Walls

Despite repeated predictions about the demise of the hierarchy and the continued search for alternative organizational configurations, today almost every large organization remains hierarchical. In a rare defence of the hierarchy as a durable organizational form, Harold Leavitt argued that 'the intensity with which we struggle against hierarchies only serves to highlight their durability . . . The organization of the knowledge economy – whether loosely coupled, networked, or federalized – seems to be no more than modifications of the same basic design. The new flatter, faster organizations certainly reflect some important changes in the way business is done, but the basic blueprint is unchanged' (p. 98).[12]

Hierarchies have many flaws, but they are also quite capable of change and adaptation. They deliver real practical and psychological value, and fulfil our deep needs for order and security. Leavitt even went so far as to argue that hierarchy may be intrinsic in our natures. Multi-level hierarchies remain the best available mechanism for doing complex work, and it is unrealistic for it to disappear in the foreseeable future.

Hierarchies, however, have evolved considerably, and some radical changes have been taking place in recent years with the widespread adoption of information systems. The different schools of management, from the human relations movement to analytical management to the use of group or project-based management and community of practice, have all left marks on the hierarchies of today. Most of all, information and communications technologies have enabled some organizations to resolve (or eliminate) many conventional problems inherent in the hierarchy, allowing radical structural changes to take place within the parameters of the hierarchy. One example of this is that many conventional organizational designs are based on a series of internal contradictions or compromises. Rather than simply changing the balance of these compromises as was done by previous organizational reforms, ICTs can be used to resolve these compromises, thereby significantly increasing the capability and flexibility of the hierarchy.

Despite the obvious limits to structural changes,[13] perhaps the search for organizational forms other than the hierarchy is a lost cause. Hierarchies add structure and regularity to our lives, they give us routines, duties and responsibilities, and they help define ourselves. The more chaotic and rapidly changing the world, the stronger the need for order, regularity, formality and boundary.[14] The hierarchies might have become flatter, more flexible, and even more informal, but as a basic form of organizational design it is unlikely to be replaced in the foreseeable future.

Structural Innovations: Emerging Trends

The traditional hierarchies are under increasing pressure to change. The many layers of middle management have become too expensive and they have often impeded information flows and the responsiveness and speed necessary for flexibility and innovation in an uncertain business environment. Advanced information systems also increasingly allow information to bypass middle management layers to communicate directly between the centre and the frontline at the lowest level. As a result, many middle management structures have been de-layered. In the meantime, power in terms of the capacity to monitor and control has increasingly been centralized; and responsibilities, decision making and many associated strategic and operational activities are increasingly decentralized to the remaining middle management layers and to the bottom of the hierarchy.

Back in 1989, Peter Drucker predicted that the business of the future will be like a symphony, where a single conductor leads many musicians without any intermediaries or assistants. This did not happen, partly because even a modest-sized organization has more employees than the largest orchestras. Most organizations remain some modified form of the basic hierarchical design. However, the hierarchies have indeed changed and organizations based on dominance and submission have increasingly been replaced by communities and other more humane and productive alternatives. Of particular significance is the impressive adaptability demonstrated by many large organizational hierarchies, and these are quite capable of change to meet the new requirements of the new business environment.

Fluid hierarchies

For example, the structure of an organization does not have to be rigid and fixed as long as people understand the relationships. Within my university, the overall hierarchy is clearly articulated, which is similarly the case amongst almost all higher education institutions in the UK. However, within the hierarchy, there are various programme or project committees, and in some of the committees I chair, some members are more senior than I am in the overall university hierarchy. However, there is almost always a clear understanding that within the realm of the specific committees even the more senior members become subordinate to the Chair. Such flexible, fluid structures enable different groups of people to accomplish various tasks within the overall hierarchy of the organization. In many commercial organizations similar structures are deployed to carry out cross-functional projects or address emerging opportunities and challenges. Some such structures are semi-permanent or permanent, while others are one-off or temporary.

Ambidextrous organizations

One other approach that some organizations are increasingly adopting is to build so-called 'ambidexterity' into the formal organizational design. The concept itself is not new but many companies are rediscovering this concept and implementing it in their own organizations.[15] For a company to succeed over the long term, it often needs to master both adaptability and alignment. However, the core business of a company today may not be sustainable in the long term and the company needs to simultaneously explore and experiment with a vast array of emerging opportunities. The problem is that the organizational requirements for the existing and emerging businesses are often fundamentally different, and require different organizational forms, culture and management styles. Many organizations deal with this issue by setting up a separate, independent business unit outside the established organization and management hierarchy. Although many such new units might become profitable quickly, they are often so isolated from the rest of the business that they cannot capitalize on the vast resources of the parent. Some businesses then spin out the new units completely and make a quick buck, but it often means that the original intention of focusing on the core business while exploring emerging opportunities was unfulfilled and some of the spin-out units may become powerful future competitors.

An alternative is to build a 'ambidextrous' organization by establishing project teams that are structurally independent units, each having its own structures, processes and cultures, but integrated into the existing management hierarchy at the top. This way, both the existing and the emerging business can focus on their main activities while at the same time capitalizing on the resources of the parent organization. By combining organizational separation with senior team integration, the organization can build ambidexterity into its organizational design. Julian Birkinshaw and Cristina Gibson outlined different types of ambidexterity and how an organization can build ambidexterity into organizational design, including the main issues that should be addressed and the potential pitfalls involved.[16] Vijay Govindarajan and Chris Trimble also discussed the processes and main issues involved in using what they called strategic experiments to build sustainable breakthrough businesses within established organizations.[17]

Bring market mechanisms inside the hierarchy

Many other measures have also been identified to address some of the problems associated with the traditional hierarchy. For example, with the rapid development of electronic trading systems, it has become increasingly easier to bring some form of market mechanism inside the hierarchy.[18] Examples include how BP used an internal trading system between different units to trade greenhouse gas emission allowances. In 1998, the Chairman and CEO of BP made a public commitment to reduce the company's greenhouse gas emissions to 10 per cent below the 1990 level by 2010. To meet this goal a target quota was allocated to each business unit. An electronic trading system was then set up within the company which allows each unit to buy and sell permits, and business units could then make their own decisions about the level of emission reductions. The incentives built into the system allowed BP to achieve its target in the first year – nine years ahead of schedule.

Malone believes that the Internet, e-mail and cheap long-distance telephone services made BP's internal market possible.[19] Such internal markets can move information quickly and efficiently, and it can dramatically streamline decision making. This concept can be applied in a range of areas, including internal selling, trading ideas, and allocating assets. An internal market brings inside the company the efficiency, flexibility and motivation of a free market. People can buy and sell to one another based on their self-interest and the result is a continuous reallocation of resources to the places where they are most valuable. The potential downsides include that the self-interest of some units may take precedence over the overall benefits to the organization as a whole; and when the company is shrinking, centralized authority might be more effective in resolving conflicts, which is usually more important than creativity and independence. Furthermore, the overall vision of the company could be undermined by an internal market when there are many different units involved. Risks and quality may also be difficult to control. Implementing an internal market is not a panacea, and it requires the organization to change its structure, incentive system, culture and information system. Nevertheless, the rapid development of Internet and related technologies has made large-scale internal markets possible, and organizations should start experimenting with this concept in selected applications.

Summary

Numerous studies have investigated how the increasing use of ICTs is affecting organizational structures, and many structural innovations have been identified and conceptualized. Back in the 1970s and early 1980s, studies demonstrated that the widespread use of the telephone led to significant changes in organizational structures; for example, high-level functions were increasingly concentrated into big cities in the core regions, and production and low-level functions were increasingly decentralized to the peripheral, low-cost regions and to developing countries. Since then, the impact of data communications via computer networks on organizational designs has become the central focus of research. There has been a continued search for new organizational forms, especially non-hierarchical organizational structures. Various guides on how to design effective organizations have also been published.[20]

This chapter illustrated some of the identified changes in organizational structures, and highlighted some of the most influential structural innovations in recent years. On the one hand, despite organizations having become flatter, more flexible, more responsive, and making increasing use of project-based or virtual teams, so far nobody has been able to identify an organization that is not a hierarchy. In the past few years I have been challenging people on my executive programmes and MBA classes to identify non-hierarchical organizations, but after careful analysis and investigation, all their examples have been proven to continue to embody fundamental characteristics of hierarchies. Hierarchies are alive and kicking, and this is likely to continue for a long time.

On the other hand, however, the characteristics of hierarchies and the way they work have gone through some radical changes. One particular reason for this is the significantly improved transparency of organizations to business leaders and managers – the higher up the hierarchy they are, the more transparent the organization has become to them. This, on the one hand, leads to further centralization of power, but at the same time enables senior managers to have the confidence to decentralize responsibilities and activities to operational managers and frontline employees. The shape of the organization may have not changed beyond hierarchies, but the functioning of the new hierarchies is radically different from traditional ones. ICTs play a key role in enabling this transformation.

Furthermore, many measures have been adopted by various organizations to improve the flexibility and responsiveness of large hierarchies whilst at the same time retaining their main advantages of scale economy, efficiency, control and long-term focus. The increased ability for large organizations to resolve the conflict between control and flexibility perhaps explains the contemporary trends towards mergers and acquisitions of increasing magnitude. In many cases, structural changes are often a response to changes in the strategy of the organization, but some recent research indicated that the relationship between strategy and structure is a complex and dynamic one, and restructuring of the organization can sometimes lead to new business strategies.[21]

Reflecting on these changes and previous research, this chapter concludes that a fundamental rule of organizational design has been redefined. In the past, most organizational reforms were to change the balance of various compromises inherent in organizational designs – that is, if you want to centralize you will lose some local autonomy, for example. However, with the support of ICTs it is possible to resolve the compromises inherent in traditional hierarchies and improve both simultaneously. For example, centralization and decentralization can both be improved; and improved geographical flexibility in relocating various activities and functions does not necessarily undermine the level of process or functional integration.

Is the organizational structure ever going to evolve beyond hierarchy? My answer is: not in the foreseeable future. However, with the rapid development of new technologies such as grid computing and the Internet, which some scholars argue are essentially non-hierarchical in nature, it might still be possible to develop non-hierarchical organizations. Only time will tell if this will ever happen.

Discussion Questions

1 Is the hierarchy still an appropriate organizational form in the network economy? Why? Support your views with evidence and explanations.

2 It has often been argued that information systems have enabled organizations to adopt radically different structures (known as structural innovations), which in turn have led to new forms of organization. Describe the main forms of structural innovations that have been introduced in recent years. Critically evaluate the rationales for these changes in the context of the new business environment.

3 It has often been argued that non-hierarchical organizations have been invented in recent years. Are you aware of any such new structures? If so, conduct some research and clearly illustrate the new structures. Discuss whether they are actually non-hierarchical structures, or are simply hierarchies in disguise.

Assignments

1. A Taxonomy of Emerging Organizational Forms

   In recent years, numerous new organizational forms have been identified and/or proposed by scholars and by business practitioners. Conduct a thorough literature search and develop a comprehensive taxonomy of emerging organizational forms, explain what each of them means, and critically evaluate their benefits and potential problems for organizations in the new business environment. Highlight the role ICTs play in these new organizational forms. Write up your findings in the format of an academic journal paper (5,000 words).

2. Case Studies

   Using the Internet and published studies as your main source of information, identify one or a few companies that have adopted a unique organizational form. Conceptualize the new organizational form and the structural innovations involved, explain its main features, and discuss its potential benefits and problems using the materials of the case studies (5,000 words).

NOTES

1   Noam, Eli (2005) How a company's tools can define its structure. *Financial Times*, Friday 20 May, p. 19.

2   Downes, Larry and Chunka Mui (1998) *Unleashing the Killer App: Digital strategies for market dominance.* Harvard Business School Press, Boston.

3   Tapscott, Don and Art Caston (1992) *Paradigm Shift: The new promise of information technology,* McGraw-Hill, London; Tapscott, Don and David Ticoll (2003) *The Naked Corporation: How the age of transparency will revolutionize business,* Free Press, New York.

4   Scott Morton, Michael (1991, ed.) *The Corporation of the 1990s: Information technology and organizational transformation.* Oxford University Press, New York.

5   Carr, Nicholas (2004) In praise of walls. *Sloan Management Review*, Spring, 10–13.

6   Eisenstat, Russell, Nathaniel Foote, Jay Galbraith and Danny Miller (2001) Beyond the business unit. *The McKinsey Quarterly*, 1, 54–63.

7   Morgan, Gareth (1997) *Images of Organizations*, 2nd edn. Sage, London.
8   Mintzberg, H. (1979) *The Structuring of Organizations*, Prentice Hall, Englewood Cliffs, NJ;
    Mintzberg, H. (1983) *Structure in Fives*, Prentice Hall, Englewood Cliffs, NJ.
9   Pettigrew, Andrew and Silvia Massini (2003) Innovative forms of organizing: trends in
    Europe, Japan and the USA in the 1990s. In Andrew Pettigrew et al. (eds), *Innovative
    Forms of Organizing*. Sage, London.
10 Rajan, Raghuram G. and Julie Wulf (2003) The flattening firm: evidence from panel data
    on the changing nature of corporate hierarchies, reported in *Sloan Management Review*,
    44(4), 5, full paper available from Wulf@wharton.upenn.edu; Pettigrew and Massini (2003)
    op. cit.
11 Venkatraman, N. (1994) IT-enabled business transformation: from automation to busi-
    ness scope re-definition. *Sloan Management Review*, 35(2), 73–87.
12 Leavitt, Harold (2003) Why hierarchies thrive. *Harvard Business Review*, March, 96–102.
13   Oxman, Jeffrey and D. Smith (2003) The limits of structural change. *Sloan Management
    Review*, Fall, 77–81.
14 Carr (2004), op. cit.; In praise of boundaries: a conversation with Miss Manners, *Harvard
    Business Review*, December, 41–45.
15 O'Reilly III, Charles A. and Michael L. Tushman (2004) The ambidextrous organization,
    Harvard Business Review, April, 74–81; Birkinshaw, Julian and Cristina Gibson (2004)
    Build ambidexterity into your organization, *Sloan Management Review*, Summer, 45(4),
    47–55; Duncan, R. B. (1976) The ambidextrous organization: design dual structure for
    innovation. In R. H. Kilmann, L. R. Pondy and D. Slevin (eds), *The Management of Organiza-
    tion Design: Strategies and implementation*, vol. 1, pp. 167–188. North-Holland, New York.
16 Birkinshaw and Gibson (2004) op. cit.
17 Govindarajan, Vijay and Chris Trimble (2005) Building breakthrough businesses within
    established organizations. *Harvard Business Review*, May, 58–68.
18 Malone, Thomas E. (2004) Bringing the market inside. *Harvard Business Review*, April,
    107–114.
19 Ibid.
20 E.g. Goold, Michael and Andrew Campbell (2002) *Designing Effective Organizations*. Jossey-
    Bass, San Francisco.
21 Slywotzky, Adrian and David Nadler (2004) The strategy is the structure. *Harvard Business
    Review*, February, 16.

FURTHER READING

Birkinshaw, Julian and Cristina Gibson (2004) Build ambidexterity into your organization. *Sloan
    Management Review*, Summer, 45(4), 47–55.
Goold, Michael and Andrew Campbell (2002) *Designing Effective Organizations*. Jossey-Bass, San
    Francisco.
O'Reilly III, Charles A. and Michael L. Tushman (2004) The ambidextrous organization. *Harvard
    Business Review*, April, 74–81.
Pettigrew, Andrew et al. (2004, eds) *Innovative Forms of Organizing*. Sage, London.
Leavitt, Harold (2003) Why hierarchies thrive. *Harvard Business Review*, March, 96–102.

Search new business journals and books to identify new references on new organizational structures and emerging forms of organizations.

Chapter 11

Process Innovations: Beyond Business Process Reengineering

Alongside the structure, the process is another important dimension of organizational design. Whilst the structure is concerned with the shape of the organization and the relationships between its different parts, the process is concerned with how things are done in the organization. Most organizations have distinctive and unique processes for almost everything they do, ranging from routine, narrowly focused processes to broad, cross-functional and strategically important ones. Many processes cut across organizational boundaries.

Process has been a key factor influencing the performance and competitiveness of organizations, and as a result, the search for process innovations – redesigning various processes either incrementally or radically to improve the performance of the organization – can go back a long time. In the 1970s and 1980s, companies across the world improved their processes as part of the quality movement, through continuous improvement and total quality management (TQM). In the 1990s the focus shifted to radical process innovations – more commonly known as business process reengineering or business process redesign (BPR). Today the process view of the organization remains profoundly influential and there has been a return to process improvements through operational innovation and six sigma programmes to extract more value out of the radically redesigned and reengineered processes. Process innovations have been a critical dimension of e-Business development. Furthermore, many key processes are increasingly commoditized, some of which are based on industrial best practice mapped and built into information systems. In most cases, information systems play a fundamental role in enabling process innovations.

Although many large organizations have been reengineered since the 1990s, there remain numerous processes that could benefit from a radical redesign, especially in many public sector organizations where some key processes were designed and put in place many decades ago. This chapter focuses on radical process innovations and the role of ICTs in these processes.

Business Processes and Types of Process Innovations

According to Michael Hammer, business process refers to the collection of activities that takes inputs and creates an output that is of value to customers. The customers can be external as well as internal. The scope of business processes varies greatly, from the narrowest view which considers processes in terms of individual work tasks (such as handling a customer inquiry), to the other end of the spectrum where business processes cut across organizational boundaries to involve suppliers and customers along the entire supply chain. Between these two perspectives, business processes can also be defined as involving several different tasks and individuals within a department or function, or as organization-wide processes that operate across several different departments.

Process innovations are essential to renewing an organization's ability to compete effectively. The organization needs to improve the way products are made or services delivered, either by being able to make and deliver products and services that others cannot, or by doing those things better than others – cheaper, faster, higher quality, more customized and so on. Process innovations can involve high risks, high costs, and high uncertainty, but if successful, the rewards can be very significant. In many cases, the organization has no choice but to implement process innovations as a competitive necessity when competitors are engaged in such initiatives.

There are many different types of process innovations, from the incremental process improvements involving frequent small changes, via generational changes in the way the process operates, to radical changes in the basic business processes and transformational changes which involve changing the rules of the game across the whole industry and beyond. In the 1970s and 1980s, the focus was on improving existing processes through incremental changes, but from 1990 attention was increasingly shifted to more radical changes through business process reengineering. Since the turn of the new millennium when 'best practice' business processes have already been implemented widely in many organizations through radical changes, attention is once again shifting towards more incremental changes to fine-tune the reengineered processes in order to extract more value out of them. However, the search for radical process innovations has continued, particularly through innovative exploitation of the Internet and related technologies.

Business Process Reengineering (BPR): The 'Clean Slate' Approach for Radical Process Innovation

Business process reengineering or redesign, widely known as BPR, was first introduced in 1990 when Michael Hammer, and Thomas Davenport and James Short, separately published their seminal papers in *Harvard Business Review* and *Sloan Management Review*, respectively.[1] Almost immediately BPR became the hottest management concept since the quality movement and it dominated management thinking for a whole decade. Even today, many organizations are still engaged in reengineering their key business processes. Although some authors regarded BPR as an extension of the principles of the quality movement,[2] or of traditional industrial engineering and Frederick Winslow Taylor's principles of scientific management,[3] the most influential view has been the radical changes promoted by Michael Hammer and James Champy, that BPR is the search for new models of organizing work which has nothing in common with other business improvement programmes.[4] By the mid-1990s, most large organizations were engaged in some BPR programmes, and every management consultancy was selling it – at some point, worldwide revenues from selling BPR solutions alone was worth several billion dollars per year to the big management consulting firms.

Unlike some other authors, Hammer and Champy regarded BPR as overturning over two centuries of tradition in the way organizations should be managed. It was derived from the practical experience of the authors in working with large organizations, rather than from existing theory of organization. In fact the authors argued that BPR is different from any other business improvement programme, including those sharing some common promises. In their influential book in 1993, Hammer and Champy used some examples to illustrate the strong need for radical process reengineering. They believed that problems are embedded in the way processes are designed, rather than how hard mangers and employees work. It is no longer enough to ask how we can do what we do faster, better and at lower cost, but why we do what we do at all.

> A set of principles laid down more than two centuries ago has shaped the structure, management, and performance of businesses throughout the nineteenth and twentieth centuries . . . the time has come to retire those principles and to adopt a new set . . .
>
> For two hundred years people have founded and built companies around Adam Smith's brilliant discovery that industrial work should be broken down into the simplest and the most basic tasks. In the post-industrial business age we are now entering, corporations will be founded and built around the idea of reunifying those tasks into coherent business processes. (pp. 1–2)[5]

For Hammer and Champy, reengineering is 'the fundamental rethinking and radical redesign of business processes to achieve dramatic improvements in critical, contemporary measures of performance, such as cost, quality, service and speed' (p. 32). It is about starting over; beginning with a clean sheet of paper; and reversing the Industrial Revolution. It is not about making incremental change. If you were to re-create this company today, given what you know and given current technology, what should it look like? Although individual tasks in a process are important, none of them matters if the whole process does not work.

Hammer and Champy also emphasized that reengineering is not about automation, which is concerned with more efficient ways of doing the wrong things. Neither is it about restructuring, downsizing, reorganizing, de-layering or flattening organizational hierarchy, because problems have not resulted from structures in the first place. Nor is it about busting bureaucracies, because bureaucracies hold our organizations together. It is not total quality management either, because TQM is about incremental improvement, which is fundamentally different from BPR. Although they fall short in developing a methodology on how BPR can be developed and implemented in different organizations, they described the problems and solutions through a series of examples.

One was about how returned goods were often lost in the system because the process involved thirteen departments and it was not a priority for any of these departments. Another was how IBM's credit department took six days to two weeks to process an application when the actual time used in processing an application was only ninety minutes. Through these examples, they also highlighted some obvious principles for reengineering. For example, organizations should be organized around outcomes, not tasks; have those who use the output of the process perform the process; subsume information processing work into the real work that produces the information; target geographically dispersed resources as though they were centralized; link parallel activities instead of integrating their results; and put the decision point where the work is performed and build control into the process.

Despite various criticisms of such radical approaches, BPR has been extremely influential in injecting process-oriented thinking and result-driven approaches into organizations throughout the world. There has been a high failure rate for BPR programmes (over 70 per cent by Hammer's own estimation). This is partly because of the inherent high risks of radical changes of such magnitude (starting from a clean sheet of paper), but also because of the lack of a robust methodology in designing and implementing it. By the second half of the 1990s, many detailed methodologies had been developed – particularly by consulting companies selling BPR solutions – and applied in different organizational contexts; and many valuable lessons were also learnt from the early rounds of BPR initiatives. Today, many of the reengineered organizations have shifted their focus to extracting more value out of the new processes through incremental improvements, but there remain many cases where a radical process redesign could lead to dramatic improvements in performance.

Processes in Need of Reengineering: a Textbook Example

In most universities in the UK, the approval of any new degree programme involves a lengthy, multi-staged process. I recently led the development of a new Master Programme on E-Business and Information Systems, jointly between the Business School and the School of Computing Science, which was a textbook example of where a radical business process redesign could lead to dramatic improvements in a number of aspects. The fact that the course was a joint programme between two schools in two separate faculties further complicated the process. The existing process had been in place for decades. First, the academics from both schools developed an outline of the programme (Part I), explaining the aims and objectives and providing evidence for market demand (amongst other information), which needed to be approved by the Teaching and Learning Committees (TLC) of both schools before they were then submitted to the Teaching and Learning Committees of both faculties. Each of these committees made suggestions for revisions and demanded additional information, and this process could go back and forth a number of times. Needless to say, managing and resolving conflicting demands from different committees was one of the main tasks.

The approval from the two faculty TLCs – separately – gave the go-ahead for preparing the full programme specifications (Part II), which involved descriptions of the programme's aims and objectives in detail, as well as the module outlines and who would teach them. An array of other administrative information was also required. This part then went through the same process, involving multiple committees at different levels, each of them requiring the lead academics to answer questions and provide additional information. Once all issues had been addressed to the satisfaction of these committees, the full programme specifications needed to be approved by the University Teaching and Learning Committee. Like other committees, this committee would normally require additional revisions, and the revised, final programme then needed to be signed off by the Pro-Vice-Chancellor in charge of Teaching and Learning. The whole process could take between six months and two years.

Reflecting on this process, we felt that developing the Part I and Part II forms took two to four academics from the two schools a maximum of one week, which perhaps would need to be spread over a month owing to the academics' various other commitments. Most of the delays were caused by waiting for the various committees to convene. After discussions with several other colleagues who had recently been through the process, we all felt that this process had taken on a life of its own, and most of the requests for revision and additional information were from administrative staff and non-specialist academics sitting on these commit-tees. We also questioned the necessity for the two-stage process involving mul-tiple committees, most of which were using sub-committees (with three members) to handle the approval, and most of the issues raised were administrative rather than academic in nature. There is no academic reason why a single committee could not deal with this issue through a one-stage process, which could reduce the lead time from 6–24 months to 1–2 months while significantly improving the quality of the new programmes by enabling academics to focus more on the academic issues rather than jumping through administrative hoops. Furthermore, none of us felt that the complicated process led to any real changes or improved the quality of the programmes in any identifiable form. This long delay means lost opportunities and a significant amount of lost revenues; and it also means that some academics simply do not bother with proposing new programmes. The university is currently considering reengineering this process. Several other processes have also been under review, such as the student application and selection process which could take as much as 47 days in 2004, compared with 24–48 hours in some leading competitors!

The Role of ICTs in BPR

Although not all BPR projects need the support of ICTs, most organizations have exploited the new capabilities afforded by advanced information systems when designing and implementing BPR. The role of ICTs in BPR is a complex one, and sometimes a distinction is made between ICTs as implementer (making a contribution to the process) and as enabler (a driving force of BPR). As an implementer, ICTs can be used for process simulation to test new processes, or for drawing process models. However, most writers have focused on ICTs' role as an enabler or driver for BPR, and sometimes the recursive relationship between ICTs and BPR is emphasized. In many cases, ICTs enable new ways of carrying out processes, and the role of ICTs in BPR can vary from automational, informational, sequential, tracking, analytical, geographical, to integrative, intellectual, and disintermediating, according to Davenport.[6]

Hammer and Champy emphasized that the critical role of ICTs in BPR is 'difficult to overstate', because ICTs allow organizations to do many things in ways impossible in the past by changing basic rules. For example, the old rule of paper-based information is that information can appear in only one place at one time, but the new rule is that shared databases allow information access simultaneously in as many places as needed. In almost all the examples cited by various authors, ICTs are described as an integral part of BPR.

Hammer and Champy emphasized that a company that cannot change the way it thinks about information technology cannot reengineer. The technologies are not simply used to automate existing processes, nor to provide technological solutions for identified business problems. Instead, they emphasized that state of the art information technology is part of any reengineering effort, which they refer to as an essential enabler that enables organizations to reengineer business processes. They also emphasized that 'the misuse of technology can block reengineer altogether by reinforcing old ways of thinking and old behavior patterns' (p. 83); and companies 'need to be aware of thinking that technology is the only essential element in reengineering' (p. 101).[7] Reengineering is to take a journey from the familiar to the unknown.

Michael Hammer: From Business Process Reengineering to Operational Innovation

During the 1990s, most large organizations were reengineered, many through multiple BPR programmes. However, the failure rate was high by any estimation, and many organizations struggled to extract the anticipated value and dramatic improvements from the reengineered new processes. Despite its enormous popularity and strong influence in management thinking and organizational designs, BPR has been criticized by academics, consultants and practitioners alike from all camps. One criticism is that process alone is not enough because organizations are far more than a series of processes that take in inputs and produce outputs. This was in fact acknowledged, albeit indirectly, by Hammer and Champy because they used the term reengineering rather than business process reengineering (BPR) in their 1993 book: *Reengineering the Corporation*. Other dimensions and aspects of the organization, including its vision, strategy, culture and technology, amongst others, need to be considered as integral to any reengineering programme.

Another criticism is the 'clean slate' approach promoted by Hammer and many other writers, which caused huge problems in the implementation of BPR programmes. Organizations are not clean sheets of paper, and they have histories and many well-established ways of doing things, which are all valuable assets that should and could not be discarded. Despite the need for radical changes as a response to the changing business environment, in many aspects continuity from the past needs to be maintained (e.g. customer relations). How to reconcile the gaps between the need for radical changes required by BPR and the need for continuity by employees and customers has been a difficult problem for many organizations. Designing the new processes, however difficult, is the easy part in comparison with the implementation of them in organizations.

Today, many organizations have shifted their focus, from designing and implementing new business processes through reengineering to fine-tuning the new business processes to extract more value out of them, although the need for radical process innovations remains strong. Recognizing the limitations of BPR from the experience of the 1990s, Hammer recently called on all organizations to implement what he calls 'operational innovation' to move a company to an entirely new level.[8]

Similar to BPR, operational innovation is fundamentally different from operational improvement or operational excellence. Operational innovation is not about achieving high performance via existing modes of operation. Instead, it means coming up with entirely new ways of doing things. Hammer used examples such as Wal-Mart, Toyota and Dell, as well as a less well-known example, Progressive Insurance, to illustrate how each of these companies fundamentally rethought how to do work in their industries, and in doing so they successfully dislodged some mighty companies.

Although Hammer continues to emphasize the critical importance of process, the focus of operational innovation is considerably broader. He emphasized that operational innovation affects the very essence of a company and how its work is done, and it requires new systems for performance measurement and reward, and new job designs, organizational structures and managerial roles. He discussed how operational innovations can result in direct improvements in performance in many aspects, such as lower costs, faster cycle time and improved accuracy; which can then lead to superior market performance such as lower costs and differentiated offerings; which can further lead to strategic payoffs such as improved customer retention and greater market shares. Furthermore, compared with other programmes that stimulate growth, for example through acquisitions, technology investments or marketing campaigns, operational innovation is relatively reliable and low cost, but can lead to major improvements in time, costs and customer satisfaction. He also emphasized that operational innovation is by nature disruptive.

Hammer estimated that less than 10 per cent of large companies had made a serious and successful effort at implementing operational innovation, because there are several organizational barriers. To make it work, companies need to look for models outside their own industries for inspiration and ideas. They should re-examine long-standing assumptions about how work should be done, and rethink critical dimensions of work, including what results are to be delivered, by whom, under what circumstances and so on. Seven main dimensions of work were summarized for organizations to reimagine processes: what results, who, where, when, whether, what information and how thoroughly.

Finally, unlike what he promoted in reengineering, Hammer emphasized the critical importance of implementation for operational innovation. In particular, unlike the clean slate approach for reengineering, he advised organizations not to try to implement an operational innovation all at once. Instead, companies should break up large-scale operational innovation into manageable phases to create momentum, dispel scepticism and anxiety, and silence critics. Based on the experience of Dell, Toyota and others, he believed that operational innovations can deliver sustainable benefits even though on the surface they may be easy for competitors to imitate. It is also interesting to note that he ended the paper by saying: 'In an economy that has overdosed on hype and in which customers rule as they never have before, operational innovation offers a meaningful and sustainable way to get ahead – and stay ahead – of the pack' (p. 93).[9]

Thomas Davenport: From Business Process Redesign to the Commoditization and Outsourcing of Business Processes

In contrast to Michael Hammer, who until recently has been a leading advocate for radical changes through a 'big bang' approach, Thomas Davenport has always had a milder approach to BPR. Also, unlike Hammer, who focused on processes that are large, organization-wide and cut across functional and organizational boundaries, Davenport adopted a more inclusive view of processes – how an organization does its work – which can be large and cross-functional, or relatively narrow, and either internal or external. As Hammer turned his attention from BPR to operational innovations, Davenport recently turned his attention to the commoditization and outsourcing of business processes. 'Business processes – from making a mouse trap to hiring a CEO – are being analysed, standardized, and quality checked. That work, as it progresses, will lead to commoditization and outsourcing on a massive scale' (p. 101).[10]

Davenport argued that, in the past, companies had outsourced only some ancillary services (such as building maintenance), but the focus has increasingly shifted to the outsourcing of major capabilities, sometimes known as transformational or strategic outsourcing. In the past few decades, outsourcing has gone through several main stages of evolution. The first major step was when some large companies outsourced their IT management. This was followed by the outsourcing of human resources, accounting and finance, and other administrative processes. Many companies also increasingly outsourced manufacturing activities, often in low-cost countries, and in the past few years such international outsourcing – more widely known as offshoring – has increasingly been extended from manufacturing to service work, including some highly skilled work. The motivations for all these changes were not only to reduce costs, but also to improve flexibility and access to specialized expertise.

Despite the recent debates about outsourcing and offshoring and their effects on job opportunities in developed economies, today most companies retain most of their processes internally; and most outsourced processes are transactional or administrative activities. Davenport believed this was largely because most processes are unique in each organization, and the lack of standardization and comparability means that organizations generally have no clear basis for comparing the capabilities provided by different external organizations or with those offered in-house. The result is that for an organization to outsource, they have to have faith in the capabilities of the external provider, and the cost has to be attractive.

However, the situation is changing because many business processes have been reengineered since the 1990s and numerous 'best practice' business processes from different sectors have been mapped out by consulting companies and then sold to other companies as BPR solutions. Software providers also built many best practice processes into various information systems (such as ERP and CRM systems), which led to further standardization of key business processes both within and between industries. The standardization of processes can facilitate communications about how business processes operate within the company, and make cross-company commerce easier. It will also make outsourcing process capabilities easier and more transparent.

Davenport believes that three sets of process standards are already emerging. The first set is in the area of process activity and flow standards, such as the supply chain operations reference model (SCOR) developed by the Supply Chain Council, the Process Classification Framework developed by the American Productivity and Quality Center (APQC), and several others. The application of these standards has already led to dramatic improvements in performance in many companies across the world. However, Davenport cautioned readers that a process standard alone cannot lead to dramatic improvements in performance and, as with any process improvement programme, firms need to change the way they do their work and the associated systems and behaviours.

The second set of standards was in the area of process performance standards, which enables companies to measure their processes and compare their results with those of external suppliers. Benchmarks for the SCOR model are already available.

The third set, Process Management Standards, is 'the easiest to create and the most widely available today'. This enables organizations to ascertain how well their processes are managed and measured. Examples of this type of standards include the Software Engineering Institute's Capability Maturity Model and ISO9000.

Davenport argued that these standards will eventually make it easier to determine whether a business capability can be improved by outsourcing it. Comparison of services provided by different firms will also be made easier and this will lead to the commoditization of business processes and revolutionize how businesses work. He believes that this will lead to a dramatically increased level and breadth of outsourcing and reduce the number of processes performed by organizations internally. To compete they will have to find other sources of differentiation and revisit the basis for competition in their businesses. Today, software development is leading the way in this process and this is rapidly proliferating into other areas.

BPR: Main Lessons and What Next?

Although some people still dismiss BPR as a management fad, its enormous influence on organizations has been evident and today process-oriented management thinking has become deeply embedded in many organizations and is extending beyond the organization's boundary to include suppliers and customers, sometimes spanning the entire supply chain. Several lessons have been learnt from over a decade's worth of BPR programmes.

The first is that business processes, however important, are only one dimension of organizations. Many other dimensions, such as culture, structure, strategy and so on, are equally important and an appropriate alignment – or fit – has to be achieved between them if the organization is to function effectively. Therefore it is essential to develop and implement process redesigns in the context of other aspects of organizations.

The second lesson is that as a philosophy or as a new business concept it is useful to look for radical process innovations. However, implementing new business processes is a different issue, requiring different skills. To be successful, it is often necessary to break up radical changes into smaller and less radical phases and implement them gradually. This will enable some continuity to be maintained and it will also allow people time to get used to the new processes. Any mistakes can also be identified and rectified before they lead to significant damage and the eventual failure of many BPR programmes.

For several decades, process innovations have strongly influenced management thinking and business performance across many different industries, and today it remains a critical dimension of e-Business development. Many business processes – especially public sector organizations – could still benefit from a radical reengineering, and process-oriented thinking is increasingly applied between organizations along the entire supply chain. The rapid development of the Internet and related technologies, such as mobile communications and RFID, may lead to further changes in business processes both within and between organizations.

Discussion Questions

1   According to Michael Hammer and James Champy (1993), reengineering is about 'starting over . . . If I were re-creating this company today, given what I know and given current technology, what would it look like?' Describe the main features of Hammer and Champy's approach to reengineering. Critically evaluate the strengths and weaknesses of this approach in the broad context of process innovations.

2   Systematically compare and contrast the ways in which Davenport's theory on business process redesign is similar to and different from Hammer's business process reengineering.

3   Is BPR still relevant to today's organizations? Explain why and support your views with evidence.

4   Critically evaluate Hammer's operational innovation, and discuss its relevance to today's organizations.

5   What is your view on the standardization and outsourcing of business processes? Critically evaluate its benefits and potential problems; and elaborate on where it might be going and why.

Assignments

1. Beyond BPR: What Next?

    You are a leading expert on process innovations, including BPR. You have been invited by a leading business magazine (such as *The Economist*, *Fortune* or *Business Week*) to contribute a short piece on future trends in this area. Since many organizations have already been reengineered many times, the logical question is – what next? Clearly illustrate the main issues in the area, and where appropriate support your views with evidence and examples (3,000 words).

2. A Collection of Successful and Failed BPR Cases

    Based on published materials, identify 10 successful and/or failed implementations of BPR in real organizations (the lecturer should coordinate this to ensure minimal overlapping amongst students on the course). Write each of them up on one side of A4 (single spaced), clearly illustrating how the processes were reengineered, the benefits achieved and problems encountered during the implementation, and the role played by ICTs. These can then be published on the course website so the materials can be shared amongst the students.

NOTES

1 Hammer, Michael (1990) Reengineering work: don't automate, obliterate, *Harvard Business Review*, July–August, 104–112; Davenport, Thomas and James Short (1990) The new industrial engineering: information technology and business process redesign, *Sloan Management Review*, Summer, 11–27.
2 Johansson, H., P. McHugh, A. J. Pendlebury and W. A. Wheeler III (1994) *Business Process Re-engineering*. John Wiley & Son, Chichester.
3 Davenport, Thomas (1993) *Process Innovation*. Harvard Business School Press, Boston.
4 Hammer, Michael and James Champy (1993) *Reengineering the Corporation: A manifesto for business revolution*. Nicholas Brealey Publishing, London.
5 Ibid.
6 Davenport (1993) op. cit.
7 Hammer and Champy (1993) op. cit.
8 Hammer, Michael (2004) Deep change: how operational innovation can transform your company. *Harvard Business Review*, April, 84–95.
9 Ibid.
10 Davenport, Thomas (2005) The coming commoditization of processes. *Harvard Business Review*, June, 100–111.

FURTHER READING

Davenport, Thomas (1993) *Process Innovation*. Harvard Business School Press, Boston.

Davenport, Thomas (2005) The coming commoditization of processes. *Harvard Business Review*, June, 100–111.

Davenport, Thomas and James Short (1990) The new industrial engineering: information technology and business process redesign. *Sloan Management Review*, Summer, 11–27.

Hammer, Michael (1990) Reengineering work: don't automate, obliterate. *Harvard Business Review*, July–August, 104–112.

Hammer, Michael (2004) Deep change: how operational innovation can transform your company. *Harvard Business Review*, April, 84–95.

Hammer, Michael and James Champy (1993) *Reengineering the Corporation: A manifesto for business revolution*. Nicholas Brealey Publishing, London.

Johansson, H., P. McHugh, A. J. Pendlebury and W. A. Wheeler III (1994) *Business Process Re-engineering*. John Wiley & Son, Chichester.

Chapter 12

New Work Organization and New Ways of Working: From Teleworking to Virtual Teams

Introduction

Emerging strategies and business models are not only translated into new structures and processes, but also the way work is organized, managed and conducted at micro-levels. The rapid development of ICTs has enabled people to work with more flexibility in terms of where, when and how – both individually and collaboratively, often in ways not possible in the past. This chapter explores new forms of work organization and new ways of working that have been developed to exploit such increasing flexibilities. Between the 1970s and mid-1990s, the focus was on teleworking and telecommuting, but since then, the focus has increasingly shifted to using ICTs to support geographically distributed virtual teams, some of which operate at the global scale.

Teleworking refers to the use of ICTs to enable work to be conducted at a distance from the place where the work results are needed or where the work would conventionally have been done (such as the central office). It can take many different forms, and the most common ones include:

- Home-based teleworking, also known as telecommuting, when an employee or contractor works from home instead of travelling to the employer's or the customer's premises.
- Mobile teleworking, when executives, professionals or service staff use ICTs to enable them to spend more time with customers and deliver services and capabilities 'on the road' that previously would have involved office-based staff or visits to the company offices.
- Telecentres, which provide local office facilities for people who prefer not to work at home but wish to avoid the cost, time and inconvenience of commuting to the city centre offices.

- Telecottages, which provide local communities with access to skills development, high-performance ICTs, and the networking and social aspects of work that may be missed by a home-based worker.
- Sometimes, the concept of teleworking is also extended to include functional relocation, where business functions previously located close to the customer (e.g. front-office activities) are concentrated and delivered at a distance (e.g. in a call centre).
- Some scholars went even further to consider many forms of outsourcing and off-shoring as teleworking, where an increasing range of work can be done from thousands of miles away and outsourced across organizational and national borders.
- In some cases, teleworking is also used to illustrate dispersed team-working across geographical and time boundaries.

The rapid and continuous conceptual expansion of teleworking is also the main cause of its downfall: its connotation has expanded so much that by the early 1990s it had become very difficult to identify any activity that could be excluded from it. This has been further exacerbated by the exponential growth of the Internet and mobile communications since the mid-1990s. Many of the reported benefits of teleworking, such as reduced congestion, although important, have never been the main motivation for organizations to implement teleworking. Some of the sub-areas of teleworking have become mainstream activities in their own right, in terms of both research and business applications, such as outsourcing and offshoring, and functional relocation.

As a result of such conceptual and practical difficulties with teleworking, the focus of research and applications is increasingly shifting from electronic home-working and telecommuting to using ICTs to improve the productivity and effectiveness of knowledge workers both individually and in groups. Using ICTs to support geographically dispersed groups to work together is often illustrated as virtual teams. There have been numerous studies of virtual teams in recent years, because in the network economy, virtual teams offer opportunities for geographically dispersed individuals to access information remotely and work together on common projects. This is particularly attractive to global organizations with geographically dispersed employees with special expertise. Virtual teams offer a new form of organizational design, which enables organizations and individuals to exploit new flexibilities enabled by advanced ICTs in terms of space and time.

Today, it has become clear that although an increasing number of people would work full time from home (especially people living in remote parts of developed countries), most people prefer working from home for only some of the time, and spending the rest of the time in the office. This is particularly the case for managerial and professional workers. The most important growth category in the past few years, and perhaps in the foreseeable future, is mobile working, where people work mainly in different places such as hotels, clients' premises, airports and on the train or plane, but using the home or the office as a base. For many people, work and leisure will be less distinct, and managing time will become a much more critical issue than before. In particular, mobile working and home working will involve a shift from personalized space (the office) to personalized time. This will require the development of new management control, which will affect the management of all employees.[1]

From Teleworking to Virtual Teams

The concept of teleworking was invented many decades ago but it only became popular after the oil crisis of the early 1970s. With the rapid growth of information workers in developed economies, it became both feasible and desirable for some office workers to work from home via computers and telecommunications linked to the central office, so their daily commuting to the city centre could be avoided. This was referred to as telecommuting,[2] a concept widely used in North America, although in Europe the term teleworking, or telework, is more widely used. Teleworking attracted enormous attention from a wide variety of domains, and its connotation has expanded rapidly and continuously. From the early 1980s, more complex organizational and locational forms of teleworking were increasingly developed to overcome various problems associated with electronic home working, including the development of neighbourhood teleworking centres and satellite offices to overcome problems such as personal isolation associated with home working. Several existing forms of work (for instance, mobile working) are also included in the definition. This conceptual expansion, however, has created enormous confusion and operational difficulties for teleworking researchers and practitioners – particularly in defining what exactly teleworking is (and is not), and in counting the number of teleworkers.[3]

In contrast to the rapid conceptual expansion, the growth of teleworking itself has been slow and fragmented. Although the remark that 'there are more people doing research on teleworking than there are actual teleworkers' was exaggerating the situation, the growth in the actual number of teleworkers has certainly fallen far short of even the modest forecasts in the 1980s. The implicit identification of teleworking with full-time home working has increasingly been challenged, and it has been argued that the primary forms of teleworking are those based on various kinds of telecentres (where full-time teleworking is appropriate) and those involving 'split-site' teleworking – that is, working part-time from home and part-time in the office. This has in fact been proved the case today.[4]

Many reasons have been identified for the slow growth of teleworking in the real world. Amongst the main reasons are two conceptual flaws inherent in the visions of teleworking. Most previous attempts to define teleworking and to apply it in practice started from two underlying, implicit assumptions:

- First, work is an individual rather than a group endeavour.
- Second, the workplace is simply a physical place where people carry out their job-related activities.

Teleworking therefore involves taking these individuals and their work out of their normal working context (e.g. the central office) through technological support, and relocating them to, mainly but not exclusively, the home. However, in reality, neither of these assumptions can be justified. The growth of the modern economy has been based on people working together in fulfilling complex tasks through the division of labour, which means that a significant proportion of work is primarily a group rather than an individual activity; and indeed, most tasks conducted by different individuals must be closely coordinated and integrated to be meaningful.

Even with activities that are primarily individual, the social environment in which these activities are located is essential to their efficiency and long-term viability. The workplace is not only a physical environment in which the work is carried out, but also, probably more importantly, a social environment in which people get inspiration, recognition and promotion, make friends and enemies, and communicate and argue with each other. In fact, studies in the 1920s and 1930s (known as the Behavioural School of Management) demonstrated that the social environment is extremely important to the productivity of workers – even when they are working on relatively 'self-contained' tasks. As Charles Handy famously pointed out: 'A room of one's own, or at least a desk of one's own, has been the security blanket for a century or more. A sense of place is as important to most of us as a sense of purpose . . . even office politics and gossip have their attractions, if only as an antidote to the monotony of much of what goes on in the name of work. Few are going to be eager advocates of virtuality when it really means that work is what you do, not where you go.'[5] This view was, unfortunately, largely neglected by most previous teleworking studies and applications.

The Importance of the Social Environment

When a young executive took over a mail order company, he was unhappy about the layout of the office, where a large number of part-time, primarily female workers, sitting around large tables, handled large volumes of letters. The tasks are simple and repetitive so the workers chat and joke with one another while carrying out the work. The executive thought that if he could stop the workers chatting and joking during working hours, perhaps productivity could be improved. So actions were taken to rearrange the tables along the walls in the large office (instead of in the middle), so the workers were no longer facing each other.

The new layout did reduce the noise and the amount of chatting and joking amongst the workers, but instead of increasing productivity, the company experienced a significant surge of absenteeism and sick leave, and the workers made more frequent visits to the washrooms and could not wait for tea and lunch breaks. In the end the executive was forced to revert to the original work layout and made special efforts to make the work less boring and the working environment more pleasant.

The moral of this example is that even for very simple, repetitive, individual tasks, the social environment is essential to the productivity of the workers: without the social interactions, such work may not even be sustainable.

As such, successful teleworking must emphasize two propositions, namely, a significant proportion of work is primarily a group activity, and the workplace is as much a physical as a social environment for the workers. By incorporating these two conditions into the design of teleworking applications, a new scenario emerges, together with a very different set of requirements for technological, organizational and socio-economic support. This was sometimes referred to as team-telework in the early 1990s.[6] Unlike most conventional visions of teleworking, which are primarily concerned with moving people from the central office to their homes by substituting telecommunications and computers for physical transport, team-telework focuses on collaborative group working on common tasks over space by innovatively exploiting the new flexibility and capability of ICTs. In doing so, the need for physical co-presence can be replaced, or at least supported or supplemented, by tele-mediated co-presence between team members.

Since the mid-1990s, such studies have increasingly converged with research and applications of team working. The rapid development of ICT infrastructure, combined with globalization and various other developments, means that organizations increasingly need, and are able, to deploy the expertise of individuals located in different places – either different parts of the same city or different parts of the world – in a group setting. Such groups are referred to as virtual teams, and this concept has been widely deployed not only in operations that have a significant digital component (such as software development), but also in a wide variety of other situations, from consultancy, joint design, and publishing to legal and medical services. Many such virtual teams involve members located on different continents, in different time zones, and belonging to different cultures and sometimes different organizations, which raises serious challenges different from those faced by conventional, physically co-located teams.

The concept of the virtual team often overlaps with concepts such as the virtual or networked organization, virtual workplace, virtual community, electronic commerce and electronic market, as well as some forms of teleworking in the academic and business literature. In some cases, virtual teams are used interchangeably with virtual organizations. However, for most researchers, virtual organization refers to inter-organizational arrangements where a group of independent organizations work together for a common goal, usually, but not exclusively, by using various telecommunications channels and information systems to coordinate their activities. This enables organizations to compete, collectively, with larger integrated organizations in the global market. In contrast, virtual team is usually used to describe micro-level work organization, where a group of geographically dispersed workers are assembled using ICTs to accomplish a common task. The workers can come from the same or different organizations depending on the nature of the task. A team can become virtual when their members are separated by organizational, geographical and/or temporal boundaries.

Living in 'Two Spaces': The New Business Environment for Virtual Teams

To understand teleworking and virtual teams in a business context, it is essential to understand one aspect of the new business environment in the networked, information economy: how the development of ICTs has affected space and time (geography) in the organization of work. Despite major progress made in research on the geography of the information economy, utopian views about the 'end of geography' remain extremely influential today, even though such views and claims are based on limited empirical evidence, or futuristic predictions about the potential impact of tele-communications in terms of what is technologically possible. It is important to recognize that even in the information economy, geography matters. The physical space and place are still fundamentally important to us at all levels of society and the economy.

The neglect of space and place is surprising given the inherent geographical nature of information and telecommunications systems. In particular, the rapid development and proliferation of ICTs has facilitated the emergence of an electronic space, but all users of the Internet are still part of a real geography – they exist somewhere in the world, as do the parts of the Internet itself. Moreover, laws are still very much organized within geopolitical boundaries and these have to be taken into account even in the information age. As the Internet expands, the governments of the world have been working together to develop laws and regulations that are supportive of electronic commerce, and which will protect citizens around the world from abuse – which can be launched from anywhere on the Internet.

The electronic space and the physical space are not mutually exclusive and they overlap with each other in the organization and execution of activities, but many rules governing these two spaces are fundamentally different. To survive in the information economy, organizations – and individuals – not only need to exploit geographical differences and overcome geographical constraints in the physical world, but they also increasingly need to exploit opportunities and face threats in the new electronic space. Indeed, a fundamental feature of the new business environment is that the rapid development of the Internet and other communications technologies has facilitated the emergence of an electronic space, which coexists, and often intertwines, with the physical space and place we live in.[7] Since the late 1980s, numerous studies have been carried out concerning the geography of the information economy. One of the main conclusions is that to understand the new spatial dynamics of corporate activities we need to shift our focus from the geography of space (geographical separation) and place (the unique characteristics of particular socio-cultural settings) to the geography of flows. ICTs allow information capital to be accessed instantly from, or transmitted to, remote locations. Therefore, the locational patterns of the (networked) information capital cannot truly represent the geographical patterns of its use.

Hepworth advanced the concept of 'communicability' to interpret the movement characteristics of networked information capital and its spatial dynamics.[8] This concept highlighted the qualitative difference between the geographical mobility of information capital through computer networks and alternative conceptions of capital mobility (e.g. the physical relocation of fixed capital or physical travel by information workers). The emergence of the electronic space, however, does not mean that the significance of the physical space has decreased. Many characteristics of the physical space will continue to affect the operation and development of organizations. As Harvey argued, with the support of advanced information systems, organizations are increasingly able to exploit minute geographical differences to good effect.[9] Small differences in what the space contains in terms of labour supplies, resources, infrastructures and the like become of increased significance. An important paradox is that the less important the spatial barriers, the greater the sensitivity of capital to the variations of place within space, and the greater the incentive for places to be differentiated in a way that is attractive to capital. In other words, geography has never been more complicated and more important to organizations and individuals! Geographical differences have in fact become an important resource to exploit for competitive advantage, which explains major contemporary trends in the business world, from globalization to offshoring.

The coexistence of 'two spaces' represents a fundamental change in the business environment. Although the electronic space perhaps has emerged since the telephone and radio were invented, it has only become essential to organizations and many individuals in the past ten years or so as advanced information infrastructures become widely available and as the information economy becomes firmly established. In particular, unlike the telephone which has improved only the geographical flexibility of labour (other geographical flexibilities have been derived from this), data communications increase the flexibility of both labour and information capital. So the level of flexibility to organizations in terms of 'who does what where and when' has increased significantly. This is especially so given the growing importance of information in capital and labour formation in all developed economies. Virtual teams are essentially developed to exploit the new geographical flexibility of information capital and information labour.

With the emergence of the electronic space, the nature and characteristics of the 'place' have also been radically redefined. At one extreme, virtual places in the electronic space are increasingly being created – enabling people physically located in different places to meet electronically (e.g. an online chat room, an important tool for many virtual teams). In essence, space and place have converged into one. This is not to say that the physical place is no longer relevant to individuals and organizations. On the contrary, local characteristics will continue to affect the effectiveness of communications between people from different places even in the 'virtual place'. Indeed, even though in the electronic space the 'friction of distance' based on the transportation model for certain information capital and labour has been eroded, other frictions of distance derived from differences between places (e.g. local culture, language) will continue to exert major effects. A new model based on telecommunications and transportation is needed to understand the new dynamics of the space economy. Even though distance between physical places for certain information capital can be overcome by telecommunications, geographical differences between places still need to be fully appreciated for people to work together effectively. This is highly relevant to virtual teams.

Also significantly affected by the emergence of the electronic space is time. A very important dimension of the industrialization process is the standardization, and our acceptance, of time in our work and social life. By changing the nature of the friction of distance, and by becoming available anytime, anywhere with the proliferation of mobile communications, the question of time and its significance in our work and everyday life is reopened. New flexibility and constraints in time (e.g. time zone) for virtual team members are very important issues that need to be considered. The boundary between work and leisure also needs to be re-examined. In the new business environment characterized by 'two spaces', time is not only a constraint (e.g. nobody wants to work at three o'clock in the morning in order to collaborate with virtual team members from other continents!), but also a resource that can be exploited for organizational benefit. Global virtual teams can pass work-in-progress around the clock between the three main economic centres (America, Europe and Asia) – for example, 24-hour collaborative designs around the clock and globe; around the clock and globe stock-trading. Even in the same time zone, work-in-progress can be suspended in time (stored), which gives virtual team members the chance to organize individual time more effectively.

Identity and Trust in Virtual Teams

Today, virtual teams have been widely adopted in different sectors, from software development and joint design (e.g. a new plane or new car), to consultancy, publishing and legal and medical services. It is a new form of organizational design to exploit our improved capability in managing issues arising from distance, time, and organizational boundaries, through the support of advanced ICTs. Virtual teams enable organizations to reach remote markets and bring dispersed talents from different locations together, transcending geographical, cultural and organizational boundaries. However, owing to various barriers and difficulties, few virtual teams have been able to achieve a performance level comparable to geographically co-located, conventional teams. Conceptually, virtual teams are still ill-defined and many difficult issues still need to be resolved. Despite the rapid development of ICT infrastructures and services, and the growing range of communication tools at our disposal, spatial, temporal, cultural and organizational boundaries and language barriers continue to prevent many virtual teams from functioning efficiently and effectively. Furthermore, compared with conventional teams, virtual teams bring a wide range of other issues which need to be carefully addressed, such as psychological distance, lack of cohesiveness, the erosion of trust and the crisis of member identity.

Identity plays an essential role in virtual teams. In communication, knowing the identity of those with whom you communicate is essential for understanding and evaluating an interaction. Yet, when team members are separated by spatial, temporal and organizational boundaries, identity is ambiguous. Many of the basic cues about personality and social role to which we are accustomed in the physical world are absent. In the physical world, there is an inherent unity to the self, for the body provides a compelling and convenient definition of identity. The norm is one body, one identity. Though the self may be complex and mutable over time and circumstance, the body provides a stabilizing anchor. The virtual world is different. It is composed of information rather than matter. Information spreads and diffuses; there is no law of the conservation of information. The inhabitants of this impalpable space also diffuse, free from the body's unifying anchor. One can have as many electronic personas as one has time and energy to create, i.e. multiple identities, which can be a replica of the identity of the person in the physical world, or carefully re-created identities that have little or no resemblance to the person who creates them. This raises serious issues about trust in the electronic virtual environment.

Trust is an important enabler of cooperative human actions. Many authors highlight the importance of trust in the success of teams, which is especially important in virtual teams where team members do not see each other, at least not as often as people do in conventional teams. Charles Handy,[10] when discussing how to manage people when you do not see them in his *Harvard Business Review* article, 'Trust and the virtual organization', argued that '[t]rust is the heart of the matter. That seems obvious and trite, yet most of our organizations tend to be arranged on the assumption that people cannot be trusted or relied on, even in tiny matters . . . If we are to enjoy the efficiencies and other benefits of the virtual organization, we will have to rediscover how to run organizations based more on trust than on control. Virtuality requires trust to make it work: Technology on its own is not enough.' This, however, requires a radical turnaround of management thinking and managerial tradition that efficiency and control are closely linked and one cannot be achieved without the other. Handy proposed seven rules of trust which should be kept in mind in a virtual setting:

- Trust is not blind.
- Trust needs boundaries.
- Trust demands learning.
- Trust is tough.
- Trust needs bonding.
- Trust needs touch.
- Trust requires leaders.

Handy further argued that virtuality calls for new forms of belonging. He believes that a sense of belonging is a basic human need, and that the concept of membership could replace the sense of belonging to a place with a sense of belonging to a community, including a virtual community. 'A shared commitment still requires personal contact to make it real. Paradoxically, the more virtual an organization becomes, the more its people need to meet in person. The meetings, however, are different. They are more about process than task, more concerned that people get to know each other than they deliver.'[11]

Some researchers also examined different types of trust in virtual teams, including familiarity-reliance-based trust, confidence-based trust, dependence-based trust and situational trust. However, to nurture trust amongst virtual team members and effectively manage the identities of the virtual team members and the virtual team itself is a daunting task, which needs to be carefully managed. Virtual teams differ in many ways, including their interaction modes, the history, future and permanency of the team, the membership of the team – are they from the same or different organizations, cultures and nationalities? All these issues affect virtual team members' situation awareness and situational trust, and comprehension of situational cues. To succeed, complex social, economic, managerial and psychological as well as technological barriers have to be overcome.

Virtual Teams in Action: Some Examples

Over the years, many virtual teams have been set up by different organizations in a variety of settings to exploit the new spatial and temporal flexibility afforded by advanced ICTs. This section describes some such examples.

Virtual Teams in Action: Some Examples

The first example is a virtual team involving a CASE (computer-aided software engineering) tool supplier and their main customer in the UK. The supplier develops a diverse range of software applications for customers in aerospace and defence, telecommunications, electronics, energy, system software and manufacturing. As part of its services the company provides constant, high-quality, technical support to its customers. In the past these services were maintained by the supplier by sending experts to the customers' premises, but a virtual team solution has enabled the company to formulate an effective way of supporting its customers with greater responsiveness and efficiency. This approach is complex and a high level of interaction between geographically dispersed team members is needed. By providing a software tool to support remote tele-interactions between an expert and the client, the previous physical co-presence of these people is replaced by tele-mediated co-presence. In doing so, the geographical flexibility of the experts and the responsiveness of services have been improved significantly. This is especially so in urgent problem situations (e.g. a system breakdown).

Another interesting virtual team was developed in a large law firm with several offices in Germany. With only small branch offices and a limited number of clients, the provision of a full range of professional legal services in remote locations is expensive. In many such situations, the result is a poorer, less extensive service in rural areas. A virtual team solution was developed involving a main office and two branch offices in northern Germany. The intention was not only to enhance services in remote locations but also to reverse the previous situation by having a range of experienced legal experts available in remote locations. Thus, a particular legal expert would not have to remain in the main office but could provide services from a branch office to clients in large cities electronically. This application requires good quality videophones and the ability to transfer copies or images of documents for simultaneous viewing. To maintain strong professional links between the legal offices, the system also supports the transmission of large volumes of case file data. Despite various difficulties, the system has significantly improved the geographical flexibility of legal experts and the responsiveness and quality of services to customers.

In France, a business services company set up an information system to support real-time communications between its central office in Paris, three satellite offices in the suburbs and several regular clients. The system enabled direct communications, parallel viewing of documents and also parallel working on word-processed documents while in simultaneous voice and visual communications. This allowed complex editing and formatting issues to be quickly resolved.

In southern Italy, a system was developed to link together several academic and research institutions to provide, collectively, a full range of research training and consultancy services needed by industries. In a market research firm in

England, a new system was developed to support the collaboration of a team of market researchers, consultants and managers working from their own homes. In Scotland, a system was developed between a large central hospital and a small clinic on a remote island. Medical experts in the central hospital use the system to transmit high quality X-ray images together with other audio, visual and text support to facilitate remote diagnosis. Similarly, in Greece, a new system was developed to provide full-time medical consultancy between a major teaching hospital in a large urban area and some small clinical units based in remote rural areas.

Teleworking, Virtual Teams and E-Commerce

The ambiguity and overlapping between the concepts, and phenomena, of teleworking, virtual teams and e-Commerce as well as a wide range of other contemporary business phenomena (such as offshoring) have created huge confusion for both researchers and practitioners. Various efforts have been made to clarify the situation, and their similarities, differences and relationships have been explored in different contexts. In Europe, a new framework is increasingly adopted to illustrate these closely related phenomena: this framework classifies business activities into three categories: teleworking, telecooperation and teletrade.

Teleworking refers to the use of ICTs to enable work to be done at a distance from the place where the work results are needed or where the work would conventionally have been done. Telecooperation is the application of ICTs by individuals and organizations to enhance communications and access to information, which often entails new skills and changes to organizational designs. Teletrade uses ICTs to market and sell goods and services, to enhance customer relationships, and to reach distant markets without the overhead of a local physical presence. Teletrade is broader than narrowly defined e-Commerce because it covers all business use of electronic networks during all phases of a business relationship. Key activities of teletrade include identification of customer needs and wants, communicating with customers about new products, marketing of goods and services online, direct online selling, and accepting payment and delivering electronically where appropriate. Teletrade also covers areas such as supply chain management and customer services and support electronically. However, e-Commerce is widely used today to illustrate the activities of teletrade.[12]

Today, teleworking has become appropriate for a large proportion of people and jobs, because organizations are effectively networked, and the managers and staff have developed telecooperation skills. For individual teleworkers, telecooperation methods provide enhanced communication with colleagues, and the ability to connect with professional and other networks of people, regardless of their location. Teletrade is possible without telecooperation, but the use of telecooperation methods opens up a much wider range of products and services to teletrade possibilities.

Emerging Issues

With the rapid development of broadband communications, ubiquitous computing and mobile communications, there has been a surge of electronic home working and mobile working. Even through the growth of full-time home workers has not reached a level predicted in the 1970s and 1980s, we have seen more and more mixed-mode teleworking. Many of us spend time working from home for some of the working week – sometimes to complete an urgent report or to avoid interruptions in the office. We can also check e-mails and respond to urgent matters easily from airports or holiday resorts.

We are also increasingly working with people electronically, either locally or across the globe. Globalization and other developments increasingly require people to work with others in virtual team settings. Many comprehensive studies have been conducted – some in controlled environments – to investigate and conceptualize different types of virtual teams, identify critical success factors, assess the role of technology in virtual teams, understand how culture affects the performance of virtual teams, and explore ways to develop the competences of effective virtual teams. Many other issues, such as the orientation process of a virtual team, how to build trust amongst team members, and how to facilitate meetings in a virtual team environment have also been studied. Some researchers are also examining the dynamics of virtual teams and key principles of working in the networked environment. Various ways to overcome problems associated with teleworking and virtual team working – such as through the support of virtual communities of practice – have also been investigated and trialled in real business environments.

As well as affecting the individual and the organization, teleworking and virtual teams also have significant economic and trade implications; for example, many jobs in computer programming that were previously done in California or Sweden are now done in Bangalore. Understanding teleworking and virtual teams in all their ramifications is essential to the future of work and jobs.

Discussion Questions

1   What is teleworking? What are the main forms of teleworking? From a *business* perspective (as opposed to an individual, trade union's or environmental perspective), critically evaluate the main benefits and problems of teleworking.

2   Identify some of the difficulties in drawing the boundaries for teleworking when counting the number of teleworkers. Discuss possible ways to overcome the ambiguities.

3   What is a virtual team? From a *business* perspective, what are the main benefits and problems of virtual teams? How could the problems be effectively addressed?

4   Systematically compare and contrast the concepts of teleworking and virtual teams: in what ways are they similar, different and overlapping?

Assignments

1. A Comprehensive Bibliography on Teleworking and/or Virtual Teams
   Conduct an online search and develop a comprehensive bibliography of books and journal papers on teleworking and/or virtual teams. Identify the most influential references and annotate them.
2. A Handbook on Teleworking and/or Virtual Teams
   Critically review the conceptual and practical issues associated with teleworking and/or virtual teams, and write a handbook for senior business executives who are interested in introducing teleworking and/or virtual teams in their organizations.
3. Article for a Business Magazine. Is Teleworking Still Relevant Today?
   The European telework online (http://www.eto.org.uk) recently closed down its website, mainly because interest in teleworking in Europe has largely been subsumed into other research areas in recent years, from virtual teams and e-Commerce to ambient working environment. Write an article for a business magazine such as *The Economist* or *Business Week* to illustrate your views on whether teleworking is still relevant today. You should also discuss what might happen next (3,000 words).
4. PowerPoint Presentation: The Benefits and Problems of Teleworking and/or Virtual Teams
   Find as many real-life examples of teleworking and/or virtual teams as you can, and investigate what made some of them successful and why others failed to live up to expectations. Write up your findings in the format of a 15-minute PowerPoint presentation; your target audience is business executives interested in introducing teleworking and/or virtual teams in their organizations.

NOTES

1 Moynagh, Michael and Richard Worsley (2005) *Working in the Twenty-First Century*. The Economic and Social Research Council, Future of Work Project, University of Leeds, Leeds.
2 Nilles, J. (1988) Traffic reduction by telecommuting: a status review and selected bibliography. *Transportation Research*, 22A (4), 301–307.
3 Huws, U., W. B. Korte and S. Robinson (1990) *Towards the Elusive Office*. John Wiley & Son, Chichester.
4 Moynagh and Worsley (2005), op. cit.
5 Handy, Charles (1995) Trust and the virtual organization: how do you manage people whom you do not see? *Harvard Business Review*, May–June, 73 (3), 40–54.
6 Li, Feng and Andrew Gillespie (1994) Team telework: an emergent form of work organization, in R. Baskerville et al. (eds), *Transforming Organizations with Information Technology*, IFIP WG8.2, North-Holland, Amsterdam, ISBN 0-444-81945-2, pp. 397–419; Li, Feng (1998) Team telework and the new geographical flexibility for information workers, in Magid Igbaria and Margaret Tan (eds), *The Virtual Workplace*. Idea Group Publishing, Hershey, pp. 301–318.
7 Li, Feng, Jason Whalley and Howard Williams (2001) Between the electronic and physical spaces: implications for organizations in the networked economy. *Environment & Planning A*, 33, 699–716.

8 Hepworth, M. (1989) *Geography of the Information Economy*, Belhaven, London.
9 Harvey, D. (1989) *The Condition of Postmodernity*, Blackwell, Oxford.
10 Handy (1995) op. cit.
11 Ibid.
12 For a more detailed discussion please refer to this website: http://www.eto.org.uk/twork/index.htm.

FURTHER READING

The top three publications you identified in Assignment 1.

Handy, Charles (1995) Trust and the virtual organization: how do you manage people whom you do not see? *Harvard Business Review*, May–June, 73 (3), 40–54.
Huws, U., W. B. Korte and S. Robinson (1990) *Towards the Elusive Office*. John Wiley & Son, Chichester.
Li, Feng (1998) Team Telework and the New Geographical Flexibility for Information Workers, in Magid Igbaria and Margaret Tan (eds), *The Virtual Workplace*, Idea Group Publishing, Hershey.
Li, Feng, Jason Whalley and Howard Williams (2001) Between the electronic and physical spaces: implications for organizations in the networked economy. *Environment & Planning A*, 33, 699–716.
Lipnack, Jessica and Jeffrey Stamps (2000) *Virtual Teams: People working across boundaries with technology*. John Wiley & Son, Chichester.
Moynagh, Michael and Richard Worsley (2005) *Working in the Twenty-First Century*. The Economic and Social Research Council, Future of Work Project, University of Leeds, Leeds.
Nilles, Jack (1998) *Managing Telework: Strategies for managing the virtual workforce*. John Wiley & Son, Chichester.

Chapter 13

Inter-Organizational Innovations through Inter-Organizational Information Systems

Introduction

Organizational innovations are not limited within the boundaries of the organization, and increasingly they are developed between organizations as well, sometimes across the entire supply chain. The process of using inter-organizational information systems to enable inter-organizational innovations is not new, and it has been going on for several decades. Back in the 1970s, some large firms placed computer terminals in their customers' offices and offered these customers direct access to certain information (such as stock availability and price) held on their central computers. These systems facilitated information exchange between suppliers and buyers, reduced costs, improved quality of services and stabilized inter-organizational relations. However, until the end of the 1980s the development of such inter-organizational information systems and innovations was slow and fragmented both in terms of sectoral penetration and in the range of applications they supported. After that time, inter-organizational systems began to diffuse rapidly in an increasing number of sectors, and new forms of inter-organizational collaboration based on such systems also began to emerge. Since the mid-1990s, the rapid diffusion of the Internet and related technologies has made it much easier – and cheaper – to establish and maintain new inter-organizational systems, which has led to a range of inter-organizational innovations. In this chapter the evolution of inter-organizational systems and the associated changes in inter-organizational relations are discussed.

Inter-organizational innovations are perhaps the most significant amongst all organizational innovations in the age of the Internet and e-Business. Indeed, after several decades of restructuring and reengineering, as well as exploring different types of new work organization and new ways of working, most potential internal efficiency gains associated with ICTs perhaps have been squeezed out of most organizations. In contrast, the rapid development of the Internet and related technologies, infrastructure and services has enabled business partners to explore inter-organizational innovations in ways not feasible, or not even imaginable, in the past. This allows organizations to extend their internal gains from computer networking and process and functional integration to business partners across the entire supply chain. Some of these inter-organizational innovations are closely linked to emerging strategies and business models discussed earlier in the book, such as the strategic reorientation from products and services to solutions and experience, the web strategy and virtual or network organizations. They are also closely linked to many emerging e-Business models, underpinning the entire e-Commerce and e-Business phenomenon ranging from B2B and B2C to the integration of internal functions and processes with inter-organizational applications.

Furthermore, many other forms of organizational innovation, such as the deconstruction and unbundling of integrated business models and processes, depend critically on robust inter-organizational systems to reintegrate the unbundled activities and processes across the newly created organizational boundaries. Inter-organizational innovations are also closely linked with a wide range of contemporary business phenomena that have been discussed in various chapters of this book, such as business process and IT outsourcing and offshoring, the commoditization and standardization of a wide range of business processes, and a number of other emerging trends.

What are Inter-Organizational Information Systems?

Inter-organizational information systems, or inter-organizational systems for short, refer to the computer and telecommunications infrastructure developed, operated and/ or used by two or more organizations for the purpose of exchanging information that supports a business application or process. These organizations can be suppliers and customers in the same value chain, or strategic partners or even competitors in the same or related market. Such systems are sometimes called inter-organizational networks, or computer-mediated inter-organizational systems. These systems can take many different forms, ranging from dedicated, closed group systems, via semi-closed group networks based on value added network services (VANS) and some B2B portals, to completely open systems based on the Internet, which is sometimes referred to as an electronic market or open e-market.

Before the commercial applications of the Internet in the 1990s, many inter-organizational systems were built with technology and interfaces proprietary to a particular group of organizations. Many such systems are still being used today amongst strategic partners or within particular sectors, even though more and more systems have been migrated to the Internet platform. As such, firms wishing to join the business network often need to invest in the special hardware and/or software for the system. The reasons for adopting this type of system were divergent. In some cases, they were intended by some firms to lock in customers and lock out competitors. In most cases, it was simply because common standards were not available, or because available open technical solutions could not provide the sophisticated technologies or the level of confidentiality required by the partners for particular applications. There are many advantages with this type of network, but problems such as high development and maintenance costs, low flexibility and so on were increasingly recognized. It is also interesting to note that some strategic collaboration between organizations (e.g. the joint design and development of new products between firms) was often based on this type of inter-organizational system.

The second category, the most widely used form in the 1980s and 1990s, is based on standard, common purpose computing facilities and communication protocols, very often, but not always, using VANS. VANS describe the electronic communication services provided, usually by a third party, to two or more trading partners that not only establish an information link between the participants, but also assist and add value to the communication process in some way. One of the most widely used standards for VANS is based on electronic data interchange (EDI). EDI has primarily been used in the subcontracting area along value chains, and it has been proven most effective in supporting operational-level applications, mainly because of its limited technical capabilities and the existence of multiple technical standards both within and between sectors. In order to support more complex and strategically more important applications and processes, some firms have preferred to maintain dedicated data links between their computer systems by themselves, using various interfaces and communication protocols capable of handling more sophisticated forms of information exchange.

The situation has been changed considerably by the Internet since the mid-1990s when such services were gradually moved onto the Internet platform, and some VAN providers have evolved into B2B exchanges or portals. Most B2B e-Commerce is an adaptation of EDI or is based on EDI principles, and even today EDI is still the method used for most electronic B2B transactions (some estimate as many as three-quarters of all B2B transactions). It is important to note that Internet EDI (also called Web EDI or Open EDI) has not replaced traditional EDI because many large companies have significant investments in the computing infrastructure they use for traditional EDI. Concerns about security issues and the inability to provide audit logs and third-party verification of transactions also significantly slowed down the proliferation of Internet EDI. Today, most VANS providers offer Internet EDI but they continue to provide traditional EDI services. However, the situation is changing rapidly as security concerns are increasingly alleviated and the open architecture of the Internet allows trading partners virtually unlimited opportunities for customizing their information exchanges. It also provides inexpensive communication channels that traditional EDI lacked, which allow more and more small companies to participate in Internet EDI.

In both of these categories, all parties involved in the systems are predetermined and all participants have agreed to trade or exchange information electronically. These types of inter-organizational systems are often referred to as 'electronic alliance'. However, the rapid development of the Internet and related technologies has opened up the opportunity for instant encounters and trade between un-predetermined members.

Today, any firm can establish electronic communications with any other firms in the world at very low cost; and a firm wishing to offer its products and services can simply store an electronic catalogue on its server (or on a third-party hosting server) for the world to look at. Such inter-organizational systems are referred to as the 'electronic market'. Clearly it takes more than just the Internet to make such open trading and communications work, and many difficult barriers have to be overcome. For example, most commercial transactions between firms are based on trust, which is currently lacking in the electronic market, but many trade organizations and international bodies have been developing various schemes to overcome these barriers. The reputation of companies also plays a key role in some instances (e.g. it is relatively reliable and safe for anyone to do business with Dell or Cisco electronically). The electronic market is increasingly used for standard, undifferentiated products and services or for trading excess stocks in many industries. The rapid growth of companies such as eBay has also made trading between small companies and between individuals straightforward.

Inter-Organizational Information Systems and the Changing Inter-Organizational Relations

Until the late 1990s, most applications of inter-organizational systems were amongst business partners that had agreed to do business electronically, and the situation has continued today even though open electronic markets have been developing rapidly for certain products and services in the form of B2B and B2C e-Commerce. In fact, many B2B transactions are based on established relations between the trading partners. Inter-organizational systems are particularly developed amongst firms along the same supply chain. Various benefits such as lower costs, shorter lead-time, lower stock levels and improved cash flows were often achieved. For small firms, the benefits and danger of being locked in and locked out of such systems were also highlighted. Most inter-organizational systems were usually initiated by a large firm at the centre of the trading network in order to interact electronically with regular suppliers and/or buyers. The main purpose was typically to reduce transaction costs, stock levels and lead-time. In some cases, these systems were developed through the natural extension of the centre firm's internal computer and communication systems. The development of such systems often entails the extension of the centre firm's internal gains from computer networking to its suppliers and/or customers, in order to reduce the total cost of the final products and to improve the responsiveness of the supply chain to market changes. Sometimes, such systems are imposed on trading partners by the large firm at the centre. The costs to each firm are normally paid back by productivity gains, increased sales or secured long-term contacts, and sometimes the development is directly subsidized by the centre firm.

The development of such inter-organizational systems can often serve to stabilize existing relations between suppliers and buyers, and raise the entry barriers for potential competitors. This is because setting up and maintaining inter-organizational systems requires close cooperation between participating firms, which helps them to foster closer partnerships and encourage the sharing of information. The use of such networks can also contribute to the removal of barriers to cooperation by reducing errors typical of paper-based communications; and should any errors happen, these networks can also facilitate problem resolution, because the problems can be more easily traced and dealt with more quickly and effectively. In addition, introducing inter-organizational systems often requires both time and money, their maintenance often requires special skills, and there are also security and reliability concerns. Switching partners (suppliers or buyers) would therefore by definition be costly and time consuming. All these factors have served to stabilize existing inter-organizational relations.

From Routine Transactions to Strategic Applications

Most inter-organizational systems have been developed to support routine, repetitive transactions between business partners, such as electronic ordering and invoicing. However, there have been two important developments in recent years. One is that some business partners use inter-organizational systems to support strategic collaborations, such as joint new product development and collaborative designs. This is particularly important in the age of virtual organizations. The other, perhaps a more significant one, is that some leading firms are using electronic transactions with suppliers and buyers to support their new business models, such as Dell, Cisco and Toyota. In fact, even though many of the applications and processes supported by inter-organizational systems are routine in nature, without seamless electronic transactions amongst their business networks, the business models that have brought these companies success would not have been possible.

Inter-organizational systems and strategic collaborations between firms

Using inter-organizational systems to support strategic applications has been going on for many years.[1] Back in the early 1990s, a fashion designer and manufacturer in the UK used EDI to exchange market and design information in addition to electronic ordering and invoicing. By adding special software in both the manufacturer's and the retailer's computers, the two companies needed to exchange only limited data between their information systems to enable the designers in the manufacturer and the purchasing staff in the retailer to exchange ideas about new designs and new market requirements, which translated into more frequent orders and new products more closely linked to market demand.

Equally, in the car manufacturing sector, EDI-based ordering and invoicing systems enabled just-in-time production which reduced costs and improved the responsiveness of the entire supply chain. However, once such routine electronic trading was established, some companies started to explore strategic applications as well. Examples include the so-called 'synchronous supply' with selected local suppliers by a car manufacturer based in the UK.

'Synchronous Supply' and Inter-Organizational Systems

The use of inter-organizational systems has enabled real just-in-time production in a leading car manufacturer in the UK. Some components (e.g. car seats) are delivered to the car assembly lines by the suppliers – with the right variants and specifications – just twelve to fifteen minutes after the car manufacturer issues the order. Apart from the locational proximity between them and the convenience of electronic ordering based on EDI, one key to this application was that the suppliers are granted direct access to production planning and forecasting information stored on the car manufacturer's computers, so the suppliers can plan their own production before receiving orders. Otherwise, this application would have not been possible. For suppliers in other parts of the UK and in Europe, the lead-time from order to delivery has also been reduced dramatically. By the mid-1990s, the car manufacturer's average inventory and stock holding for European-originated parts was reduced to less than one day. Essential to the improvement is the sharing of business information between business partners via inter-organizational systems.

Other strategically important applications include the joint development of new products. In the car industry, some component suppliers are technically very competent, and it is in the car manufacturer's interest to tap into this expertise. As a result, since the 1990s, some car manufacturers have decided to work with selected suppliers in new car developments. The car manufacturer provides the supplier detailed CAD data on the space the component occupies and its technical specifications; the supplier will then begin to design the component, passing it back to the car manufacturer via inter-organizational systems for feedback and modifications (to ensure total compatibility). Such interactive communications enable emerging problems to be resolved quickly. Online simulations between different components can also be conducted before the design is finalized.

Whilst the in-bound material flows in most car manufacturers are very efficient today, out-bound logistics has not been able to achieve the same level of responsiveness, with high levels of inventory for finished cars, which ties up a huge amount of working capital. The key to improving the inventory level of finished cars is to improve the relations between dealers and manufacturers, enabling the sharing of stock movement and production planning information between the car manufacturer and the dealers and between the dealers themselves through inter-organizational systems. Today, when a customer walks into a dealership, the sales person can check stock availability easily by accessing production planning information and the finished car database not only within different branches of the car dealer itself, but also from the manufacturer's production plan and the stocks of other, sometimes competing dealers.

Inter-organizational systems and new business models

In additional to supporting strategically important applications between organizations, it is important to note that inter-organizational systems have underpinned, or enabled, the business models of many well-known, successful companies that are based on special relations with their partners and customers. Toyota is one such example that developed lean production systems amongst its partners and suppliers. The inter-organizational information systems are essential in enabling the sharing of information and the effective integration of their operations. This enables Toyota to use operational excellence as a strategic weapon: it designed cars faster, with more reliability, yet at a competitive cost, making it the third largest car manufacturer in the world after General Motors and Ford, and it has been expanding faster than its larger competitors.

Toyota's Lean Production System and Inter-Organizational Systems

According to Jeffrey Liker, the Toyota Production System is Toyota's unique approach to manufacturing.[2] It is the basis for much of the lean production movement that has dominated manufacturing trends for many years, and it was heralded as the Japanese secret weapon which has spread rapidly throughout the world.[3] Lean production welds everyone's activities into a tightly integrated system that responds quickly to market demands. Liker summarized lean manufacturing as a five-part process that includes defining customer value, defining the value stream, making it flow, pulling from the customer back, and striving for excellence. To be a lean manufacturer requires organizations to adopt a way of thinking that focuses on making the product flow through value-adding processes without interruption, a pull system that cascades back from customer demand by replenishing at short intervals only what the next operation takes away, and a culture in which everyone is striving continuously to improve the system. Pull means the ideal state of just-in-time manufacturing: giving the customer what they want, when they want it, and in the amount they want. All these processes would not be possible without the support of robust inter-organizational information systems that are closely integrated with the internal systems of all parties involved in the entire supply chain, both to support routine transactions and to share strategic and operational information.

Another well-known business model based on integrated inter-organizational systems is the Cisco model, which made the company very responsive to market changes and allowed it to close its books in 24 hours throughout the year (see box below). A further example is Dell's direct sales model. Dell is the largest direct supplier of computer systems, and it sells to both individual and business customers. By using the Internet to sell customized computers directly to customers, Dell eliminated the need for a wholesale and retail network and costly mark-ups. In addition, Dell is able to ship customized computers as fast as mail order companies shipping from inventory, at a cost not much higher – or even lower – than their non-customized competitors. However, the model requires Dell's operation to be closely integrated with that of its suppliers, contractors and logistical service providers throughout the supply chain. The support of a robust inter-organizational system is essential.

Cisco's Business Model and Inter-Organizational Systems

Cisco's supply chain consists of a group of contract manufacturers who ship directly to customers on demand. These manufacturers depend on other large manufacturers of components for their supply, and these latter companies in turn depend on a large network of global suppliers. To improve the responsiveness of the supply chain, Cisco developed an eHub with its suppliers that works with its Partner Interface Process system. These systems operate in real time and they significantly increase transparency for orders. The Partner Interface Process system sends demand forecasts to both the contract manufacturers and the component makers in the supply chain, and ultimately Cisco is able to automate the whole product fulfilment process; a customer's online transaction will simultaneously update Cisco's financial database and supply chain. Essential to the business model is a flexible, robust IT system that integrates and coordinates the entire manufacturing, supply chain and logistical systems. Furthermore, to harness the expertise of its customer base, Cisco has extended its links further downstream by creating Cisco Connection Online, which provides a suite of interactive, networked services with quick open access to Cisco's information, resources and systems. The system enables Cisco customers to engage in dialogue and help solve one another's technical problems.

Many other companies are following these market leaders – a trend sometimes referred to as mass customization. For example, Toyota is able to ship custom-built cars in a week; and the car industry is hoping to save billions of dollars each year from reduced inventories alone by producing cars made to order. Similarly, Nike allows customers to customize shoes, and De Beers allows customers to design their own engagement rings. These innovations would not have been possible without the support of inter-organizational information systems which enables the close integration of operations across the entire supply chain, from suppliers all the way to the final consumers. Many of these new business models are based on the effective integration of the electronic market downstream (customers) with the electronic alliances upstream (suppliers).

From Lean Production to Lean Services and Lean Consumption

Lean production has undoubtedly transformed manufacturing, and in recent years the same principles have been successfully applied in some service industries. In her paper published in *Harvard Business Review*, Cynthia Swank described how Jefferson Pilot Financial, a US life insurance and annuities company, successfully applied the principles of lean production to significantly improve operations and increase revenue.[4] Just like the assembly line for cars, an insurance policy goes through a series of processes from application, risk assessment and underwriting to policy insurance. Each step adds value to the final 'product'. The main advantage of implementing a lean production initiative over business process reengineering, for example, is that the new system can be introduced without significantly disrupting operations. Through this initiative, the company transformed its operations from batch processing to continuous flow processing, and applied various lean production principles, which significantly reduced the build-up of work in progress. Although lean production is generally seen as a manufacturing concept, Swank believed that many of its tools were originally developed in the service industries: like retailing, customers pulled what they wanted from the shelves, which were then replenished for subsequent customers. The application of lean production principles in services may lead to similar changes – including inter-organizational innovations – we have witnessed in the manufacturing sectors.

More significantly, James Womack and Daniel Jones believe that after the transformation of manufacturing (and services) by lean production, the next step is to apply lean thinking to the process of consumption.[5] This new theory is closely linked to the concept of 'experience' – a strategic reorientation discussed earlier in the book.[6] With the unstoppable trend towards deregulation in a growing number of areas, people's freedom has increased dramatically, but with this comes new responsibilities. Today, consumers have access to a growing range of products at lower cost, higher quality and more variety, but this also means they have a growing range of decisions to make, about what product or service to purchase, from which supplier, through different channels and so on. In this process, the boundary between production and consumption is blurred by ICTs. Consumers need to do an increasing amount of work – unpaid – on behalf of providers (e.g. entering data into order forms and tracking their own orders). 'And these consumers are spending more and more time and energy to obtain and maintain the computers, printers, PDAs, and other technological tools needed to solve routine problems – for themselves and for providers' (p. 60).[7] The situation is further exacerbated by the changing characteristics of consumers, such as the growing number of two-wage families and single parent households, and aging populations, which all mean that people have declining energy and time to confront expanding choices.

According to Womack and Jones, lean consumption is not about reducing the amount customers buy, but about providing the full value that customers desire from their goods and services with the greatest efficiency and least pain. By minimizing customers' time and effort and delivering exactly what they want, when and where they want it, companies can benefit from the process. However, for lean consumption to work, a fundamental change needs to happen in the way retailers, service providers, manufacturers and suppliers think about the relationship between provision and consumption and the role their customers play in the process. Customers and providers must collaborate in order to minimize total cost and wasted time and create new value, and the processes of provision and consumption need to be tightly integrated and streamlined.

Like lean production, lean consumption has a series of corresponding principles, including solving the customer's problem completely by ensuring that all the goods and services work and work together; not wasting the customer's time; providing exactly what the customer wants, where and when it is wanted; and continually aggregating solutions to reduce the customer's time and hassle. To implement these principles, providers need to work together to perfect the entire consumption process rather than deal with their own individual piece of the solution, and solve problems at the source. Companies should use 'pull' (e.g. Nike can profitably deliver customized bags overnight anywhere in North America), rather than large inventory, to satisfy customer needs. For consumers, by sharing their plans with a producer and ordering in advance (e.g. a car), it is possible to obtain a customized product for a reduced price; and manufacturers could save significantly in reduced inventory costs. However, the current system of manufacturing and purchasing often penalizes customers for planning ahead.

The real challenge for lean consumption is for the retailers, service providers, manufacturers and suppliers to look at the total costs from the consumer's point of view, and eventually to work with customers to optimize the process of consuming. This requires not only changing mindsets on the part of all stakeholders involved, but also the underpinning of a robust information system that links together the operations of these stakeholders and enables the effective sharing of information. Lean production has in recent years become the dominant model of production, and the proliferation of lean consumption will lead to new forms of inter-organizational relations across the entire supply chain – all the way to the consumers.

The Internet and B2B Electronic Marketplaces

The rapid development of the Internet since the mid-1990s facilitated the emergence of B2B electronic marketplaces. There are several different types of electronic marketplace, although some of them perhaps are more precisely described as 'electronic alliances', with predetermined trading partners only. Schneider briefly illustrated several categories of e-marketplaces:[8]

- Independent industry marketplaces, which are also known as industry marketplaces (focused on a single industry), independent exchanges (not controlled by one of the established buyers or sellers), and public marketplaces (open to new buyers and sellers). Examples include Chemdex and ChemConnect for bulk chemicals.
- Private stores and customer portals: for example, Cisco and Dell offer private stores for each of their major customers within their selling website to ensure they meet the needs of their key customers better than industry marketplaces would.
- Private company marketplaces, where a large company purchasing from many vendors can open an e-marketplace for its own procurements, sometimes known as e-procurement.
- Industry consortia-sponsored marketplaces: a marketplace formed by several major companies in an industry, such as Covisint in the auto industry sponsored

by DaimlerChrysler, Ford and General Motors, together with several thousand suppliers; and Avendra, formed by Marriott, Hyatt and three other major hotel chains.

Today, all these models are being used in various industries. It is not clear which of these models will dominate B2B e-Commerce in the future, although so far the industry consortia-sponsored marketplaces appear to be most successful.

In a similar fashion, Laudon and Traver classified B2B e-marketplaces into net marketplaces and private industrial networks.[9] Net marketplaces can be further classified into four categories:

- e-distributors: a single-firm version of retail and wholesale stores, such as Grainger.com, FindMRO.com and Staples.com;
- e-procurement: a single firm creating a digital market where thousands of sellers and buyers transact for indirect inputs, such as Ariba.com and CommerceOne.com;
- exchanges: independently owned digital marketplaces for indirect inputs, such as IMX.com and eSteel.com; and
- industrial consortia: industry-owned vertical e-markets open only to selected suppliers, such as Covisint.com and Plasticsnet.com.

Private industrial networks include single-firm networks to coordinate the supply chain with a limited set of partners (e.g. Wal-Mart, Proctor & Gamble), and industry-wide networks to coord-inate supply and logistics for the industry (Nistevo and Globalnetexchange.com).

Turban et al. also illustrated different types of e-marketplaces, but their discussions included both B2B and B2C e-Commerce, from electronic storefronts and malls to private and public e-marketplaces and information portals.[10] They also discussed the various business models used in these e-marketplaces.

Some of these e-marketplaces are perhaps more precisely described as electronic alliances, which are similar to electronic trading networks based on VANS or direct inter-organizational systems, although the open standards of the Internet make it easier and cheaper than before to establish and maintain the electronic links. Others are similar to open markets enabled by Internet-based communications. In some cases, these developments have significantly increased the transparency of the market in various contexts, and in all cases the efficiency of trading between organizations is significantly improved. Some of the electronic marketplaces serve to enhance and stabilize inter-organizational relations, but in others the systems encourage competition between suppliers of the same products.

Today, B2B e-Commerce still captures the lion's share of total e-Commerce in terms of transaction value, even though B2C e-Commerce has been growing steadily and rapidly. In some cases the distinctions between B2B and B2C are becoming blurred. The Internet has made it increasingly easy and affordable for almost anyone to set up electronic links with anyone else, which without doubt will facilitate further growth of electronic trading between organizations, between organizations and individuals, and between individuals themselves. The rapid development of companies such as eBay and various services offered by companies such as Yahoo, MSN and Amazon.com allow small companies as well as individuals to set up online shops easily to sell anything to other companies or to final consumers, either through auctions or at fixed prices. Price comparison sites, such as Froogle from Google and Kelkoo, enable organizations and individuals to identify the cheapest or most suitable providers easily, significantly increasing the transparency of the market. Companies such as Overstock.com enable organizations to sell excess stocks quickly and easily. Priceline.com enables buyers to name their own price and enable providers to sell their products at suitable prices. Other models of e-Commerce and e-marketplace continue to be invented, and rapid developments are likely to continue in the foreseeable future. This is still a rapidly evolving area and further studies are needed to make sense of the latest developments and to understand their implications for inter-organizational relations.

Barriers to Inter-Organizational Systems and Innovations

There are many barriers to inter-organizational systems and innovations, not only serious technical barriers but also cultural and political barriers which are extremely difficult to overcome. Examples include sharing sensitive business information with suppliers, customers and even competitors; the integration of business processes between firms; the control of one firm by another; the coexistence of competition and collaboration; the integration of production with consumption; and many other related issues. Many of these barriers have to be overcome before some inter-organizational innovations in strategic areas can be developed. In fact, the full potential of inter-organizational systems probably cannot be achieved without radical changes in the institutional framework in which most organizations operate, and in the perception and assumptions of business leaders about the nature of firms and markets in the network economy.

The main barriers to the future development of inter-organizational systems and innovations exist at three levels. At the bottom level, there are technical barriers that organizations have to overcome, in terms of system reliability, security and in managing incompatible standards and networks. Such technical problems – and the lack of trust in such systems – have prevented some firms from developing new collaborations in strategic areas. Although recent developments in technology, infrastructure and services have significantly relieved these problems, technical barriers will continue to constrain the development of inter-organizational systems and new applications based on such systems.

A more difficult barrier exists at a second level, which requires radical changes in the understanding of the nature of firms and markets and the new rules of the game in the information economy. Issues such as sharing sensitive business information (e.g. stock availability, forecasting and production planning data) with suppliers, buyers and even rival companies still worry some business leaders. However, if such issues are not resolved, many strategic inter-organizational collaborations are simply impossible to develop and the full potential of inter-organizational systems and innovations cannot be achieved. A study by Dyer and Hatch highlighted how Toyota achieved sustainable advantage by partnering with suppliers and partners and sharing knowledge with them through organized networks.[11]

Even when firms are prepared to share certain business information with each other, the success of inter-organizational innovations is still not guaranteed. Successful collaborations between firms require more than the exchange of information. Differences between the collaborating organizations in terms of aims, culture, structure, procedures, professional and natural languages, accountabilities, and the sheer amount time and effort required to manage the logistics of communication often militate against success. Of particular importance for effective collaboration between organizations is perhaps the development of 'common knowledge', which is essential to successful collaboration, but it is an extremely difficult endeavour between organizations. As such, the success of inter-organizational innovation through inter-organizational systems is much more difficult than many people have perceived. This to some extent explains why the enormous potential of inter-organizational system has been difficult to materialize so far.

For open electronic marketplaces, there are still serious concerns about security, trust, third-party verification, payment and so on. Many organizations are working hard to address such issues. Most of the barriers are non-technical in nature and their removal will facilitate further growth in e-Commerce.

Inter-Organizational Systems and Changing Inter-Organizational Relations: What Next?

In the age of the Internet and e-Business, inter-organizational systems and inter-organizational innovations will continue to develop rapidly. The Internet has made it increasingly easier, and cheaper, to set up and maintain electronic links between organizations, and between customers and organizations. This has not only facilitated the increasing adoption of inter-organizational collaborations in routine and strategic applications, but also enabled the adoption of new business models that have brought success to an increasing number of companies.

Inter-organizational innovations are closely linked to some of the strategies and business models discussed earlier in the book, and are an essential aspect of e-Commerce and e-Business. They are also closely linked to many contemporary business phenomena, ranging from the deconstruction and unbundling of the integrated business model and processes to the outsourcing and offshoring of routine and strategic activities, functions and business processes. Many inter-organizational innovations have been implemented to extend the benefits of internal gains through restructuring and reengineering to business partners, suppliers and customers; and increasingly, some organizations are exploiting core competences based on unique relations and applications between organizations. In fact, it has been argued that in the age of the Internet and e-Business, companies are increasingly seen as portfolios of capabilities and relationships positioned within a global network of business processes, and it is the dynamic creation of value within the entire network that frames our thinking.[12] The integration of operations across value chains has enabled the adoption of new business models in a growing number of industries, which are further leading to significant restructuring of value chains and value networks, and new forms of competition and collaboration between business partners and new relationships between businesses and consumers, including lean consumption and the co-construction of value and experience with business partners and consumers. Continued research is clearly needed in this area.

Discussion Questions

1 What is an inter-organizational system? From a business management perspective, in what ways are inter-organizational systems similar to or different from intra-organizational systems?

2 Inter-organizational innovations based on inter-organizational systems have evolved from routine applications to strategically more important ones. Outline the main types of inter-organizational innovations and illustrate each of them with a real-life example.

3 Describe the concept of lean consumption by James Womack and Daniel Jones. Illustrate its possible application in a particular industry you are familiar with, and discuss the key issues involved.

4 What are the main types of e-marketplace? Illustrate each with a real-life example.

5 What are the main barriers to the development of inter-organizational systems and inter-organizational innovations? What possible measures could be taken to overcome these barriers?

Assignments

1. Case Study
   Using the Internet and other published materials, study the business model of Cisco (or other suitable companies such as Dell, Amazon.com and so on). Describe the business model and discuss the role played by inter-organizational systems.

2. Lecture on Inter-Organizational Systems and Inter-Organizational Innovations
   Imagine you are responsible for teaching 'inter-organizational systems and inter-organizational innovations' to your class. Conduct some independent research (including both relevant theories and examples) and develop a one-hour lecture on this topic using PowerPoint.

3. Strategic Assessment of E-Marketplace
   You are a consultant on the e-marketplace. You have been commissioned by the CEO of a leading company from a particular industry you are familiar with to produce a briefing report to the board of directors about the current developments and potential benefits and problems of e-marketplace in this industry. The report should be no more than three pages of A4, single spaced. Please bear in mind that the target audience is senior business executives who are primarily interested in strategic issues.

NOTES

1 Li, Feng and H. Williams (1999) Inter-firm collaboration through inter-firm networks. *Information Systems Journal*, 9(2), 103–117.

2 Liker, Jeffrey (2004) *The Toyota Way: Fourteen management principles from the world's greatest manufacturer*. McGraw-Hill, New York.

3 Womack, James P., Daniel Jones and Daniel Roos (1990) *The Machine that Changed the World*. Rawson Associates, New York.

4 Swank, Cynthia Karen (2003) The lean service machine. *Harvard Business Review*, October, 123–129.

5 Womack, James P. and Daniel T. Jones (2005) Lean consumption. *Harvard Business Review*, March, 59–68.

6 Pine II, Joseph and James Gilmore (1998) Welcome to the experiences economy, *Harvard Business Review*, 76(July–August), 97–105; Prahalad, C. K. and V. Ramaswamy (2003) The new frontier of experience innovation, *Sloan Management Review*, Summer, 12–18.

7 Womack and Jones (2005) op. cit.

8 Schneider, Gary (2006) *Electronic Commerce*, 6th annual edn. Thomson Course Technology, Canada.

9 Laudon, Kenneth C. and Carol Guercio Traver (2003) *E-Commerce: Business, technology and society*, 2nd edn. Pearson Addison Wesley, Boston.

10 Turban, Efraim, David King, Jae Lee and Dennis Viehland (2004) *Electronic Commerce: A managerial perspective*. Pearson Prentice Hall, New Jersey.

11 Dyer, Jeffrey H. and Nile W. Hatch (2004) Using supplier networks to learn faster. *Sloan Management Review*, Spring, 57–63.

12 E.g. Venkatraman, N. Venkat (2004) Offshoring without guilt. *Sloan Management Review*, Spring, 14–16.

FURTHER READING

Dyer, Jeffrey H. and Nile W. Hatch (2004) Using supplier networks to learn faster. *Sloan Management Review*, Spring, 57–63.

Liker, Jeffrey (2004) *The Toyota Way: Fourteen management principles from the world's greatest manufacturer*. McGraw-Hill, New York.

Prahalad, C. K. and V. Ramaswamy (2003) The new frontier of experience innovation. *Sloan Management Review*, Summer, 12–18.

Schneider, Gary (2006) *Electronic Commerce*, 6th annual edn. Thomson Course Technology, Canada.

Venkatraman, N. Venkat (2004) Offshoring without guilt. *Sloan Management Review*, Spring, 14–16.

Womack, James P. and Daniel T. Jones (2005) Lean consumption. *Harvard Business Review*, March, 59–68.

Womack, James P., Daniel Jones and Daniel Roos (1990) *The Machine that Changed the World*. Rawson Associates, New York.

Chapter 14

Conclusions and Emerging Issues

What Is E-Business and Does It Matter? Strategic Innovations and Organizational Transformation in the New Business Environment

From an organizational perspective, this book systematically examined the phenomenon of e-Business in the context of the changing business environment, emerging strategies and business models, and various organizational innovations. E-Business is not just about using the Internet to create dot.com companies, which is an important but limited part of the concept. Fundamentally, e-Business is about using information and communications technologies to enable organizations in private and public sectors to do things differently, in more superior ways than what was possible or imaginable before. This could be achieved either by creating entirely new organizations or by transforming existing organizations in the way they are organized and managed, the way they interact with suppliers, buyers and other stakeholders, and the way people work independently and/or with one another. From an organizational perspective, e-Business is primarily about developing and implementing strategic and organizational innovations in the context of the new business environment, by innovatively deploying ICTs in general and the Internet and related technologies in particular.

The business environment has been undergoing a radical transformation, and the main driving forces are the rapid development and proliferation of ICTs and the changing nature of the economy, from the industrial economy to the knowledge-based, information economy. The transformation is ongoing, and just when we think things might calm down for a while, something even more exciting emerges, which spurs another round of frantic activities and adjustments. The knowledge-based, networked, information economy has now become firmly established; the transformation from the industrial economy to the information economy has been measured quantitatively, and it is clearly reflected in a wide range of mainstream social, economic, political and personal activities today.

Indeed, I am increasingly convinced that things are different just by observing how my teenage son does his homework each day ('I can't do my homework without my computer'); how he maintains contact with his friends locally and globally, by using the house telephone, mobile phone, e-mails, online chat via MSN Messenger, Yahoo Messenger and AOL Messenger – simultaneously; how he listens, manages, shares and swaps music, as well as video clips and photos; how he plays online games or shares tips about various online and offline games on the Internet with people from around the world, and how he participates in and contributes to various online forums; and most of all, how he learnt to play the electric guitar almost entirely by using free resources on the Internet and tips from other guitar enthusiasts on the Internet – using the webcam and online chat (he refused my offers to find him a professional guitar teacher because it would turn this into a task and 'ruin the fun'). He is equally comfortable borrowing our credit cards to buy things online, ranging from books and CDs to badminton racquets and musical instruments, even including my last birthday present.

For many people under a certain age, there has never been an ICT Revolution – for them it is just how things have always been. Most of them are already big spenders, and many of them have – or soon will have – their own income. As they increasingly reach employment age, they expect organizations to work differently, and some of them have and will continue to set up businesses that will work differently. My son sneered at me when I told him about a major project I was working on with a multi-national company, with a budget of several hundred thousand pounds, to develop a system for 200 senior directors of the operating companies around the world to communicate more effectively – and the various difficulties involved. He told me about an online trading card game he was playing (Duel Monsters). The popular card game itself was developed by a Japanese company, but a teenager in Taiwan developed and hosted an online forum for players from around the world to play the game in real time, with online spectators, using free resources on the Internet. These children did not have a budget and they had never met in person, but they managed to put together a robust system to enable them to interact globally through multiple channels in an orderly fashion. Just imagine what they could do when they grow up and with a few hundred thousands pounds' budget to play with.

Many previous studies have investigated and quantified the growing proportion of information workers in the composition of the labour force in different economies; the information content in products and services and production processes; and the contribution of information activities in terms of 'value-added' to the GDPs of different economies. Some researchers also illustrated the rapid development of information and communications technologies, including the explosive growth of the Internet and mobile communications in recent years, and how ICTs are increasingly embedded in almost all economic and social activities in many countries – at work, on the road and at home. Extensive research has also been conducted to measure the contribution of investments in ICTs to productivity growth, and theories such as transaction cost economics have been used to illustrate how the increasing deployment of ICTs can affect organizational boundaries and explain some of the significant organizational transformations – from mergers and acquisitions to business unbundling and the formation of new alliances. Many other changes in the business environment have also been identified and illustrated, and these changes together are leading to the emergence of a whole set of new 'rules' radically different from those of the industrial economy. Indeed, perhaps even the new information economy itself has now been so firmly established that we are embarking on yet another round of radical transformation, from the information or knowledge economy to the 'creative economy' or 'experience economy'. All these changes significantly shape the strategies, business models and organizational designs of both private and public sector organizations.

The rapidly changing business environment, underpinned by the rapid development and proliferation of ICTs and the changing nature of the economy, requires organizations large and small, from both the public and private sectors, to re-evaluate their strategies and business models. A range of new strategies and business models, including the web strategy, various disruptive strategic innovations in different sectors, the experience innovation and the deconstruction of the integrated business models and the unbundling of integrated business processes, together with a series of e-Business models, have been introduced in both new and established organizations. These new strategies and business models challenge conventional thinking by taking advantage of the new features of the new economy and the new capabilities from advanced ICTs. Their introduction in different sectors significantly intensifies competition and leads to radical changes in the landscape of those sectors – and indeed, the boundaries between sectors are increasingly eroded (for example, what is the telecom industry today?). These new strategies and business models are also increasingly reflected in the way public and private sector organizations are organized and managed and the way people work. Some of these changes have been implemented in leading organizations and conceptualized as structural innovations, process innovations, new work organization and new ways of working, and innovations in inter-organizational relations.

Although some of the changes represent continuation from the past, many radical changes have also been introduced. These changes challenge many conventional business management theories that have been developed in the context of the industrial economy, and a new generation of theories is increasingly needed for organizations in the information economy. The implications are profound, not only for businesses and public sector organizations, but also for public policies and for individuals.

The dot.com burst in the stock market during 2000–1 certainly did not mark the end of e-Business; e-Business has since become a mainstream activity in a wide range of industries and sectors, and it is proliferating rapidly from developed countries to developing countries. Today, ICTs continue to develop at breathtaking speed, and advanced infrastructure and services continue to proliferate rapidly. Organizations and individuals are also getting more and more comfortable – and experienced – in using ICTs and in extracting value from these technologies. Although we have all benefited from the process, perhaps we have only scratched the surface of the phenomenon and more changes are yet to come. Strategic and organizational innovations through ICTs will continue to dominate business thinking for the foreseeable future, and it will form the basis for a new generation of organization and management theory for the new economy.

Strategic and Organizational Innovations: What Really Works?

Many other strategic and organizational innovations were not explored in the book; for example, various production innovations transforming mass production into mass customization, and innovations in logistics, supply chains and supply constellations or networks. It should be pointed out that although the changing business environment requires organizations to introduce strategic and organization innovations at different levels, simply copying what others have done is not enough. Those innovations only worked under specific circumstances and it is important to understand what your circumstance is before designing and implementing strategic and organizational innovations. Business process reengineering perhaps only worked because many organizations were so focused on their organizational structures that they lost sight of the links between different parts of the organization, and why people were doing what they were doing. A process orientation gives people focus in making sense of how their own work fits into the mechanisms of the whole organization. After over ten years of BPR, however, many organizations are shifting their focus back to structures to provide order in the organization, which enables people to respond effectively to the uncertain, chaotic environment. As the ancient Chinese proverb says, 'you can have too much of a good thing' – and this includes new business ideas.

Good ideas also need to be implemented and executed properly to ensure success. Many of the new ideas introduced in this book perhaps should be seen as examples of strategic and organizational innovations that have been deployed by some leading organizations to address emerging opportunities and challenges under specific circumstances, and they may, or may not, be suitable for your own organization. Although it is necessary to have radical visions given the radical changes in the business environment, their effective implementation needs to be much more moderate, and perhaps staged, to give people – including employees, suppliers, customers and the management themselves – time to adapt to the new way of working and thinking.

In 2003, Nitin Nohria, William Joyce and Bruce Roberson published their paper 'What really works' in *Harvard Business Review*.[1] They examined more than 200 well-established management practices as they were employed over a ten-year period by 160 companies. Their research found that most of the management tools and techniques they studied had no direct causal relationship to superior business performance. However, what does matter is having a strong grasp of the business basics. Based on the detailed findings, they developed a '4+2 model' to help organizations achieve better performance. Companies that outperformed their industry peers excelled at what they call the four primary management practices: strategy, execution, culture and structure. They also supplemented their skill in those four areas with a mastery of any two out of four secondary management practices: talent, innovation, leadership, and mergers and partnerships. One way to explain their findings is perhaps that any new idea could work effectively if it is appropriate for the particular 'circumstance' of the organization, and if the implementation is executed effectively.

Equally, we should also be aware of the potential downsides of various strategic and organizational innovations with honourable intentions. In his book on *The New Ruthless Economy: Work and power in the digital age*, Simon Head vividly illustrated a long list of new economy promises that failed to pan out.[2] He argued that most American companies used ICTs not to empower employees but to further their regimentation. In manufacturing, companies followed the lead of Japanese transplants and instituted faster assembly lines that reduce tasks to their simplest components. With reengineering, managers ended up dictating the one best way to their workers and increasingly used intrusive technology to enforce that way. Standardized, off-the-shelf enterprise resource planning systems (ERP) have codified decisions that previously had allowed employees to exercise judgement and creativity. He went further, arguing that this de-skilling of the workforce allowed nearly all the productivity gains of the 1990s to flow to managers and investors instead of to ordinary employees. Despite the one-sidedness of his portrayal of the workplace in the network economy, it does prompt some caution when we evaluate the virtue of various strategic and organizational innovations.

Owing to the limited volume of the book, many important issues surrounding e-Business have been left out. Some of those issues have been systematically examined by other scholars in specialized books, while others have so far been neglected partly because of the rapidly evolving nature of the contemporary period. This chapter highlights some of the key issues that are not covered by this book, and many of these issues would make interesting topics for student assignments or independent studies.

E-Business Technologies

E-Business is supported by a plethora of technologies, infrastructure and services. The changing technological platforms and key developments in wireless communications, grid computing, Wi-Fi, RFID, Internet 2.0 and pervasive computing will all have profound implications for what will be possible in the near future. These technologies are not examined in this book but they have been the focus of many other books.[3] It should be pointed out that many e-Business studies about emerging strategies, business models and organizational innovations are based on the assumption that technologies are given, but in reality the relationship between ICTs and strategic and organizational innovations is an extremely complex one. New technologies shape, and are shaped by, the applications they support. Many new business applications are not possible – or not even imaginable – without the support of new technologies. At the same time, many new technologies are developed to address specific demands by organizations and individuals or to solve particular problems or tackle emerging business opportunities. Today, technologies continue to develop at an astonishing pace. Many new technologies and services have been developed, waiting for new applications to support. At the same time, many complex business problems require more advanced technologies to underpin or enable new solutions. Today, a void remains between many business managers, who, for the most part, lack the technical expertise of computer and communications scientists, and these scientists, who often lack the business acumen of managers. Bridging this gap remains one of the most difficult challenges today.

E-Business Applications in Different Sectors

This book also did not specifically explore how organizations in different sectors are responding to challenges posed by the changing business environment, although many of the theories and ideas have been conceptualized from in-depth research in real organizations. The changing business environment is having profound implications for almost all sectors, and a wide range of strategic and organizational innovations have been developed and implemented by different organizations.

Internet banking

Financial services have always been in the vanguard of using ICTs to improve their operations, and for several decades many financial institutions such as banks would not even have been able to function without the support of their information systems. The Internet and related technologies have facilitated profound changes in the banking industry since the late 1990s, not only as a cheap new channel that enables banks to handle transactions much more cheaply than any other existing channels, but more importantly as the basis for strategic innovations. These strategic innovations include using Internet technologies (such as web services) to integrate legacy systems supporting different applications and enabling banks to view their customers as 'whole persons'; or exploiting the connectivity of the Internet to enable some players to unbundle integrated banking services and focus on specific niche markets or specific stages of the value chain where they have unique advantages. A wide range of new business models have been implemented; some of them are extensions of the existing banking model, while others are radically different. These strategic innovations and new business models are increasingly reflected in the changing organizational designs of these organizations. This is still a rapidly evolving area and new developments are taking place rapidly. Examining the evolving Internet banking will make an interesting student assignment, which provides the opportunity for students to explore how emerging strategies and business models are being introduced in the banking industry.[4] Radical changes have also been introduced in other financial services such as stock trading and the insurance industry.

E-Tailing and e-Supermarkets

Another sector that has experienced similar changes is e-Tailing, where the Internet has not only become a new channel to sell products and services but also enabled the development of new business models. Apart from Amazon.com and many other famous e-Tailors, the evolution of e-Supermarkets for online grocery shopping is an interesting area which has experienced a roller-coaster ride since the late 1990s, with some modest yet steady success in some cases (e.g. Tesco.com has now become the largest e-Tailor in the UK) and spectacular failures in others (e.g. Webvan). These applications need to be studied and conceptualized.

Unbundling of the telecommunications industry

Telecommunications is another area that deserves some special attention, because it not only provides the infrastructure and services for e-Business applications in all sectors, but is also in the vanguard of experimenting with new strategies and business models by exploiting advanced ICTs. For several decades, since the deregulation of the telecommunications industry across the world, many companies have experienced profound changes, and it was also one of the hardest-hit sectors during the dot.com burst. Some of the changes in the sector are extremely radical. For example, the unit cost of bandwidth has been diving towards zero for many years, and with the enormous over-capacity in the industry, it has become increasingly difficult for companies to make profits and generate revenue under conventional pricing models – cost plus profit margin. As basic telecommunications services are rapidly commoditized, how to survive the extremely competitive market has been a key issue for the incumbents; they need to explore radically different business models – especially new pricing models to generate sufficient revenue and profit. In a special issue of *Telecommunications Policy* I edited in 2002 on 'Mapping the evolving telecommunications value chain and market structure', many key issues in the area were investigated.[5]

Today, radical changes continue to be introduced in the sector, not least in mobile communications such as 3G. In fact, British Telecom in 2005 embarked on a £10 billion (about $18 billion), five-year project to develop its '21CN' (21st Century Network).[6] This project will save an estimated £1 billion in year-on-year operating costs, by transforming its core network from the old circuit-switched, narrow-band technology to modern IP (Internet Protocol), broadband transmission. The anticipated savings are a direct result of the lower maintenance, operating and running costs associated with collapsing the current sixteen separate service-specific networks into one multi-service infrastructure. Several rivals are said to have similar plans, and their implementation will transform the industry once again. Such developments will contribute to improved quality of services for users, especially the ability for seamless integration of various information systems, which may transform the way people work. Mobile communications – and their operators and providers – are another area that needs watching.

E-Government and E-Public Services

Another significant area that has not been examined is e-Government, and more broadly, e-Public Services (because public services are increasingly provided by the private sector in some countries such as the UK and the USA). This book regards e-Public Services as a subset of e-Business – the use of Internet and related technologies to transform public services and the organizations providing them. However, owing to the profoundly different issues – and challenges – in public services compared with e-Business in the commercial sense, e-Government and e-Public Services are increasingly becoming an area of study in its own right.

E-Business in the private sector is profoundly different from e-Government in several ways. For private sector businesses, the dominant logic is relatively clear and simple – any business needs to make more money than it spends in the long term, it needs to generate adequate returns for its investors, and it needs sufficient cash to keep it going. There are many other stakeholders – such as employees, managers and the government, amongst others, but the dominate logic for private sector business is simple. That is to generate profit for its shareholders, even though it has responsibilities for employees and for the wider community. Recently, considerable attention has been paid to issues such as corporate social responsibilities, but the dominate logics of business in the private sector remain unchanged.[7] In contrast, the logics in the public sector are much more complicated. There are multiple, sometimes equally powerful stakeholders, and the reason for the existence of many public sector organizations is to protect the weak and disadvantaged. Many public services have no alternatives, so they have a captive audience. The differences, and sometimes conflicts, between the different logics – and between different strategic objectives – are often difficult to reconcile. What works in the private sector rarely works in the public sector in the same fashion, even after serious adaptation and adjustment.

For example, in the UK the implementation of e-Government could lead to substantial job losses (one in five by the government's own estimation, which translates into 800,000 civil servants), but this would be in direct contradiction to the government's priority for full employment.[8] The public sector is generally more unionized and has more rigid salary scales and conditions of service than the private sector. It has often been more difficult and time consuming to achieve changes in working practices because of the need for these changes to be agreed through negotiation and collective bargaining. There are many other difficult issues. Public sector organizations need to be more cautious than private companies because the information about individuals they deal with is both more extensive and more sensitive. The public generally trusts public sector organizations with this information, and a failure to deal adequately with issues relating to the security and confidentiality of information transferred electronically is likely to erode this trust. The 'digital divide' and the lack of access by certain fractions of society are also a major concern.

There are also many difficult issues in the realm of e-Health, which is becoming an important area of study in its own right. Other areas that have been transformed by the Internet and e-Business include e-Music, e-Holidays and e-Tourism, and e-Learning. All these issues are currently being researched in different contexts.

Other Key Areas and Emerging Issues

A long list of other areas also needs to be investigated, including e-Marketing, especially CRM (customer relations management) and online advertising, e-Procurement, e-Payment, m-Commerce and m-Business. The rapid development of e-Business also raises serious issues about privacy, online security, and many legal, ethical and social issues. Most of these issues are extremely complex and they have been the subject of specialized studies. In the increasingly networked economy and society, our privacy can be easily breached and existing laws and regulations may not be sufficient to protect us. Identify theft has been causing serious concerns and financial losses. The range of issues is extremely divergent, from unsolicited e-mails and e-mail bombing, the collection of information about individuals and the protection of individual privacy and intellectual property rights, to fraud on the Internet and the digital divide. Many of these issues are being investigated but we still do not fully appreciate the implications of e-Business. In 2004, an edited book on *The Social and Cognitive Impacts of E-Commerce on Modern Organizations* was published to address some of these issues.[9] In 2005, the *Journal of E-Commerce in Organizations* also dedicated an entire special issue to the social aspects of e-Business.[10] More research is expected on these issues in the next few years.

The development of the Internet and the global Internet economy also raises serious cultural and regulatory issues, and the ideological foundation of various national systems. The development of the Internet is a global cultural movement, and at least in the early part of its development it was marked by the transportation of the Silicon Valley Model to other countries with different cultures and institutional frameworks. The Internet is an intrinsically global technology, but its development occurs within the physical and institutional geography of nations. As Bruce Kogut put it: 'The Internet has borders.' The rapid expansion of Internet-related businesses challenges national systems consisting of firms, governments, consumers and workers. However, the Internet appears deeply engrained in the American model of entrepreneurship and new firms, and thereby it threatens the ideological foundations of these national systems across the globe. Many such issues were carefully explored in different national contexts in an edited book on *The Global Internet Economy* in 2003, but many difficult questions remain unanswered.[11]

Within different countries, many profound changes are taking place. The rapid proliferation of blogs (web logs) challenges the dominance of the established media and the government in controlling what information we receive, when and in what form, although the long-term implications of blogs are still not clear.

What Next?

This book systematically investigated the phenomenon of e-Business in the context of the changing business environment, emerging strategies and business models and various organizational innovations. However, many issues remain unresolved and further research is needed. For example, in examining the transition from the industrial to the information economy, there has been strong evidence to support this proposition. However, this may not fully explain the value-added involved in some cases, and perhaps other concepts, such as the conceptual economy, creative economy and experience economy, may be better suited to explain some of the emerging phenomena. It is not sufficient just to create value: it is equally important to capture the value created. Michael Jordan, the American basketball player, is worth more than the

GDP of the Kingdom of Jordan. The Chinese basketball player currently in the USA, Yao Ming, is worth US$100 million – the value of a very large company employing thousands of people in China. J. K. Rowling, the author of the Harry Potter books, managed to accumulate a personal wealth of £500 million within a few years, and in the process she also created opportunities for many other organizations and individuals to generate wealth many times that. Do such examples indicate that the nature of the economy has changed yet again? Further research is clearly needed to conceptualize the essence of the new economy.

Also, in terms of productivity gains through investments in ICTs, there was no supporting evidence until the period 1995–2000, when there was finally quantitative evidence to demonstrate productivity gains. However, the gains were concentrated in six sectors in the USA, where the use of IT led to organizational innovations and stronger competition, which in turn led to increased productivity. However, just when the evidence eventually emerged, Michael Hammer argued that knowledge worker productivity is not meaningful, because unlike manual workers making physical products that can be counted, knowledge worker productivity only makes sense in the context of business processes. Indeed, it can be argued that making a brilliant ten-second advertisement for US$1 million is far more productive than making five hours of useless film for nothing. What are we measuring? More importantly, what shall we be measuring in the new economy?

In such an uncertain business context, we also need to continue our search for strategic and organizational innovations. What really works? Under what conditions and circumstances? For how long? We also need to make clear distinctions between developing strategic and organizational innovations, and implementing and executing them effectively. The skills required are very different. The research by Nitin Nohria, William Joyce and Bruce Roberson found that it did not matter what strategies and organizations were implemented, but if an organization followed the 4+2 formula in the context of eight key factors, it was likely to achieve above average performance. Leaving aside the validity of the research, perhaps each of the strategies and organizations worked because they were chosen under specific circumstances: if they had been introduced at the wrong time, or implemented and executed badly, perhaps the results would have been different. This raises serious issues for academics and practitioners alike.

Today, new technologies and new business concepts continue to be developed and implemented. The full implications of many such developments remain unclear. However, the limited evidence available about various developments perhaps can shed considerable light for us, and it is very important for us to continue to identify novel applications and try to make sense of what is actually happening. For example, the study of m-Business and m-Commerce has so far been confined to using mobile devices for information and transactions, but more recently an executive MBA student working in the mobile industry pointed out that perhaps the real significance of m-Business in the near future is not in the area of transactions and information but in the seamless integration of people and activities within large organizations. We should carefully monitor new technological and conceptual developments and identify ways that value can be extracted from them that would benefit the majority of the stakeholders. At least nobody can say that we are living in a boring time.

Discussion Questions

1   What is e-Business and does it still matter today? Explain why and support your views with evidence.

2   In what ways has the business environment changed? What evidence do you have about such changes? Critically evaluate the implications of these changes to contemporary organizations.

3   The rapid development of ICTs, combined with radical changes in the nature of the economy, has enabled organizations from different sectors to adopt new strategies and business models. Illustrate one of the most significant strategies or business models that has emerged in recent years. Explain why you think this new strategy or business model is significant. Critically evaluate its relevance to today's organizations.

4   The changing business environment and the development of new strategies and business models have also challenged organizations to come up with new organizational designs, sometimes known as 'organizational innovations'. Illustrate three of the most significant organizational innovations that have emerged in recent years. From a business perspective, critically evaluate their potential benefits and problems.

5   The e-Business phenomenon has evolved considerably over the past ten years. Highlight three of the most significant issues for e-Business in the next five years and explain why.

Assignments

1. Report: Important Areas Not Covered in the Book
    In this book, many important issues were not addressed. Choose one topic from the following list and write a 5,000-word report. The report should clearly define the concept and illustrate the main schools of thought in the literature; and discuss in what ways it is relevant to contemporary organizations. You may wish to choose a different topic but please discuss it with your lecturer. The target audience is students in your class.

    *   E-Marketing
    *   E-Learning
    *   E-Government
    *   E-Health
    *   M-Commerce and M-Business
    *   E-Logistics and E-Supply Chain
    *   Social Implications and Challenges of E-Business

2. Report: E-Business Developments in Different Sectors (or Countries)
    E-Business has developed in different ways in different sectors, and there are also significant national and geographical variations. Choose a sector (or country)

you are familiar with and investigate e-Business development in the sector (or country). Write up your findings in the format of a 5,000-word report, clearly illustrating the main issues and significant developments in the sector (country). Below is a list of possible sectors where e-Business development has been particularly significant, but you may wish to choose a different topic. The target audience is students in your class or on your course. Where appropriate, you should illustrate the main issues with real examples.

- Internet Banking
- E-Insurance
- E-Stock Brokerage
- E-Tailing
- E-Supermarkets
- E-Music
- E-Holidays

3. Case Study
   Using the Internet and other published sources, study the strategies, business models and organizational designs of leading companies in e-Business, either dot.com companies or established companies successful in deploying Internet and related technologies to transform themselves. Write up the case study in the format of a report (5,000–6,000 words) clearly outlining the key theoretical issues covered in this book. The following are some suggestions but you may wish to choose your own case, perhaps from your local area or your own country.

- Amazon.com
- eBay
- Yahoo
- Google
- Dell
- Cisco
- Lastminute.com
- Experdia.com
- Esure.com
- Egg.com

NOTES

1 Nohria, Nitin, William Joyce and Bruce Roberson (2003) What really works? *Harvard Business Review*, 81(7), 42–52.
2 Head, Simon (2003) *The New Ruthless Economy: Work and power in the digital age*. Oxford University Press, London.
3 E.g. van Slyke, Craig and France Belanger (2003) *E-Business Technologies: Supporting the net-enhanced organization*, John Wiley & Son, New York; Beynon-Davis, Paul (2004) *E-Business*, Palgrave Macmillan, Basingstoke.

4   Li, Feng (2002) Internet banking in the UK: from new distribution channel to new business models. *Journal of Financial Transformation*, 6, 53–65. http://www.capco.com/pdf/j06art10.pdf; Li, Feng (2002) Internet banking: from new distribution channel to new business models, *International Journal of Business Performance Management*, 4(2/3/4), 134–160; Li, Feng (2001) The Internet and the de-construction of the integrated banking model, *British Journal of Management*, 12, 307–322.

5   Li, Feng and J. Whalley (2002) The deconstruction of the telecommunications industry: from value chains to value networks, *Telecommunications Policy*, 9, 1–22. This paper is part of a special issue of the journal dedicated to mapping the evolving telecommunications value chains and market structure.

6   Awde, Priscilla (2005) BT's 21CN explained. *Financial Times*, 15 June, http://news.ft.com/cms/s/f22449ea-dcde-11d9-b590-00000e2511c8,dwp_uuid=fb0d80f4-2663-11d8-81c6-0820abe49a01.html.

7   Bakan, Joel (2004) *The Corporation: The pathological pursuit of profit and power*. Constable, London.

8   Li, Feng (2003) Implementing e-government strategy in Scotland: Current situation and emerging issues. *Journal of E-Commerce in Organizations*, 1(2), 44–65.

9   Khosrow-Pour, Mehdi (2004) *The Social and Cognitive Impacts of E-Commerce on Modern Organizations*. Idea Group Publishing, Hershey.

10 Li, Feng (2005, ed.) Social aspects of E-Business, special issue of *Journal of E-Commerce in Organizations*, 3(2).

11 Kogut, Bruce (2003, ed.) *The Global Internet Economy*. The MIT Press, Cambridge, MA.

FURTHER READING

Beynon-Davis, Paul (2004) *E-Business*. Palgrave Macmillan, Basingstoke.

Khosrow-Pour, Mehdi (2004) *The Social and Cognitive Impacts of E-Commerce on Modern Organizations*. Idea Group Publishing, Hershey.

Kogut, Bruce (2003, ed.) *The Global Internet Economy*. The MIT Press, Cambridge, MA.

Nohria, Nitin, William Joyce and Bruce Roberson (2003) What really works? *Harvard Business Review*, July, 42–52.

van Slyke, Craig and France Belanger (2003) *E-Business Technologies: Supporting the net-enhanced organization*. John Wiley & Son, New York.

Appendix I

Developing a Launch-Ready E-Business Plan: Putting Theory into Practice (Assignment I)

This book has mainly focused on the theoretical issues in e-Business, but studying e-Business is like learning to drive: the only way to learn is to get into a car and drive it; the theories alone will not be enough. Over the years of teaching e-Business classes in different postgraduate and undergraduate programmes, I have used this group assignment to address practical issues of e-Business, with considerable success. Students on my various courses have won many local and national business plan competitions. Some of the winners of these competitions were quickly snatched up by big employers; and several groups even launched their own e-Businesses after graduation. Even for those students who have no intention to launch their own businesses, this assignment would enable them to apply all their knowledge and skills, and develop essential transferable skills valued by employers.

The Assignment

Depending on the class size, work in groups of 3–5 on an e-Business idea and develop it into a launch-ready business plan (a report). As part of this business plan you should also prepare a 10-minute presentation using PowerPoint slides to outline your key selling points; and develop a prototype e-Business system (a site map) to support your business idea. You should describe the key functional features of this system in one section of your report.

In addition to an executive summary, the business plan should contain (but not be restricted to) the following aspects. You need to do some background research to justify your arguments and projections.

1. Detailed description of the business idea (your strategy and possible business models).
2. Key people – highlighting the main skills you possess and matching them with the key skill requirements for the business. Identify skill gaps.
3. Product/service – what is/are your main product/services; where/how to obtain them; the main value added from your business; product life cycles etc.
4. Pricing strategy – how to price the products/services; where will your main revenue come from?
5. Customers – who are they? Market projection, etc.
6. Competition – existing and potential new entrants.
7. Premises and equipments required (with cost and other implications).
8. Cash flow (initial capital requirements; future projection, etc.).
9. Action plan.
10. The most critical issues for the venture to succeed.

The Preparation

The key to the success of this assignment is to do it *for real*. To maximize the benefits of this class, everyone should do some thorough preparation in their own time. It would also be useful to organize some external speakers to talk to the students about various aspects of setting up a business – lawyers, accountants, bank managers, regional development agencies, entrepreneurs and so on. These talks could be part of the course. For one of the modules I teach, 50 per cent of the module was made up of external speakers and the business plan (the other 50 per cent through conventional lectures assessed by an exam). This is a very demanding piece of work and all students should do the following preparation in advance.

1. Each student should come up with at least one e-Business idea that can be developed into a business plan for this assignment. This could be either a new e-Business venture or an idea that will help an existing business or address an existing business problem/opportunity. Do some background research, and it would be very helpful if you could obtain the support of an external sponsor.
2. Prepare a short description of your personal strengths and weaknesses as a member of a founding team for an e-Business. Also think about what quality and skills you will need to obtain from the rest of the team to make your e-Business idea a success. This will be discussed in the class or in seminars and will provide the basis for team formation. Be very careful about whom you choose to work with, because you could potentially develop a very significant idea that would eventually be launched.
3. Visit some successful e-Business websites and do some background research on these companies. Also think about why some e-Business ventures have failed.
4. Go to the library or visit a bookshop to read some books on launching a new business or entrepreneurial venture in general and launching an e-Business venture in particular. Also scan through some booklets on how to write a business

plan (in order to obtain initial funding). The following books are merely suggestions and there are hundreds of similar books available. There are also numerous books on writing business plans and I will not suggest a specific one.

- Allen, Kathleen R. (1999) *Launching New Ventures: An entrepreneurial approach*, 2nd edn, Houghton Mifflin Company, Boston, about £20
- Morrath, Peter (2000) *Success@e-business*, McGraw-Hill, London, about £21
- Lynn, Jacquelyn (2005) *Start Your Own E-Business*, The Entrepreneur Press, Newburgh

5. Do some research and find out about relevant free resources and initial financial/ professional support available for new business start-ups both in your local region and elsewhere. Please use any support you can obtain in developing your business plan.

To give students extra incentives to work on the business plan, each year I have worked with the Enterprise Centre of my university to have the quality of the business plans judged by a professional panel; the winners are awarded a cash prize (from various sponsors) and a certificate, and selected business plans are encouraged to enter into various business competitions.

Appendix II

Developing an Online E-Business Resource Portal: Who is Who in E-Business (Assignment 2)

Since e-Business is still an emerging area, most scholars active in the area are coming from other more established disciplines such as strategy, marketing or information systems. The views in the area are often incoherent and sometimes contradictory, which creates serious problems for students, academics and business practitioners. It would be particularly beneficial to students, researchers and business executives if a comprehensive e-Business resource portal could be developed to store and disseminate up-to-date, comprehensive research findings in the e-Business area.

One way to structure such a portal is to develop a searchable 'Who is Who in E-Business' database, with links to summaries of their contributions, their most influential publications and their contact details. This way, if someone has questions about, say, e-Business strategy, the portal could provide relevant information on the key researchers in this area in the global context, as well as pointers such as what their main views are, links to their most influential work and brief annotations of their selected publications, as well as comments and criticisms by other readers. Other features could also be added to the portal, such as a forum for discussions as well as questions and answers; a Wikipedia on key concepts of e-Business; and blogs kept by participants. The portal could become a valuable learning resource for current and future students. Students contributing to the portal not only benefit from their own in-depth research on a specific area of e-Business, but also from the research by others.

The Assignment

This could be either an individual or small group assignment. First, a discussion should be organized for the whole class to identify some of the most significant sub-areas of e-Business. Then each of the topics is assigned to individuals or groups. The people involved will then conduct comprehensive research in the sub-area; identify the top ten most influential scholars in the sub-area; summarize the views and main contributions of each of the top ten scholars; and annotate their most influential publications (papers, books or reports). Then submit their assignment in the form of a report consisting of:

* a summary of the definitions and key issues in the selected sub-area in the overall context of e-Business;
* a short profile for each of the top ten scholars in the sub-area, why they have been selected, their main contributions to the sub-area, followed by brief annotations of their most influential publications;
* bibliographical details for further reading.

The work by the class can then be collated electronically on the course website, so that each individual can benefit from the research by others in the class. Below is a list of possible topics for student assignment.

* E-Business
* E-Commerce
* E-Business Strategies
* E-Business Models
* E-Business Transformation and New Organizational Designs
* E-Supply Chain/E-Logistics
* E-Marketing
* E-CRM (customer relation management)
* E-Business Infrastructure and Technology (such as web services, ERP, portals, RFID)
* M-Business and M-Commerce
* E-Government and E-Public Services
* E-Learning

The list is not exhaustive and could be further broken down into more specific sub-areas. The assignment could also be structured around different application areas or along other dimensions. For example:

* Internet Banking
* E-Holidays
* E-Tailing
* E-Music
* E-Auction

- E-Publishing/E-Books
- E-Business Consultants
- E-Business Solution Providers (companies)
- E-Business Resource Centres (websites containing E-Business-related materials)
- Web Metrics (e-Business measurements)
- E-Business Practitioners
- E-Business Textbooks

An example of such a portal is available at: http://www.newcastle-ebusiness.com.

Appendix III

Developing an E-Business Resource Portal and Online Forum: E-Business Wikipedia (Assignment 3)

This assignment requires the collaboration and contribution of all students studying the module. It can be undertaken either in parallel to the main lectures, or as one of the main assignments after the course. This assignment could also be used as 50 per cent of an e-Business module. For example, after teaching all the theories in the first half of the module, students are then required to develop a comprehensive Wikipedia on e-Business independently, with guidance and support from the lecturers and tutors.

Wiki and Blogs

Wiki is a piece of server software that allows users to freely create and edit webpage content using any web browser. It supports hyperlinks and has a simple text syntax for creating new pages and cross-links between internal pages on the fly; and it allows the organization of contributions to be edited in addition to the content itself. Most of all, it allows everyday users to create and edit any page in the website. A free licence for Wiki is available at http://www.gnu.org/copyleft/fdl.html and http://www.mediawiki.org/wiki/MediaWiki. It may be necessary for the lecturer to set up mediawiki on a server for students to use.

Web logs or blogs are a type of web content typically created by independent writers (although some reporters for media companies create blogs on newspaper or magazine sites). Some are personal journals/diaries; others resemble newsletters or columns. Often, they contain links to other sources of content. Although most early web logs were manually updated, tools to automate the maintenance of such sites made them accessible to a much larger population, and the use of some sort of browser-based software is now a typical aspect of 'blogging'. For this assignment, blogs can be used by students on the course to share ideas and regularly comment on various relevant issues. For this assignment, we can use Google's blog service: http://www.blogger.com/.

This Assignment

Using Wiki, develop a comprehensive Wikipedia on e-Business. The class should have a discussion to identify the main issues that should be covered, and the specific tasks are then assigned to individuals. Each student should undertake research and write up the sections they are assigned. Depending on the number of students in the class and the nature of the issues, each student may be asked to be responsible for several issues – write 500–1,000 words on each issue.

In addition, each student is also required to read and comment on other people's writings on various issues, and contribute to those sections by editing them or adding additional information. They should also give a rating on each piece of work written by others, and write up their reflections on a personal web log.

The lecturer will mark the students' work on the basis of:

1. the quality of each student's writing in the Wikipedia as judged by the lecturer (50%);
2. the reflections by each student on various issues in their personal web log (20%);
3. the contributions each student makes to other people's entries in the Wikipedia (15%);
4. the rating of each student's work given by others in the class (15%).

Bibliography

Abell, D. F. (1980) *Defining the Business: The starting point of strategic planning*. Prentice Hall, Inc., New Jersey.

Adams, Gerard F. (2004) *The E-Business Revolution & the New Economy: E-Conomics after the dot-com crash*. Thomson (South-Western), Mason, Ohio.

Afuah, A. and C. L. Tucci (2000, 2003) *Internet Business Models and Strategies: Text and cases*. McGraw-Hill, Boston.

Allmendinger, Glen and Ralph Lombreglia (2005) Four strategies for the age of Smart Services. *Harvard Business Review*, October, 131–145.

Alt, R. and H. Zimmermann (2001) Introduction to special section – business models. *Electronic Markets*, 11(1), 3–9.

Amit, R. and S. Zott (2000) Value Drivers of e-Commerce Business Models. *Knowledge at Wharton*. 2000. http://knowledge.wharton.upenn.edu.

Amit, R. and C. Zott (2001) Value creation in e-business. *Strategic Management Journal*, 22, 493–520.

Applegate, L. M. (2001) E-business models: making sense of the Internet business landscape. In G. Dickson, W. Gary, and G. DeSanctis (eds), *Information Technology and the Future Enterprise: New models for managers*. Prentice Hall, Upper Saddle River, NJ.

Applegate, L. and M. Collura (2000) *Overview of E-Business Models*, HBS Note (vol. 9-801-172, pp. 1–18). Harvard Business School, Boston, MA.

Auer, C. and M. Follack (2002) Using action research for gaining competitive advantage out of the Internet's impact on existing business models. In *Proceedings of the 15th Bled Electronic Commerce Conference – eReality: Constructing the eEconomy*, Bled, Slovenia, 17–19 June, pp. 767–784.

Awde, Priscilla (2005) BT's 21CN explained. *Financial Times*, 15 June. http://news.ft.com/cms/s/f22449ea-dcde-11d9-b590-00000e2511c8,dwp_uuid=fb0d80f4-2663-11d8-81c6-0820abe49a01.html.

Bakan, Joel (2004) *The Corporation: The pathological pursuit of profit and power*. Constable & Robinson, London.

Barnett, Christopher (1995) Office space, cyberspace and virtual organization. *Journal of General Management*, 20(4), 78–91.

Bell, D. (1973) *The Coming of the Post-Industrial Society*. Basic Books, New York.

Bessant, John and David Francis (2004) *Developing Parallel Routines for Radical Product Innovation*. AIM Research Working Paper Series, 010-August-2004.

Beynon-Davis, Paul (2004) *E-Business*. Palgrave Macmillan, Basingstoke.

Birch, D. and E. Burnett-Kant (2001) Unbundling the unbundled. *The McKinsey Quarterly*, 1, 4–23.

Brian, Arthur W. (1994a) *Increasing Returns and Path Dependence in the Economy*. University of Michigan Press, Ann Arbor.

Brian, Arthur W. (1994b) Positive feedbacks in the economy. *The McKinsey Quarterly*, no. 1, 81–95.

Birkinshaw, Julian and Cristina Gibson (2004) Build ambidexterity into your organization. *Sloan Management Review*, Summer, 45(4), 47–55.

Brynjolsson, E. and L. Hitt (2002) *Intangible Assets: Computers and organizational capital*. MIT Sloan School of Management, Center for eBusiness, Working Paper, October.

Burns, T. and G. Stalker (1961) *The Management of Innovation*. Tavistock Publications, London.

Burtler, P., Ted W. Hall, A. M. Hanna, L. Mendonca, B. Auguste, J. Manyika and A. Sahay (1997) A revolution in interaction. *The McKinsey Quarterly*, no. 1, 4–23.

Carr, Nicholas G. (2004) *Does IT Matter? Information technology and the corrosion of competitive advantage*. Harvard Business School Press, Boston.

Carr, Nicholas (2004) In praise of walls. *Sloan Management Review*, Spring, 10–13.

Carr, Nicholas (2005) Top-down disruption. *Strategy + Business*, Issue 39, Summer, http://www.strategy-business.com/magazine.

Chandler, A. (1962) *Strategy and Structure*. MIT Press, Cambridge, MA.

Chaffey, David (2002) *E-Business and E-Commerce Management*. Pearson Education Ltd, Harlow.

Chesbrough, H. W. and Teece, D. J. (1996) When is virtual virtuous? Organizing for innovation. *Harvard Business Review*, January–February, 65–73.

Charitou, Constantinos and Constantinos Markides (2003) Responses to disruptive strategic innovation. *Sloan Management Review*, 44(2), 55–63.

Child, J. (1972) Organization structure, environment and the performance: the role of strategic choice. *Sociology*, 6, 1–22.

Child, J. (1974) Managerial and organizational factors associated with company performance (Part I). *Journal of Management Studies*, October, 175–189.

Child, J. (1975) Managerial and organizational factors associated with company performance (Part II) – a contingency analysis. *Journal of Management Studies*, February, 12–27.

Child, J. (1984a) *Organizations*. Paul Chapman, London.

Child, J. (1984b) New technology and development in management organization. *Omega*, 12(3), 211–223.

Christensen, Clayton M. (1997) *The Innovator's Dilemma*. Harvard Business School Press, Boston.

Christensen, Clayton M. and Michael Raynor (2003) *The Innovator's Solution: Creating and sustaining successful growth*. Harvard Business School Press, Boston.

Christensen, Clayton M., Eric A. Roth and Scott D. Anthony (2004) *Seeing What Next: Using theories of innovation to predict industry change*. Harvard Business School Press, Boston.

Channon, D. (1973) *The Strategy and Structure of British Enterprise*. Macmillan, London.

Coase, Ronald (1937) The nature of the firm. *Economica N. S.*, 4, 386–405.

Cohn, Jeffrey M., Rakesh Khurana and Laura Reves (2005) Growing talent as if your business depended on it. *Harvard Business Review*, October, 62–71.

Cropper, S., C. Eden, L. Gunn and K. van der Heidjen (1995) *General Strategic Management: Business policy*. Strathclyde Graduate School of Business, University of Strathclyde, Glasgow, UK.

Cross, Michael (2005) Public sector IT failures. *Prospect*, October, 48–53.

Crost, Jane and Andrea Felsted (2005) Pru eager to see when Egg will get cracking. *Financial Times*, Tuesday 8 March, p. 4.

Daverport, Thomas and James Short (1990) The new industrial engineering: information technology and business process redesign. *Sloan Management Review*, Summer, 11–27.

Davenport, T. (1993) *Process Innovation*. Harvard Business School Press, Boston.

Davenport, Thomas H. (2005) The coming commoditization of processes. *Harvard Business Review*, June, 100–111.

Delong, Brad and Konstantin Magin (2005) Comment: The last bubble was brief, but it was still irrational. *Financial Times*, 19 April, p. 19.

Downes, Larry and Chunka Mui (1998) *Unleashing the Killer App: Digital strategies for market dominance*. Harvard Business School Press, Boston.

Drucker, Peter (1973) *Management: Tasks, responsibilities and practices*. Harper & Row, New York.

Drucker, Peter (2002) *Managing in the Next Society*. Truman Talley Books, New York.

DTI (2003) *Business in the Information Age: International benchmarking study 2003*. Booz Allen Hamilton, London.

Dubosson-Torbay, M., A. Osterwalder and Y. Pigneur (2002) E-Business model design, classification, and measurements. *Thunderbird International Business Review*, 44(1), 5–23.

Duncan, R. B. (1976) The ambidextrous organization: design dual structure for innovation. In R. H. Kilmann, L. R. Pondy and D. Slevin (eds), *The Management of Organization Design: Strategies and implementation*, vol. 1, pp. 167–188. North-Holland, New York.

Dyer, Jeffrey H. and Nile W. Hatch (2004) Using supplier networks to learn faster. *Sloan Management Review*, Spring, 57–63.

Eisenstat, Russell, Nathaniel Foote, Jay Galbraith and Danny Miller (2001) Beyond the business unit. *The McKinsey Quarterly*, 1, 54–63.

Ethiraj, S., I. Guler and H. Singh (2000) The impact of Internet and electronic technologies on firms and its implications for competitive advantage. *Knowledge at Wharton*. Available from: http://knowledge.wharton.upenn.edu.

Evans, Philip and Bob Wolf (2005) Collaboration rules. *Harvard Business Review*, July–August, 96–105.

Farrell, Diana (2003) The *real* new economy. *Harvard Business Review*, October, 105–112.

Farhoomand, Ali (2005) *Managing (e)Business Transformation: A global perspective*. Palgrave Macmillan, Basingstoke.

Fox, C. (2000) *E-Commerce Business Models*. http://www.chrisfoxinc.com/eCommerceBusinessModels.html.

Gilbert, Clark (2003) The disruption opportunities. *Sloan Management Review*, 44(4), 27–32.

Goddard, John (1975) *Office Location and Urban and Regional Development*. Oxford University Press, London.

Goddard, J. (1992) New technology and the geography of the UK information economy. In K. Robins (ed.) *Understanding Information: Business, technology and geography*. Belhaven, London.

Goold, Michael and Andrew Campbell (2002) *Designing Effective Organizations*. Jossey-Bass, San Francisco.

Gordijn, J., H. Akkermans, H. V. Vliet and E. Paalvast (2000b) *Electronic Commerce and Web Technologies*, Lecture Notes in Computer Science, Vol. 1875. Springer-Verlag, Berlin, pp. 48–62.

Govindarajan, Vijay and Chris Trimble (2005) Building breakthrough businesses within established organizations. *Harvard Business Review*, May, 58–68.

Hacki, Remo and Julian Leighton (2001) The future of the networked company. *The McKinsey Quarterly*, no. 3, 26–39.

Hagel III, John (1996) Spider versus spider, *The McKinsey Quarterly*, 1, 4–19.

Hagel III, John and Marc Singer (1999) *Net Worth: Shaping markets when customers make the rules*. Harvard Business School Press, Boston.

Hagel III, John and Marc Singer (1999) Unbundling the corporation. *Harvard Business Review,* March–April, 77(2), 133–141.

Hamel, G. (2000) *Leading the Revolution.* Boston: Harvard Business School Press.

Hammer, M. (1990) Reengineering work: don't automate, obliterate. *Harvard Business Review,* July–August, 104–112.

Hammer, Michael (2004) Deep change: how operational innovation can transform your company. *Harvard Business Review,* April, 84–95.

Hammer, Michael and James Champy (1993) *Reengineering the Corporation: A manifesto for business revolution.* Nicholas Brealey Publishing, London.

Handy, Charles (1995) Trust and the virtual organization: how do you manage people whom you do not see? *Harvard Business Review,* May–June, 73(3), 40–54.

Harrison, Crayton (2004) Tech firms tout utility computing. *The E-Commerce Times,* 14 July, http://www.ecommercetimes.com/story/35105.html.

Harvey, D. (1989) *The Condition of Postmodernity.* Blackwell, Oxford.

Hawkins, R. (2001) *The 'business model' as a research problem in electronic commerce.* STAR (Socio-economic Trends Assessment for the digital Revolution) IST Project, Issue Report No. 4, July, SPRU – Science and Technology Policy Research.

Head, Simon (2003) *The New Ruthless Economy: Work and power in the digital age.* Oxford University Press, London.

Hepworth, M., A. Green and A. Gillespie (1987) The spatial division of information labour in Great Britain. *Environment & Planning A,* 19, 793–806.

Hepworth, Mark (1989) *Geography of the Information Economy.* Belhaven, London.

Huws, U., W. B. Korte and S. Robinson (1990) *Towards the Elusive Office.* John Wiley & Son, Chichester.

Jelassi, Tawfik and Albrecht Enders (2005) *Strategies for E-Business: Creating value through electronic and mobile commerce.* Pearson Education Ltd, Harlow.

Johansson, H., P. McHugh, A. J. Pendlebury and W. A. Wheeler III (1994) *Business Process Re-engineering.* John Wiley & Son, Chichester.

Jutla, D. N., P. Bodorik and Y. Wang (1999) WebEC: A benchmark for the cybermediary business model in e-commerce. *IMSA 1999,* 388–392.

Kaplan, Robert S. and David Norton (2004) *Strategic Map.* Harvard Business School Press, Boston.

Kelly, Kevin (1998) *New Rules for the New Economy: 10 radical strategies for a connected world.* Viking Penguin, Harmondsworth.

Kelly, Kevin (1997) New rules for the new economy: twelve dependable principles for thriving in the turbulent world. *Wired,* Issue 5.09, September, 140–197, http://www.wired.com/wired/archive/5.09/newrules.html.

Khosrow-Pour, Mehdi (2004) *The Social and Cognitive Impacts of E-Commerce on Modern Organizations.* Idea Group Publishing, Hershey.

Kogut, Bruce (2003, ed.) *The Global Internet Economy.* The MIT Press, Cambridge.

Laudon, Kenneth C. and Carol Guercio Traver (2003) *E-Commerce: Business, technology and society,* 2nd edn. Pearson Addison Wesley, Boston.

LeClaire, Jennifer (2005) Online retailers learned valuable e-lessons in 2004. *E-Commerce Times,* 24 January, http://www.ecommercetimes.com/story/39785.html [accessed 26 January 2005].

LeClaire, Jennifer (2005) Experts predict where search will go in 2005. *E-Commerce Times,* 9 March, http://www.ecommercetimes.com/story/41141.html.

Liker, Jeffrey (2004) *The Toyota Way: Fourteen management principles from the world's greatest manufacturer.* McGraw-Hill, New York.

Linder, Jane C. (2004) Transformational outsourcing. *Sloan Management Review*, 45(2), 52–58.

Leavitt, Harold (2003) Why hierarchies thrive. *Harvard Business Review*, March, 96–102.

Li, Feng and Andrew Gillespie (1994) Team telework: an emergent form of work organization. In R. Baskerville et al. (eds), *Transforming Organizations with Information Technology*, IFIP WG8.2, pp. 397–419. North-Holland, Amsterdam, ISBN 0-444-81945-2.

Li, Feng (1995) *The Geography of Business Information: Corporate networks and the spatial and functional corporate restructuring*. John Wiley & Son, Chichester.

Li, Feng (1997) From compromise to harmony: organizational innovations through information systems. *International Journal of Information Management*, 17(6), 451–464.

Li, Feng (1998) Team telework and the new geographical flexibility for information workers, in Magid Igbaria and Margaret Tan (eds), *The Virtual Workplace*. Idea Group Publishing, Hershey.

Li, Feng (2001) The Internet and the de-construction of the integrated banking model. *British Journal of Management*, 12, 307–322.

Li, Feng (2002) Internet banking: from new distribution channel to new business models. *International Journal of Business Performance Management*, 4(2/3/4), 134–160.

Li, Feng (2002) Internet banking in the UK: from new distribution channel to new business models. *Journal of Financial Transformation*, Winter, http://www.capco.com/pdf/j06art10.pdf.

Li, Feng (2003) Implementing E-government strategy in Scotland: current situation and emerging issues. *Journal of E-Commerce in Organizations*, 1(2), 44–65.

Li, Feng (2005, ed.) Social aspects of e-business. Special Issue of *Journal of E-Commerce in Organizations*, 3(2).

Li, Feng and H. Williams (1999) Inter-firm collaboration through inter-firm networks. *Information Systems Journal*, 9(2), 103–117.

Li, Feng, Jason Whalley and Howard Williams (2001) Between the electronic and physical spaces: implications for organizations in the networked economy. *Environment & Planning A*, 33, 699–716.

Machlup, F. (1962) *The Production and Distribution of Knowledge in the United States*. Princeton University Press, Princeton, NJ.

Malone, Thomas W., Joanne Yates and Robert I. Benjamin (1987) Electronic markets and electronic hierarchies. *Communications of the ACM*, 30(6), 484–497.

Malone, Thomas E. (2004) Bringing the market inside. *Harvard Business Review*, April, 107–114.

Mansfield, G. M. and L. C. H. Fourie (2004) Strategy and business models – strange bedfellows? A case for convergence and its evolution into strategic architecture. *South African Journal of Business Management*, March, 35(1), 35–44 (AN 12952944).

Marchand, Donald A. (2004) Extracting the business value of IT: It is usage, not just deployment that counts! *Journal of Financial Transformation*, September, 125–131.

Margretta, Joan (2002) Why business models matter. *Harvard Business Review*, May, 80(5), 86–92.

Martin, Roger L. and Mihnea C. Moldoveanu (2003) Capital versus talent: the battle that's reshaping business. *Harvard Business Review*, July, pp. 36–41.

Mintzberg, H. (1979) *The Structuring of Organizations*. Prentice Hall, Englewood Cliffs, NJ.

Mintzberg, H. (1983) *Structure in Fives*. Prentice Hall, Englewood Cliffs, NJ.

Morgan, Gareth (1997) *Images of Organizations*, 2nd edn. Sage, London.

Moynagh, Michael and Richard Worsley (2005) *Working in the Twenty-First Century*. The Economic and Social Research Council. Future of Work Project, University of Leeds, Leeds.

Nilles, J. (1988) Traffic reduction by telecommuting: a status review and selected bibliography. *Transportation Research*, 22A (4), 301–307.

Noam, Eli (2005) How a company's tools can define its structure. *Financial Times*, Friday 20 May, p. 19.

Nohria, Nitin, William Joyce and Bruce Roberson (2003) What really works? *Harvard Business Review*, July, 42–52.

O'Reilly III, Charles A. and Michael L. Tushman (2004) The ambidextrous organization. *Harvard Business Review*, April, 74–81.

Osterwalder, A. (2004) *The Business Model Ontology: A proposition in a design science approach.* PhD Thesis, Ecole Des Hautes Etudes Commerciales, University of Lausanne, Lausanne.

Osterwalder, Alexander and Tves Pigneur (2002) An E-Business Model Ontology for Modelling E-Business. *15th Bled Electronic Commerce Conference – E-Reality: Constructing the E-Economy.* Bled, Slovenia, 17–19 June.

Oxman, Jeffrey and D. Smith (2003) The limits of structural change. *Sloan Management Review*, Fall, 77–81.

Perez, C. (2002) *Technological Revolution and Financial Capital: The dynamics of bubbles and golden ages*, Edward Elgar, Cheltenham.

Peters, Tom (2003) *Re-imagine! Business excellence in a disruptive age.* Dorling Kindersley, London.

Petrovic, O., C. Kittl and D. Teksten (2001) Developing Business Models for eBusiness. Paper presented at the *International Conference of Electronic Commerce*, Vienna, Austria, 31 October–4 November.

Pettigrew, Andrew and Silvia Massini (2003) Innovative forms of organizing: trends in Europe, Japan and the USA in the 1990s. In Andrew Pettigrew et al. (eds), *Innovative forms of Organizing.* Sage, London.

Phillips, Wendy, Hannah Noke, John Bessant and Richard Lamming (2004) Beyond the Steady State: Managing discontinuous product and process innovation. *AIM Research Working Paper Series 009-August-2004.*

Pine II, B. Joseph and James Gilmore (1999) *The Experience Economy: Work is theatre and every business a stage.* Harvard Business School Press, Boston.

Pine II, B. Joseph and James Gilmore (1998) Welcome to the experiences economy. *Harvard Business Review*, 76(July–August), 97–105.

Pooley-Dyas, G. (1972) *Strategy and Structure of French Enterprise.* PhD Thesis, Harvard Business School, Cambridge, MA.

Porat, M. (1977) *The Information Economy: Definition and measurement.* US Department of Commerce, Office of Telecommunications, Special Publication 77–12(1), USA.

Porter, M. E. (2001) Strategy and the Internet. *Harvard Business Review*, March, 63–78.

Prahalad, C. K. and V. Ramaswamy (2003) The new frontier of experience innovation. *Sloan Management Review*, Summer, 12–18.

Prahalad, C. K. and Venkat Ramaswamy (2004) *The Future of Competition: Co-creating unique value with customers.* Harvard Business School Press, Boston.

Rajan, Raghuram G. and Julie Wulf (2003) The flattening firm: evidence from panel data on the changing nature of corporate hierarchies. Reported in *Sloan Management Review*, 44(4), 5. Full paper available from Wulf@wharton.upenn.edu.

Rappa, M. (2000) *Business Models on the Web.* http://ecommerce.ncsu.edu/business_models.html.

Rappa, M. (2004), *Business Models on the Web.* http://digitalenterprise.org/models/models.html.

Rayport, J. F. (1999) The truth about Internet business models. *Strategy and Business*, third quarter, no. 16.

Ridderstrale, Jonas and Kjelle Nordstrom (2000) *Funky Business.* FT Prentice Hall, London.

Sawhney, M., S. Balasubramanian and V. Krishnan (2004) Creating growth with services. *Sloan Management Review*, Winter, 34–43.

Schlenker, Lee and Alan Matcham (2005) *The Effective Organization: The nuts and bolts of business value*. John Wiley & Son, Chichester.

Schneider, Gary (2006) *Electronic Commerce*, 6th annual edition. Thomson Course Technology, Canada.

Schwartz, Peter (2000) The future of the new economy. Global Business Network Scenarios Columns by Peter Schwartz. 1 July 2000, http://www.gbn.org [accessed 4 February 2005].

Scott Morton, Michael (1991, ed.) *The Corporation of the 1990s: Information technology and organizational transformation*. Oxford University Press, New York.

Shapiro, Carl and Hal R. Varian (1999) *Information Rules: A strategic guide to the network economy*. Harvard Business School Press, Boston.

Singer, Marc (2001) A new business model may forever change the way companies compete. *The McKinsey Quarterly*, no. 3, 1–3.

Slywotzky, Adrian and David Nadler (2004) The strategy is the structure. *Harvard Business Review*, February, p. 16.

Solow, Robert (1987) We'd better watch out. *New York Times Books Review*, 12 July.

Suzuki, Y. (1980) The strategy and structure of top 100 Japanese industrial enterprises: 1950–1970. *Strategic Management Journal*, 1, 265–291.

Sviokla, John and Anthony Paoni (2005) Every product's a platform. *Harvard Business Review*, October, 17–18.

Swank, Cynthia Karen (2003) The lean service machine. *Harvard Business Review*, October, 123–129.

Tapscott, Don and Art Caston (1992) *Paradigm Shift: The new promise of information technology*. McGraw-Hill, London.

Tapscott, Don and David Ticoll (2003) *The Naked Corporation: How the age of transparency will revolutionize business*. Free Press, New York.

Tapscott, Don, David Ticoll and A. Lowy (2000) *Digital Capital: Harnessing the power of business webs*. Nicholas Brealey Publishing, London.

Timmers, Paul (1998) Business models for the electronic markets. *Electronic Markets*, 8(2), 3–8.

Timmers, Paul (1999) *Electronic Commerce: Strategies and models for business-to-business trading*. John Wiley & Son, Chichester.

Tucker, Sundeep (2005a) Show of hands packs punch in boardroom. *Financial Times*, Wednesday 26 January, p. 3.

Tucker, Sundeep (2005b) Fund managers choose to engage in dialogue rather than confrontation. *Financial Times*, Wednesday 26 January, p. 3.

Tucker, Sundeep and David Turner (2005) Lobby groups cool on executive pay pact. *Financial Times*, Wednesday 26, p. 3.

Turban, Efraim, David King, Jae Lee and Dennis Viehland (2004) *Electronic Commerce: A managerial perspective*. Pearson Prentice Hall, New Jersey.

Uday Karmarkar (2004) Will you survive the services revolution? *Harvard Business Review*, June, 101–107.

Vassilopoulou, K., X. Ziouvelou, A. Pateli, and A. Pouloudi. (2003) Examining e-business models: applying a holistic approach in the mobile environment. In C. Ciborra et al. (ed.) *New Paradigms in Organizations, Markets and Society. Proceedings of the 11th European Conference on Information Systems (ECIS 2003)*, 16–21 June, Naples, Italy.

van der Heidjen, Kees (1996) *Scenarios*. John Wiley & Son, Chichester.

van Slyke, Craig and France Belanger (2003) *E-Business Technologies: Supporting the net-enhanced organization*. John Wiley & Son, New York.

Venkatraman, N. (1994) IT-enabled business transformation: from automation to business scope re-definition. *Sloan Management Review*, 35(2), 73–87.

Venkatraman, N. Venkat (2004) Offshoring without guilt. *Sloan Management Review*, Spring, 14–16.

Weill, P. and M. R. Vitale (2001) *Place to Space; Migrating to eBusiness models*. Harvard Business School Press, Boston, MA.

Womack, James P., Daniel Jones and Daniel Roos (1990) *The Machine that Changed the World*. Rawson Associates, New York.

Womack, James P. and Daniel T. Jones (2005) Lean consumption. *Harvard Business Review*, March, 59–68.

Williamson, Oliver E. (1975) *Markets and Hierarchies: Analysis and antitrust implications*. Free Press, New York.

Williamson, Oliver E. (1985) *The Economic Institutions of Capitalism*. Free Press, New York.

Williamson, Oliver E. (1991) Comparative economic organization: the analysis of discrete structural alternatives. *Administrative Science Quarterly*, 36(2), 269–296.

Woodward, J. (1965) *Industrial Organization Theory: Theory and practices*. Oxford University Press, London.

Yates, JoAnne and John Van Maanen (2001, eds) *Information Technology and Organizational Transformation: History, rhetoric, and practice*. Sage, Thousand Oakes, CA.

Yip, G. S. (2004) Using strategy to change your business model. *Business Strategy Review*, 15(2), 17–24.

Yousept, Irene (2006) *Internet and Emerging E-Business Models: Developing an integrated analytical framework for UK Internet banking and online grocery shopping*. PhD Thesis, University of Newcastle upon Tyne, UK.

Zuboff, Shoshana and James Maxmin (2002) *The Support Economy: Why corporations are failing individuals and the next episode of Capitalism*. Allen Lane, The Penguin Press, London.

Index